Modern Diplomacy in Practice

Robert Hutchings • Jeremi Suri
Written and Edited by

Modern Diplomacy in Practice

Written and Edited by
Robert Hutchings
Lyndon B. Johnson School of Public Affairs
The University of Texas at Austin
Austin, TX, USA

Jeremi Suri
Lyndon B. Johnson School of Public Affairs
The University of Texas at Austin
Austin, TX, USA

ISBN 978-3-030-26935-7   ISBN 978-3-030-26933-3 (eBook)
https://doi.org/10.1007/978-3-030-26933-3

© The Editor(s) (if applicable) and The Author(s), under exclusive licence to Springer Nature Switzerland AG 2020
This work is subject to copyright. All rights are solely and exclusively licensed by the Publisher, whether the whole or part of the material is concerned, specifically the rights of translation, reprinting, reuse of illustrations, recitation, broadcasting, reproduction on microfilms or in any other physical way, and transmission or information storage and retrieval, electronic adaptation, computer software, or by similar or dissimilar methodology now known or hereafter developed.
The use of general descriptive names, registered names, trademarks, service marks, etc. in this publication does not imply, even in the absence of a specific statement, that such names are exempt from the relevant protective laws and regulations and therefore free for general use.
The publisher, the authors and the editors are safe to assume that the advice and information in this book are believed to be true and accurate at the date of publication. Neither the publisher nor the authors or the editors give a warranty, express or implied, with respect to the material contained herein or for any errors or omissions that may have been made. The publisher remains neutral with regard to jurisdictional claims in published maps and institutional affiliations.

Cover illustration: Patra Kongsirimongkolchai / EyeEm / Getty Images

This Palgrave Macmillan imprint is published by the registered company Springer Nature Switzerland AG.
The registered company address is: Gewerbestrasse 11, 6330 Cham, Switzerland

Preface

This book was several years in the making and has benefited from a number of distinct but related initiatives. In 2011, the two of us launched a project at the University of Texas (UT), immodestly called "reinventing diplomacy," with the aim of reinvigorating the study, teaching, and practice of diplomacy. Former German foreign minister Joschka Fischer gave the keynote address, and during the same visit helped us inaugurate the new Austin Council on Foreign Affairs. Since that time, we and our colleagues at UT have created several new courses at the graduate and undergraduate levels, provided postdoctoral fellowships to nurture the next generation of scholars, and published numerous articles and several new books, including one that we co-edited, called *Foreign Policy Breakthroughs: Cases in Successful Diplomacy*.[1] We also created and have led an annual Austin Forum on Diplomacy and Statecraft that for each of the last five years has brought together some two dozen mid-career diplomats from Europe, Latin America, and the United States to engage in an intense set of strategic dialogues here on the UT campus. Each of these activities has enriched all of the others.

One of our most ambitious efforts was a year-long research project undertaken by 15 talented graduate student researchers in the academic year 2016–2017 to survey and compare the diplomatic services of eight key countries around the world. Our partner in the project was the American Foreign Service Association and particularly its president, Ambassador Barbara Stephenson, who saw this multi-country comparative study as useful to the US Foreign Service at a time of great flux and uncertainty. The resulting report, entitled "Developing Diplomats,"[2] was published in May 2017 and profiled in the December 2017 issue of *The Foreign Service Journal*.[3] Shortly thereafter, we were approached by Dr. Anca Pusca, a senior editor with Palgrave Macmillan, who invited us to submit a book proposal based on the student-led report but with substantial additional input from us. We are grateful to Ambassador Stephenson for joining with us in this project in its initial stages and to Dr. Pusca, who saw in the original project a potential that we might have missed but for her encouragement. We also thank Katelyn Zingg, editorial assistant at Palgrave Macmillan, for her expert help in turning the manuscript into a completed book.

In our discussions with Palgrave Macmillan, we agreed to commission two new chapters, on Japan and the United States, and to revise, update, and expand the original eight chapters. We are indebted to Ambassador (retired) Ronald McMullen, our former colleague as Diplomat in Residence here at UT, and to Kazushi Minami, a recent PhD from UT's History Department and a newly minted assistant professor, for producing superb chapters on the US Foreign Service and Japan's Ministry of Foreign Affairs. The two of us divided the remaining eight chapters between us and added our names as co-authors, but we also have listed as co-authors the original student researchers, all of whom have since graduated. They deserve great credit for doing the original digging into the inner workings of these varied diplomatic services, enabling us to build on their work and add to it our own research and analysis. We are also grateful to Diana Bolsinger, a third-year PhD student at the Lyndon B. Johnson School of Public Affairs, for her invaluable assistance in helping us turn this multi-author study into a coherent final product.

The result is this first-ever book that assesses and compares the world's ten largest diplomatic services: those of Brazil, China, France, Germany, India, Japan, Russia, Turkey, the United Kingdom, and the United States. We considered other combinations that would have given greater cross-regional balance or included some smaller but high-performing services, but we ultimately decided that for comparative purposes, focusing on the ten largest made the most sense. In each chapter, we have followed the same structure so as to facilitate cross-country comparisons. Each begins with an Executive Summary and then proceeds through several sections: History and Culture, Profile (size, budget, and organizational structure), Recruitment and Selection, Professional Development, Leadership, Role in Policy-Making, and Preparations for the Future. In addition to updating, and fact-checking the middle sections, the two of us focused most of our attention on the histories and cultures of the services, their roles in foreign policy decision-making, and how well they are preparing for the future.

This has been a fascinating experience, one of the most interesting either of us has ever undertaken. Plumbing the histories and diplomatic cultures of ten very different services, and their changing roles in the decision-making arenas, has been a challenge and a pleasure. Trying to penetrate the inner workings and procedures of other countries' foreign ministries has been even more daunting. Some, notably the Chinese and Russian, do not publish much on their internal policies on recruitment, training, and promotion. Even the more open diplomatic services often operate according to unspoken rules, procedures, and customs that are known mainly to those on the inside, and even they are often mystified by the goings-on in their own institutions. This is the "inside history" of organizations, as distinct from their "public history," that Richard Neustadt and Ernest May wrote about many years ago.[4]

To meet these challenges, we have read as widely as possible, and we have consulted dozens of diplomats and scholars. Some were kind enough to read and critique earlier drafts of the chapters; others provided important inside information that helped us gain an understanding beyond what is to be found in print or online. We are indebted to these diplomats and scholars, many of whom are acknowledged at the end of each chapter. Of course, they bear no responsibility for any errors of fact or interpretation that may remain.

It has been a privilege and pleasure working on this book in consultation with so many practicing diplomats from around the world. We began this project favorably disposed to the work of diplomacy and diplomats, and we conclude it with even more positive feelings. We dedicate this book to those diplomats, and we hope that the book will contribute not only to a better understanding of the practice of modern diplomacy but also to a deeper appreciation of the vital role diplomacy plays in providing for the peaceful resolution of conflict among states and the maintenance of a workable international system.

Austin, TX

Robert Hutchings
Jeremi Suri

Introduction

On October 26, 1776, four months after signing the Declaration of Independence, Benjamin Franklin set sail from Philadelphia to France, where he became the first American diplomat. Franklin was a cosmopolitan inventor, businessman, politician, and writer. He was also a skilled representative of his new nation, negotiating the first American alliance with France. This was the only formal American alliance concluded for the next century-and-a-half—until the Second World War.

Franklin and his contemporaries understood that international diplomacy—the cultivation and management of relations with other states—was crucial for national survival and prosperity. He was part of a broader transatlantic community of learned, wealthy gentlemen who used their personal skills to manage relations between rival governments in an era of aggressive empires. Diplomacy was not an alternative to war or peace, but instead an essential part of eliciting support from potential allies, and, when necessary, balancing against potential foes in a complex international system.

Diplomacy meant delicate negotiations in between the extremes of war and peace, which Franklin and others recognized as the crucial daily maintenance of contacts and communications between states and other international actors. British, French, Prussian, and Russian diplomats had mastered this game in Franklin's day. He followed suit, and brought the wisdom of his experience back to his newly emerging nation.[5] For Franklin and his many successors, foreign relations meant a mix of cooperation, competition, and negotiations to maximize the emerging power of the United States and minimize its weaknesses. In a complex world with diverse actors, no country could survive alone. Diplomacy was survival through interdependence, and the pursuit of the national interest through direct communication, intelligence gathering, and manipulation, when necessary. The founders and successive generations concentrated their foreign policy activities on the work of diplomats, not the military, and the most talented American statesmen served their country in this capacity, following Franklin's footsteps. They expected that their successors would do the same.[6]

The twentieth century was, in some ways, the era when this vision came to fruition. The United States and its counterparts on other continents expanded their diplomatic services, placing greater emphasis than ever before on sending some of their most talented and best-trained citizens abroad to negotiate treaties, manage daily relations, and report on potential dangers. Embassies proliferated around the world, diplomatic conferences became more numerous and specialized, and organizations (especially the League of Nations and the United Nations) turned intensive diplomatic deliberations into a form of global governance. On the eve of the Second World War, the United States possessed a small divided military (the Army and Navy were entirely separate), and a growing, highly educated, and increasingly active foreign service. The diplomats largely determined American foreign policy in the mid-twentieth century.[7]

The same was true for counterpart agencies in Great Britain and France, except their foreign ministries were also imperial offices, managing empires. American diplomats, in George Kennan's first-hand account of the period, worked to reform the world through law, negotiation, and cooperation; the diplomats from old and new empires sought to protect their holdings. Washington's diplomats were the front line of American idealism and influence in an increasingly competitive international system that descended into a Second World War, when the work of the diplomats would become married to a larger and, for the first time, permanent American global military presence. Nonetheless, at least through the postwar decade of European and Japanese reconstruction, American diplomats led policy-making as strategists, negotiators, and managers on the ground.[8]

This unprecedented expansion in America's global presence, and its underlying internationalist goals (including democratization and free trade), required a more skilled, highly organized, and professionalized diplomatic corps. Professionalization occurred across all areas of society in the twentieth century (medicine, law, education, etc.), but it was especially pronounced in the field of diplomacy. The technically trained and carefully vetted representative of the state supplanted the aristocrat-turned-diplomat of old. Governments, including the United States, built large bureaucracies to train and organize the work of men (and eventually women), hired full-time to manage different elements of each nation's foreign activities in trade, travel, military affairs, education, and other matters. The new professional foreign service officers were selected on merit (usually through competitive examinations), they were highly trained (usually with advanced degrees), and they were specialized (by field or region).[9]

The venerable British diplomat, Harold Nicolson, described this as the "new diplomacy." Leisurely confidential aristocratic dialogues in royal courts were the ornaments of the past; highly disciplined negotiations, supported and surveilled by tightly organized government bureaucracies, were the wave of the future. Diplomacy changed from palace intrigue to a game of information gathering and sensitive policy application in changing circumstances.[10]

The professionalized diplomacy of the twentieth century dominated the Cold War, and it continues to shape the twenty-first century world. American diplomats (George Kennan, Averell Harriman, Dean Acheson, Henry Kissinger, and many others) were at the center of US policy-making, as were their Western European, Soviet, Chinese, Japanese, and postcolonial counterparts. Since at least 1945, every major country has strived to hire, train, and employ the most skilled foreign service professionals for a variety of tasks, including economic cooperation, counter-terrorism, cultural exchange, and, of course, conflict management. Diplomats work with diverse counterparts from their own governments, foreign governments, the business community, social movements, non-governmental organizations, and the media. And the list of potential partners continues to grow as the range of international actors expands in the early twenty-first century.[11] Diplomats often receive less public attention than soldiers, but they are ever-present and essential for the management of complex relationships across widely varying contexts. To travel, trade, and adjudicate unavoidable cross-boundary conflicts requires diplomats more than ever before. As jet travel and social media have transformed the job, diplomacy has grown in importance for translation and coordination in the face of disorienting changes. Diplomats keep the forces of global entropy under control; they help to build order out of chaos. In the terms used by political scientist Hedley Bull, diplomats socialize the relations among international actors, nurturing a system of rules, norms, and common expectations—even between adversaries.[12]

This comparative study is an effort to understand the similarities and differences in how countries recruit, train, and promote their diplomats. Our point of departure is the vital importance of diplomacy in the modern world—especially as violent conflicts spread across and within states during the early decades of the twenty-first century. We emphasize the need for more shared thinking about diplomacy and the potential gains from more common work to coordinate the development of first-class diplomats. The United States is only one of ten countries that we examine in this study. We believe that all nations, including the United States, can improve the preparation and performance of their diplomats by drawing on the best practices of counterparts abroad. National uniqueness is necessary and inevitable; but learning from others is crucial for cooperation and improvement—perhaps more than ever before.

Different nations train their doctors, lawyers, and even professors in similar ways—with shared bodies of knowledge and common standards of performance. Air travel worldwide is made safer by the common core training all commercial pilots receive, regardless of nationality. The same is not true for diplomats whose backgrounds and educational experiences vary as much as ever. Although their work is self-consciously global, diplomats are nationally selected, trained, and evaluated. Diplomatic training remains particularistic and nationalistic; it resists serious and deep efforts to make it more global, despite the global problems all diplomats must confront.

The best evidence for the resistance to globalization in diplomatic training is the paucity of comparative studies. We know of only two detailed studies of foreign service recruitment and training across societies.[13] Other comparative discussions exist, but they lack detail.[14] Even the best foreign services are remarkably insular in the ways they prepare for their core missions.

This study is a detailed and focused effort to broaden how we understand and conceptualize the recruitment, training, and development of professional diplomats in the twenty-first century. The goal is not to criticize processes in different countries, but to create a common foundation for comparing, learning, and even integrating training and career development models across nations. This is particularly valuable for American readers, who are frequently ill-informed about the workings of other countries.

We have focused on ten major foreign services: Brazil, China, France, Germany, Great Britain, India, Japan, Russia, Turkey, and the United States. We chose these services based on their size, influence, and historical role in their regions. We also chose them for their geographical and cultural differences, as well as their accessibility for research. (We included Russia as one of our case studies, although it was the least accessible of the group.)

A number of themes emerged from the final case studies, and they run through the chapters that follow. Our analysis of the ten diplomatic services interrogates these themes closely. Although the diversity of practices across services is wide, the challenges are, in fact, quite similar. The future of international diplomacy in the twenty-first century will reflect how large, powerful countries address these common diplomatic themes, with many opportunities for learning and cooperation.

Recruitment and Retention

All diplomatic services strive to recruit, promote, and retain the best talent. As discussed in the chapters of this report, foreign services employ numerous methods to attract the highest qualified individuals, while weeding out less qualified applicants. Almost all of the services rely on an examination system and various other requirements, including foreign language proficiency, specialized education, psychiatric evaluation, and extensive knowledge of economics, law, and related disciplines. France especially focuses on elite education, selecting many of its officers from the *École Nationale d'Administration*, the nation's premier public administration school.

Most of the services continue to recruit top talent, but the competition for that talent is increasing. Other government institutions, non-governmental organizations, and especially private businesses offer ambitious young citizens increasingly lucrative and attractive opportunities for public influence. Concerns about excessive bureaucracy and politicization in government also discourage some top recruits from joining government. This is particularly true in Russia, India, and, in part, the United States. Foreign services in major countries can no longer assume that the best citizens will come to them—they must do more to reach out and offer attractive working environments.

After new recruits are hired, the next challenge becomes retention. How do you engage these top candidates in early work that will encourage them to stay within the organization and maintain high working morale? Some countries, like Russia, have begun to increase salaries in an attempt to stem falling retention rates. Others, like France, continue to rely on the domestic prestige of their diplomatic corps to attract and retain talent.

The nature of promotion through the organization, "up and out" service contracts, and the responsiveness of the bureaucracy to family needs are all key factors affecting long-term development of high-quality personnel. These issues need more attention, especially as the nature of family relationships and the expectations for work–life balance change with a new generation of talented, diverse young diplomats.

Training

Beyond initial training at recruitment, all of the foreign services in this study offer further opportunities for professional development; however, the length and execution of mid-career education varies greatly. Some services mandate periodic moments of intensive study throughout the careers of their foreign service officers, some offer optional coursework and training programs as a prerequisite for promotion, and others utilize training programs only after promotion decisions have already been made.

The training of early employees varies significantly between services from a matter of weeks to a high of three years. Depending on the type of recruitment and education required, the services build their internal training upon that foundation. Services with a high barrier of entry tend to offer less early training; services that have a low barrier of entry, provide considerably more on-the-job training. The distinction blurs somewhat in the case of nations, like France, where the foreign ministry recruits some officers directly from its public administration school. Early training creates norms for a nation's diplomats, and how they will define the work they do for their country.

Several services mandate professional development and an examination as a part of their promotion process. Countries like Brazil and China have strict promotion processes that incentivize employees to attend training courses if they wish to advance their careers. China, for example, uses a "points" system to promote officers. To gain points or course credits, employees must take and pass a certain number of classes concurrent with their daily work requirements. Once enough points are accrued, officers become eligible for more advanced positions. Other services, especially Turkey, give rigorous meritocratic examinations to officers before they can advance to senior or expert-level positions.

Some services mandate refresher courses or professional development sessions after officers have worked for a certain period of time. In India, for example, foreign service officers are required to complete in-service training after their first five years of service—the goals of which are to prepare the officers for geographical specializations. France mandates mid-career training after 15 years of service, aiming to strengthen managerial and leadership skills for officers taking on upper management roles. Other services like those of Germany and Russia hold short trainings for officers between assignments, often after a term abroad.

Challenges to professional development in these services include budget limitations and current crises that take priority. These limitations often restrict the ability of services to offer extensive professional development programs.

In all services, on-the-job training and mentoring are crucial, often more important than formal classroom experiences. Nonetheless, there is a direct relationship between the different modes of learning. Services that value on-the-job training and mentoring also build in the necessary time for reflection and analysis that temporary out-of-post activities uniquely afford. Sequencing assignments for maximum learning, nurturing internal relationships that encourage growth, and allowing space for reflection away from daily pressures are interdependent elements of any serious training program.

In a rapidly changing world, with emerging actors in every region and influential new technologies, continuous training is crucial for all diplomats. Most foreign services lack sufficient personnel, resources, and internal incentives for this commitment to education, especially for mid-career diplomats. This is particularly true in the United States and Japan, where diplomats generally receive less continuous training than their military and business counterparts.

Domestic Politics

Discussion of budget limitations inevitably raises the issue of domestic politics. Each of the foreign services under examination struggles to maintain domestic support for its work. Diplomats confront perceptions of elitism and growing skepticism toward their cosmopolitanism among nationalist voters. Many foreign services are giving ever-greater attention to direct engagement with their own citizens, but that is a potential diversion for the work of international diplomacy. There is also a deep tension between the natural professionalizing tendency of diplomatic services (emphasizing special knowledge and experience) and populist tendencies that value ordinariness, localism, and authenticity.

In this study of ten leading diplomatic services, domestic tensions ranging from funding debates to diversity challenges play a central role in the effectiveness of each service within the international community. Effective diplomats must operate with the respect and support of their citizens, and this is often lacking. In Great Britain, for example, the impact of the Foreign and Commonwealth Office appears constrained by alternative international departments, a political climate shifting away from previously held globalist attitudes, and a budgetary crisis. The Turkish foreign ministry has extended its global reach in the last decade, but it faces increasing politicization and curtailed autonomy under the current president.

The Indian Foreign Service is an extreme outlier in personnel size—over-stretched in its efforts to connect with over a billion citizens and an expansive diaspora community. In Europe, the French and German foreign ministries face an uncertain domestic landscape that questions consensus assumptions about European integration and free trade. Amidst these disparate and cacophonous national voices, diplomacy faces a growing challenge to affirm its relevance at home and abroad.

Even well-informed citizens in each country lack sufficient understanding about the importance of diplomacy. Foreign ministries must do a better job of explaining the value of their work to citizens. They must communicate better through schools, media, and public associations (including business groups). They must explain why their efforts are essential for peace and prosperity, as well as growth and innovation. In the end, foreign ministries will need more resources, not less, in coming years. They will need to make more effective claims on constrained national budgets.

Diversity

One of the biggest domestic challenges is diversity—making the foreign service of a diverse nation represent that diversity. Every foreign service examined in this report comes up short, but each comes up short in its own unique way.

Most of the diplomatic services value diversity for the additional skills and perspectives it brings to diplomacy, as well as the legitimacy it provides in domestic debates. Most of the services have extensive plans to expand their diversity, defined in different ways, with different tactics.

The Constitution of India, for example, calls for proportional weighting of potential recruits by regional, caste, and tribal background; these efforts have led to disadvantaged groups comprising 46% of all new recruits in the past five years. Current efforts in India are also focused on religious and linguistic representation.[15]

In Brazil, a country of vast racial and cultural diversity, the foreign service has undertaken many efforts to increase diversity, with attention to gender, race, and socioeconomic background. Following widespread criticism of its largely insular, parochial, and European-style diplomats, Brazil has implemented several reforms; chief among these efforts are a restructuring of the recruitment process in order to make the *Itamaraty's* Foreign Service Examination more accessible, the institution of quotas for recruits of Afro-Brazilian ethnicity, and the administration of the entrance exam outside of Brasilia for distant regional applicants.

In Germany, the "Charter of Diversity" seeks to guarantee that German diplomats come from diverse backgrounds. The data on Germany's diplomatic workforce indicate impressive successes in increasing diversity, especially around gender. The same is true for France, where 53% of the diplomatic workforce is comprised of women. On racial, ethnic, and religious diversity, all of these services still have a long way to go.

Technology

If diversity is a common challenge, the rapid pace of technological change is probably the most serious source of uncertainty for each service. The pace and significance of technological change has undermined traditional assumptions about communication, influence, and power as a whole.

Most foreign services have taken advantage of the increased popularity of social media platforms such as Facebook, Twitter, and YouTube to conduct public diplomacy. Today, diplomatic services can sustain an open dialogue with the public—foreign and domestic—through social media posts that answer questions, discuss changes, and address specific issues. For example, the director of the press service for the Russian Ministry of Foreign Affairs often uses her personal Twitter account to inform the Russian public and release talking points. In this sense, services are using technology to expand their contact with the public.

As social media have extended the reach of public diplomacy efforts, they have the potential to undermine diplomatic professionalism. For instance, several reports claimed that diplomatic officers from Britain's Foreign and Commonwealth Office may have used a social media messaging application to discuss sensitive and inappropriate topics while posted abroad. This has been a problem for the US Foreign Service as well.

The information technology revolution has opened up the possibility of real-time diplomatic communications that were unthinkable before. While these capabilities enhance the ability of diplomats to provide timely information to their counterparts and report back to their home governments, some diplomats lament how communications allow government figures at home to micromanage relations far away. Modern communication systems have contributed to a sense among many diplomats that their current role is to repeat the talking points emanating from the executive, adding few expert insights.

The information technology revolution also poses a threat to the relevance of diplomatic reporting. Historically, diplomats have contributed critical information to the decision-making bodies within their home governments. In recent years, government decision-makers have marginalized diplomatic reporting because they wish to act fast and they have numerous alternative sources of direct information from abroad. The proliferation of information sources has, in some cases, contributed to the perception that decision-makers are relying on inaccurate, or at least incomplete, information. The challenge for modern diplomatic services is to harness the capabilities of the information technology revolution to reassert the power of on-the-ground reporting.

Role in Foreign Policy-Making

Technology and domestic politics have encouraged a complex mix of centralization and fragmentation within governments. Presidents and foreign ministers now possess capabilities to manage distant events from the nation's capital, with little attention to local, on-the-ground expertise. They can find their own experts outside traditional diplomatic institutions, who will affirm their biases and preferences. They can enforce personal loyalty over professionalism.

Similarly, the spread of communications technologies and general knowledge allow diverse groups to claim access and authority over diplomatic issues formerly reserved for professional diplomats. In the United States, for example, military, intelligence, and treasury officials often assert more influence than diplomats in large US embassies. As political leaders centralize their control over policy, more groups outside the foreign ministry can intervene in national decision-making. This might be the most significant challenge for each major foreign service.

The cultivation of local relationships and the nurturing of mutual interests are still what diplomats are trained to do best. They have the experience and skills to see beyond the latest headline-grabbing information, promoting shared wisdom between long-time friends and allies. Diplomats manage the enduring discussions and negotiations between countries that anticipate crises and carve out common ground, where it would not exist otherwise. They report on deeper cultural dynamics and they create basic norms of engagement to manage competition, even between violent adversaries. Each of the foreign services in this study must reassert its role in its nation's policy-making. Otherwise, foreign policy will become more crisis-driven, and less diplomatic.

The themes running through this study are contemporary, and also historical. They represent age-old challenges and opportunities, redefined by the contours of our current era. Studying these themes in a comparative context provides a foundation for rebuilding our diplomatic institutions, at a time when they are most in need of renewal.

Although diplomacy has evolved considerably from Benjamin Franklin's era, it remains as essential as ever to the security and prosperity of nations, as well as other international actors. Like its peers, the United States has a long and venerable diplomatic tradition that can and will adjust to the new challenges and opportunities of our times. Adjustment, however, will require closer study of other foreign services, and a general commitment to help each nation's diplomats develop the knowledge and resources to serve their country best. Each of the foreign services in this study has the opportunity to improve as it globalizes its vision of educating the next generation of high caliber diplomats. We hope this study helps in that worthy and essential mission.

Lyndon B. Johnson School of Public Affairs　　　　　　　　Jeremi Suri
The University of Texas at Austin
Austin, TX, USA

Notes

1. Robert Hutchings and Jeremi Suri, eds., *Foreign Policy Breakthroughs: Cases in Successful Diplomacy* (Oxford: Oxford University Press, 2015).
2. *Developing Diplomats: Comparing Form and Culture Across Diplomatic Services*, Policy Research Project Report on Reinventing Diplomacy, No. 194 (Austin: University of Texas, 2017): https://repositories.lib.utexas.edu/handle/2152/62371.
3. Robert Hutchings and Jeremi Suri, "The Making of an Effective Diplomat: A Global View," *The Foreign Service Journal*, December 2017, 22–29.
4. Richard E. Neustadt and Ernest R. May, *Thinking in Time: The Uses of History for Decision Makers* (New York: The Free Press, 1986), 212–13.
5. For more on Benjamin Franklin and the origins of American diplomacy, see Jonathan R. Dull, *A Diplomatic History of the American Revolution* (New Haven: Yale University Press, 1987). For a fuller discussion of modern diplomacy, its importance, and some of its successes in the twentieth century, see Robert Hutchings and Jeremi Suri, eds., *Foreign Policy Breakthroughs: Cases in Successful Diplomacy* (New York: Oxford University Press, 2015).
6. On the American diplomatic tradition, and its early origins, see, among many others, Felix Gilbert, *To the Farewell Address: Ideas of Early American Foreign Policy* (Princeton: Princeton University Press, 1961); Robert Dallek, *The American Style of Foreign Policy: Cultural Politics and Foreign Affairs* (New York: Oxford University Press, 1990); and David Milne, *Worldmaking: The Art and Science of American Diplomacy* (New York: Farrar, Straus, and Giroux, 2015).
7. On this point, the literature on American foreign policy during the interwar years is most revealing. Despite public isolationism, diplomats crafted and managed a coherent American internationalist vision that included increased trade, cultural influence, and political cooperation abroad. See, among others, Emily Rosenberg, *Spreading the American Dream: American Economic and Cultural Expansion, 1890–1945* (New York: Hill and Wang, 1982); and Frank Costigliola, *Awkward Dominion: American Political, Economic, and Cultural Relations with Europe, 1919–1933* (Ithaca: Cornell University Press, 1984).
8. See, among many others, George Kennan, *Memoirs, 1925–1950* (Boston: Little, Brown, 1967); Melvyn P. Leffler, *A Preponderance of Power: National Security, the Truman Administration, and the Cold War* (Stanford: Stanford University Press, 1992); William Hitchcock, *France Restored: Cold War Diplomacy and the Quest for Leadership in Europe, 1944–1954* (Chapel Hill: University of North Carolina Press, 1998); and Jeremi Suri, *Liberty's Surest Guardian: American Nation-Building from the Founders to Obama* (New York: Free Press, 2011), chapters 4–5.

9. See Harry W. Kopp and Charles A. Gillespie, *Career Diplomacy: Life and Work in the U.S. Foreign Service* (Washington DC: Georgetown University Press, 2011), 63–160.
10. See Harold Nicolson, *Peacemaking, 1919* (Boston: Houghton Mifflin, 1933).
11. See Pauline Kerr and Geoffrey Wiseman, eds., *Diplomacy in a Globalizing World: Theories and Practices* (New York: Oxford University Press, 2013).
12. See Hedley Bull, *The Anarchical Society: A Study of Order in World Politics* (New York: Columbia University Press, 1977).
13. See Henry Kittredge Norton, *Foreign Office Organization: A Comparison of the Organization of the British, French, German and Italian Foreign Offices with that of The Department of State of The United States of America* (The American Academy of Political and Social Science, 1929); Gianluigi Benedetti, Daniela Di Prima, Antonietta di Salvatore, Darragh Henegan, and Pietro Prosperi, eds., (comparing the foreign offices of France, Italy, UK, Germany, Spain), Directorate General for Administrative Affairs, Budget and Assets, Italian Ministry of Foreign Affairs (no date). The American Foreign Service Association (AFSA) recently completed its own benchmarking exercise, examining selection and entry level training in eight other foreign services: Brazil, China, the United Kingdom, Germany, France, Canada, Mexico, and India. This AFSA report was based on interviews. We have seen a 12-page summary of this report, and we have incorporated it in our research.
14. See Paul Webster Hare, *Making Diplomacy Work: Intelligent Innovation for the Modern World* (Thousand Oak, CA: CQ Press/Sage, 2016), chapter 9; Lowy Institute (London): https://www.lowyinstitute.org/global-diplomacy-index/.
15. See the text of the Constitution of India: https://india.gov.in/my-government/constitution-india/constitution-india-full-text.

References

Bull, H. 1977. *The Anarchical Society: A Study of Order in World Politics*. New York: Columbia University Press.

Costigliola, F. 1984. *Awkward Dominion: American Political, Economic, and Cultural Relations with Europe, 1919–1933*. Ithaca: Cornell University Press.

Dallek, R. 1990. *The American Style of Foreign Policy: Cultural Politics and Foreign Affairs*. New York: Oxford University Press.

Dull, J. R. 1987. *A Diplomatic History of the American Revolution*. New Haven: Yale University Press.

Gilbert, F. 1961. *To the Farewell Address: Ideas of Early American Foreign Policy*. Princeton: Princeton University Press.

Hare, P.W. 2016. *Making Diplomacy Work: Intelligent Innovation for the Modern World*. Thousand Oak, CA: CQ Press/Sage.

Hitchcock, W. 1998. *France Restored: Cold War Diplomacy and the Quest for Leadership in Europe, 1944–1954*. Chapel Hill: University of North Carolina Press.

Hutchings, R., & J. Suri, eds. 2015. *Foreign Policy Breakthroughs: Cases in Successful Diplomacy*. New York: Oxford University Press.

Kennan, G. 1967. *Memoirs, 1925–1950*. Boston: Little, Brown.

Kerr P., and G. Wiseman, eds. 2013. *Diplomacy in a Globalizing World: Theories and Practices*. New York: Oxford University Press.

Kopp, H.N., and C.A. Gillespie. 2011. *Career Diplomacy: Life and Work in the U.S. Foreign Service*. Washington, DC: Georgetown University Press.

Leffler, M.P. 1992. *A Preponderance of Power: National Security, the Truman Administration, and the Cold War*. Stanford: Stanford University Press.

Milne, D. 2015. *Worldmaking: The Art and Science of American Diplomacy*. New York: Farrar, Straus, and Giroux.

Morgan, W.D., and S. Kennedy. 2004. *American Diplomats: The Foreign Service at Work*. New York: iUniverse, Inc.

Nicolson, H. 1933. *Peacemaking, 1919*. Boston: Houghton Mifflin.

Norton, H.K. 1929. *Foreign Office Organization: A Comparison of the Organization of the British, French, German and Italian Foreign Offices with that of the Department of State of the United States of America*. The American Academy of Political and Social Science.

Rosenberg, E. 1982. *Spreading the American Dream: American Economic and Cultural Expansion, 1890–1945*. New York: Hill and Wang.

Suri, J. 2011. *Liberty's Surest Guardian: American Nation-Building from the Founders to Obama*. New York: Free Press.

Contents

1. **Brazil** — 1
Maria Pereyra-Vera, Daniel Jimenez, and Robert Hutchings

2. **China** — 21
Michael Deegan, Joel Keralis, and Robert Hutchings

3. **France** — 43
Bryce Block, Catherine Cousar, and Jeremi Suri

4. **Germany** — 59
Marne Sutten, Catherine Cousar, and Robert Hutchings

5. **India** — 81
Leena Warsi, Joshua Orme, and Jeremi Suri

6. **Japan** — 99
Kazushi Minami

7. **Russia** — 125
Jessica Terry, Zachary Reeves, and Jeremi Suri

8	**Turkey** Zuli Nigeeryasin, Evan W. Burt, and Jeremi Suri	143
9	**United Kingdom** Adam Crawford, Annika Rettstadt, and Robert Hutchings	161
10	**United States** Ronald McMullen	189

Conclusion 225

Index 237

Notes on Contributors

Bryce Block holds a Master of Arts degree (2017) in Global Policy Studies from the University of Texas at Austin.

Evan W. Burt holds dual Master of Arts degrees (2018) in Global Policy Studies and Middle Eastern Studies from the University of Texas at Austin.

Catherine Cousar holds a Master of Arts degree (2017) in Global Policy Studies from the University of Texas at Austin.

Adam Crawford holds dual Master of Arts degrees (2018) in Global Policy Studies and Middle Eastern Studies from the University of Texas at Austin.

Michael Deegan holds dual Master of Arts degrees (2018) in Global Policy Studies and Russian, East European, and Eurasian Studies from the University of Texas at Austin.

Robert Hutchings is the Walt and Elspeth Rostow Chair in National Security and Professor of The Public Affairs at the Lyndon B. Johnson School of Public Affairs, The University of Texas at Austin. His combined diplomatic and academic career has included service as chairman of the US National Intelligence Council and as special advisor to the secretary of state, with the rank of ambassador.

Daniel Jimenez holds Master of Arts degrees in Global Policy Studies (2017) and Russian, East European, and Eurasian Studies (2015) from the University of Texas at Austin.

Joel Keralis holds dual Master of Arts degrees (2017) in Global Policy Studies and Asian Studies from the University of Texas at Austin.

Ronald McMullen is a former career diplomat who served in his last post abroad as US ambassador to Eritrea. He is Ambassador in Residence at the University of Iowa and served as Diplomat in Residence at the University of Texas at Austin from 2010 to 2012. He holds a PhD in Political Science from the University of Iowa.

Kazushi Minami is an associate professor in the Osaka School of International Public Policy, Osaka University. He holds a PhD in History (2019) from the University of Texas at Austin. His research focuses on modern and contemporary US–East Asian relations. His articles have appeared in *Cold War History and Diplomatic History*.

Zuli Nigeeryasin holds dual Master of Arts degrees (2018) in Global Policy Studies and Asian Studies from the University of Texas at Austin.

Joshua Orme holds dual Master of Arts degrees (2018) in Global Policy Studies and Asian Studies from the University of Texas at Austin.

Maria Pereyra-Vera holds a Master of Arts degree (2018) in Global Policy Studies from the University of Texas at Austin.

Zachary Reeves holds dual Master of Arts degrees (2018) in Global Policy Studies and Russian, East European, and Eurasian Studies from the University of Texas at Austin.

Annika Rettstadt holds dual Master of Arts degrees (2018) in Global Policy Studies and Middle Eastern Studies from the University of Texas at Austin.

Jeremi Suri is the Mack Brown Distinguished Chair for Leadership in Global Affairs at the University of Texas at Austin, where he is a professor in the Department of History and the Lyndon B. Johnson School of Public Affairs. He is the author and editor of nine books on diplomacy, foreign policy, and political leadership.

Marne Sutten is a US Army colonel and was an Army Fellow at the University of Texas at Austin in 2016–2017. She holds a master's degree in Policy Management from Georgetown University and a master's degree in Military Arts and Sciences from the School of Advanced Military Studies.

Jessica Terry holds dual Master of Arts degrees (2018) in Global Policy and Russian, East European, and Eurasian Studies from the University of Texas at Austin.

Leena Warsi holds dual Master of Arts degrees (2018) in Global Policy and Middle Eastern Studies from the University of Texas at Austin.

CHAPTER 1

Brazil

Maria Pereyra-Vera, Daniel Jimenez, and Robert Hutchings

EXECUTIVE SUMMARY

The Ministry of Foreign Affairs, in Portuguese *Ministerio das Relações Exteriores*, has a particularly rich history. Colloquially referred to as *Itamaraty*, after the palace that has housed the ministry since its inception in the nineteenth century,[1] the Brazilian Ministry of Foreign Affairs began as an institution reserved primarily for the aristocracy. Though still an elite institution, *Itamaraty* has since become more open and modern, with respected diplomats who are widely regarded as among the most distinguished and effective in the world. The early French influence on Brazilian

---

M. Pereyra-Vera
2018 Master of Arts Degree, Global Policy Studies, The University of Texas at Austin, Austin, TX, USA

D. Jimenez
2017 Master of Arts Degree, Global Policy Studies, and 2015 Master of Arts Degree, Russian, East European, and Eurasian Studies, The University of Texas at Austin, Austin, TX, USA

R. Hutchings (✉)
Lyndon B. Johnson School of Public Affairs, The University of Texas at Austin, Austin, TX, USA
e-mail: rhutchings@austin.utexas.edu

governmental institutions is still reflected in both the prerequisites and core curriculum of the Brazilian diplomatic academy, the *Instituto Rio Branco* in Brasilia, through which every Brazilian diplomat must pass.

Brazilian diplomats typically enjoy a high degree of autonomy and capacity for independent judgment, especially in smaller or less sensitive postings. Unique among the countries covered in this book, Brazil requires that rising diplomats complete rigorous academic course work at several points in a career, including the equivalent of a master's thesis (additional to whatever degrees already earned) for promotion to the highest level.

Because of its prominence in Brazilian history, *Itamaraty* traditionally has played a strong role in the making and execution of foreign policy, with relatively little political interference during the period of democratic and authoritarian rule alike. "Presidentialism" and *Itamaraty's* leading role have gone hand in hand, even under strong and assertive presidents. *Itamaraty's* distinctive role is beginning to change, however, as foreign policy has come under increased public scrutiny and as decision making has become more centralized in the office of the president.

Although Brazil is sometimes accused of having an inconsistent foreign policy, owing to its turbulent political history, its diplomatic culture is informed by a coherent and durable set of core principles. Article 4 of the 1988 Brazilian Constitution articulates the basic tenets, which include adherence to international law, peaceful settlement of disputes, multilateralism, equality of states, sovereignty, and non-intervention. These principles flow naturally from Brazil's colonial history, its geographical situation with more national borders than any other state save China and Russia, and relatively weak capacity for military and economic power projection. Thus, Brazil has long been among the most active proponents of multilateralism and global governance, and has at the same time been a sharp critic of US domination of international institutions and of what former foreign minister Celso Amorim called "multilateralism in the service of unipolarity." Under former President Luiz Inácio Lula de Silva, Brazil embarked on a more active and assertive foreign policy under the banner of "acting globally," the title of Amorim's memoir,[2] and often as part of an informal "BRIC" (Brazil–Russia–India–China) grouping that coordinates primarily on economic and financial issues. It is an open question whether that tenuous grouping, which otherwise reflects very different positions on political and human rights issues, will survive the cross-pressures facing each of those countries and whether Brazil will be able to play the larger global role it set for itself just a few years ago.

History and Culture

The Brazilian diplomatic tradition can be traced back to the eminent Portuguese diplomat Alexandre de Gusmão, whose negotiation of the 1750 Treaty of Madrid secured for Portugal most of the borders of present-day Brazil, and whose legacy survives today via the eponymous *Fundação Alexandre de Gusmão* (FUNAG) in Brasilia. After independence and following territorial disputes with neighboring states, these borders were secured for the newly independent Brazilian state by José Maria da Silva Paranhos, Sr., Baron of Rio Branco. Considered the "father of Brazilian diplomacy," Rio Branco successfully negotiated the peaceful consolidation of Brazil's numerous borders before and during his tenure as foreign minister from 1902 to 1912. Indeed, because of Brazil's highly partisan political system, Rio Branco had demanded as a condition of his accepting the position of the foreign minister that he be empowered to create a professional diplomatic service removed from the highly charged political scene.[3] Brazilian diplomacy was thus nearly synonymous with Brazilian statehood, conferring on it prestige and domestic legitimacy that continues to this day.

The Brazilian diplomatic service, like other Brazilian institutions, was strongly influenced by French culture and institutions. The Spanish and Portuguese colonies in continental Latin America all gained independence in the immediate post-Napoleonic era and based their legal systems on the Napoleonic Code. They also drew on the US Constitution, but France and French culture served as an attractive counterweight to US domination of the western hemisphere. Nineteenth century liberalism came to Brazil in the form of the positivism of the French philosopher August Comte, whose writings inspired the motto *Ordem e Progresso* on the Brazilian flag. *Itamaraty's* website on France begins with this acknowledgment: "Since the independence of Brazil, France has held a central position in the Brazilian cultural, intellectual and institutional development. Political, philosophical, and religious ideas were sought in that country, as well as school, university and military models that would be employed in Brazil."[4] Indeed, Brazil's diplomatic academy, the *Instituto Rio Branco*, was modeled directly on the French *Grandes Écoles* and named after the Baron, who was himself an ardent Francophile.

After independence and the creation of the Empire of Brazil under Emperor Dom Pedro I in 1822, *Itamaraty*, like other governmental institutions, was a preserve of the nobility. With the proclamation of the

Republic of Brazil in 1889, the aristocracy was abolished along with titles of nobility, though a few prominent individuals were allowed to retain their titles. Among those was the Baron of Rio Branco, who nonetheless (and ironically) played a key role in the evolution of Brazil's diplomatic service by seeking to "equalize members of the service in terms of social origins and ideological bias, [favoring] the creation of a relatively cohesive and homogenous group." This groundwork of "institutional unity and ideological homogeneity" eventually led to institutional changes, including the adoption of public examinations and not long after, the merger of the State Department, Consular Service, and Diplomatic Service under the Mello Franco and Oswaldo Aranha reforms. On April 18, 1945, as part of the centennial celebration of the birth of the Baron of Rio Branco, the institute the bears his name was created by then President Getulio Vargas. Since that time, the institute has trained every Brazilian diplomat, giving *Itamaraty* a uniquely cohesive diplomatic corps all the way from third secretaries to ambassadors.

Like other Brazilian institutions, *Itamaraty* played a delicate, controversial, and somewhat compromised role during the military dictatorship that lasted from 1964 to 1985. Most of the oppressive measures under the *ditadura* were performed by the military itself or by CIEX (Information Center Abroad), a powerful intelligence agency under the supervision of the SNI (National Intelligence Service), but recent investigative reports, some drawn from the work of the National Truth Commission from 2012 to 2014, have implicated *Itamaraty* in spying on exiles and mounting counterpropaganda campaigns.[5] Much of the history of this period remains murky, however, and *Itamaraty* survived this dark period in Brazilian history with its reputation relatively unscathed. In a perverse way, the restrictions on political participation may actually have strengthened (at least temporarily) the autonomy of *Itamaraty* by shielding it from Congressional or public scrutiny.[6]

Certainly, Brazilian diplomats themselves consider their patterns of diplomatic thought and action to be uniquely theirs. Such was the premise of the three-volume *Brazilian Diplomatic Thought* published by the Alexandre de Gusmão Foundation, which posed and then answered in the affirmative the question, "Is there a Brazilian diplomatic thought?"[7] (There are parallels with a similar question posed by and to British diplomats: is there such a thing as a "Foreign Office mind," discussed in Chap. 9 of this book.) The Brazilian diplomat and scholar Paulo Roberto de Almeida summed it up this way:

Historically, Brazilian diplomacy has its own set of ideas—its own patterns of thought—which support its actions. These patterns of thought include concepts such as: an undeniable adhesion to international law; the absence of the recourse to force, to resolve disputes among States; nonintervention in the internal affairs of other countries; the observance of human rights; and a set of values unique to our civilizing heritage.[8]

PROFILE

Historically, *Itamaraty* has been well-funded, in keeping with its privileged place among Brazilian institutions, but the past decade has seen huge fluctuations in its operating budget. To support President Lula's ambitious foreign policy agenda, funding for the ministry soared, and the number of new diplomats entering the service annually more than tripled.[9] Under his successor Dilma Rousseff, beset by scandal and recession, funding went into a free fall, declining by more than 50% from 2010 to 2015, when it sank to 1.89 billion Brazilian *Reals* (approximately $600 million).[10] The budget recovered somewhat in subsequent years, but the 2018 accession of the populist and anti-globalist administration of Jair Bolsonaro introduced new uncertainties about future funding levels.

The Ministry of Foreign Affairs is the primary governing institution for the implementation of diplomatic relations with states and relevant international organizations. Headquartered in Brasilia, it is the main body providing direct support to Brazil's Minister of Foreign Affairs, as well as the Secretary General of Foreign Affairs. *Itamaraty* is organized through seven under-secretariats, both regional and functional.[11] The Rio Branco Institute, Alexandre de Gusmão Foundation (FUNAG) and International Relations Research Institute (IPRI) also fall under its authority.[12]

According to the Ministry's website, "the Brazilian Foreign Service consists of three careers: diplomat, chancery officer and chancery assistant. In April 2014, the board of employees counted with 1581 diplomats, 872 chancery officers and 603 chancery assistants."[13] The relatively small size of the service—compared, that is, to most of the services surveyed in this book—is a reflection both of the budget constraints of the time and of its elite character. Similar to the US Foreign Service, the Brazilian Foreign Service is divided into four cones—Geographic, Thematic (Functional) and Multilateral Negotiations, Consular, and Administrative—with some possibility for officers to move between them during the course of a career. Diplomats enter as Third Secretary and may be promoted sequentially to

Second Secretary, First Secretary, Counselor, Second Class Minister, and First Class Minister (Ambassador). Abroad, Second Class and First Class Ministers may exercise the function of Ambassador.[14]

In terms of *Itamaraty's* presence abroad, the Ministry of External Relations boasts a network of 226 official representations in 138 countries. This can be further broken down into 152 diplomatic missions, and 70 consular missions. The Ministry's more than 200 diplomatic representations abroad provide a range of services: they promote Brazil's interests abroad, provide various consular services to Brazilian ex-patriots and Brazilians living outside the country, offers key logistical and administrative support to Brazilian companies located abroad, and other similar functions.

Recruitment and Selection

Selection into the Brazilian diplomatic corps is extremely competitive. As an historical average, there are only around 30 slots available yearly, for which there are around 6000 applicants of which roughly 1000 will be competitive. During the Lula reforms, incoming classes increased from 30 to 100; however, after four years, incoming class sizes were cut back to their original average number. According to the Director of the *Instituto Rio Branco*, the scaling back of applicants admitted to the Institute to their original numbers has increased the magnitude and intensity of competition among potential diplomats.[15]

To be eligible to enter the Brazilian Foreign Service, a candidate must be 18 years old, Brazilian born, up-to-date with electoral obligations, have a college education, have met any military obligations, and pass physical and mental examinations. Once these requirements have been fulfilled, an applicant can begin preparing for the entrance examination, administered in three parts. The first part of the exam is in the form of multiple choice or true/false questions in the following areas: [Spoken] Portuguese Language, the History of Brazil, World History, International Politics, Geography, English Language, Economics, and Public International Law. After this initial screening, successful candidates pass to the second round, which assesses both written Portuguese through an essay and two interpretation exercises, in addition to analysis and commentary of text, and written English, through an essay, a translation, and a summary of an extended text. The third part is also written and tests candidates on the History of Brazil, the English Language, Geography, International

Politics, International law, Economics, and both Spanish and French language skills.[16] According to officers who have recently passed through the process, the English language exam is considerably more difficult than those in Spanish and French.

Brazil's elite diplomatic corps been criticized for lack of diversity and representativeness, challenges that the service is working to address.[17] Brazil's diplomats are turned out without exception via one channel: the Rio Branco Institute. The selection process for admission, while not *de jure* discriminatory, has heavily favored applicants who hail from the upper middle class to upper class with access to the kind of secondary and post-secondary education necessary for an acceptable score on the entrance exam. Moreover, until recently the exam was not held in most of Brazil's 26 states, which made it inaccessible to many would-be applicants. To address these "barriers to entry" and improve diversity, *Itamaraty* and the Rio Branco Institute have introduced reforms to the exam, expanded the number of cities in which it is administered, offered scholarships to lower income applicants, and instituted a quota of 20% for candidates of African descent. These changes led to a dramatic increase in applications, from 2556 in 1999 to 8869 in 2010.[18]

Professional Development and Training

Professional development and training for Brazilian diplomats begins immediately after matriculation into the Rio Branco Institute. The Institute's Diplomatic Training Program spans three semesters of theoretical and practical coursework. The program includes a core curriculum of required disciplines, including Law, Economics, Diplomacy and Politics, Diplomatic Language, English, Spanish, French, and elective classes.[19] In their third semester, diplomats finalize their formal training at the Rio Branco Institute by completing part-time internships in various divisions and departments of the Ministry of Foreign Affairs.[20]

The Rio Branco Institute also offers two professional development and training classes for diplomats at other levels of the career, Diplomacy Refresher Course (*Curso de Aperfeicomento de Diplomatas*—CAD) and Advanced Studies Course (*Curso de Altos Estudos*—CAE). The successful completion of the CAD is a requirement for promotion from the level of Second Secretary to First Secretary. The CAD traditionally included lectures at the Institute by senior ministry officials on issues of diplomacy and foreign policy, as well as academic lectures by university professors on contemporary politics and the Brazilian economy. In the past few years, as a cost-saving measure, the CAD consists of readings in five subject areas and essays submitted via email.

Similarly, the Advanced Studies Course (CAE) is a requirement for promotion from the position of Counselor to Second Class Minister. It is a highly demanding examination that screens out many officers from promotion to the most senior ranks. Unique among the services covered in this book, to fulfill the CAE and qualify for promotion, all officers must complete a major research paper—the equivalent of a master's thesis—of between 150 and 200 pages on a topic of "practical relevance and usefulness" to Brazilian diplomacy that contributes to "historiography or Brazilian diplomatic thinking."[21] Many of the best of these are publicly available on the website of the Alexandre de Gusmão Foundation.

Another unusual element of professional training at *Itamaraty* are its diplomatic "country visits." Similar to the practice in the Indian Foreign Service of a 12-day visit to a remote village and the *Bharat Darshan*, a tour of major cultural, commercial, and historical sites, these visits are a method of better connecting diplomats with the citizens they serve. Diplomats visit different states in Brazil, particularly those that are remote or impoverished. This exercise is also meant as a way of encouraging more applications, or at least more familiarity, from underserved areas of the country.

Like every other diplomatic service we studied, competition is fierce all the way through the ranks. The shift from an elite to a more meritocratic service, along with more recent affirmative action efforts, has created certain tensions. Additionally, during the expansion in Lula/Amorim years, certain promotion criteria were temporarily lifted, in what was known as the "trigger" (*gatilho*). As a result, there are too many people at the lower levels and too few places at the top. With the change of the mandatory retirement age from 70 to 75 for all government officials, there is even less room at the top. Where promotion to Second Secretary used to occur between two and three years after joining the service, it is now common for this promotion to take as long as six or seven years. Unless some legislative reform is undertaken, it will become nearly impossible for diplomats who entered the service in the past few years to have a chance of progressing beyond the level of Counselor. This is a topic of considerable contention within *Itamaraty*, as it is in many other institutions, with opinions naturally breaking down by age and seniority.[22]

Leadership is obviously highly valued in the Brazilian diplomatic service, but formal leadership training is not as prominent as in say, the British Foreign and Commonwealth Office (FCO). If the FCO has erred too far in the direction of what its critics call "managerialism," *Itamaraty* may be guilty of prizing diplomatic over management training, relying instead on informal mentorship and on-the-job learning as diplomats progress through the ranks. Certainly, the CAD and CAE examinations are more notable for their intensive preparation in language, history, and the arts of diplomacy than in modern management and leadership training.

LEADERSHIP

Unlike most countries covered in this book, Brazil's foreign minister is typically not a politician but a career diplomat, Second in command is the Secretary-General, a position always reserved for a senior career diplomat. *Itamaraty* is thus among the most professional of all the diplomatic services.

While Brazil does not have an "up or out" policy like the US Foreign Service, the required CAE (Advanced Studies Course) serves to "select out" many officers at an earlier stage—advanced mid-career or 12 to 15 years into a career—than advancement into the Senior Foreign Service in the United States. All Brazilian diplomats of ambassadorial rank are career diplomats. Most senior Brazilian diplomats hail from wealthy or well to do families; this is evidenced through the fact that many Brazilian diplomats obtained their post-secondary education abroad, from such prominent universities as the London School of Economics, Cambridge, the Sorbonne, Sciences Po, and Harvard. The typical Brazilian ambassador will have an advanced degree in French, Public Administration, International Affairs, Economics, or Law.

The gender disparity at *Itamaraty* is conspicuous. Those in prominent positions today are almost men; representation of women at the upper echelons of their diplomatic corps is sparse. Female representation is limited at all levels, but underrepresentation gets worse at the top. Around 22% of all diplomats and 10% of ambassadors are women. A recent social media campaign, *#maismulheresdiplomatas* ("#morefemalediplomats") aims to get more women to apply to the Foreign Service. Female diplomats have also mobilized in recent years, mostly through an informal group which has protested low levels of promotions of women and funded a documentary in celebration of the 100th anniversary of the admission of the first female diplomat.[23] During his tenure, Foreign Minister Amorim established a system to promote the advancement of female diplomats to the higher echelons of the service, an initiative that has been continued by his successors.

In addition to seniority and merit, there are other requirements which diplomats must fulfill in order to reach the highest levels of the foreign ministry in Brazil. These include having spent a minimum of three years abroad in each position they have held, and completion of specific courses and examinations in order to reach certain positions (for instance the CAD for promotion from Second Secretary to First Secretary and the CAE for promotion from Counselor to Second Class Minister). Furthermore, promotions, with the exception of the first, are voted on by diplomats' peers and superiors. Evaluations to the most senior levels are also subject to approval of the Foreign Minister or even the President. In order to become an ambassador, it is law that a diplomat must have served at least 20 years, of which ten must have been spent abroad.[24]

Role in Foreign Policy-Making

Despite Brazil's long tradition of "presidentialism"—and with the exception of the period of military dictatorship—*Itamaraty* has been the lead agency not only in the implementation but also in the making of Brazilian foreign policy. This seeming contradiction has been explained this way:

> On the one hand, Brazilian presidentialism concentrates too much agency in the president's hands, giving him/her, when particularly attentive to foreign policy issues, a great latitude for action. On the other hand, the long-standing professionalism of Brazilian diplomats thanks to the process of institutionalization of Brazilian diplomacy gives it a highly complex, bureaucratic, and professional profile, and therefore, a strong authority to formulate foreign policy even when the presidency was being conducted by strong hands.[25]

Additionally, Brazil's brand of presidential rule has been characterized as "coalition presidentialism," meaning that *Itamaraty* is often able to play a bridging role among the different (and antagonistic) political parties that make up the coalition. As an example, President Fernando Henrique Cardoso (1995–2002) governed through a heterodox alliance of his own Social Democratic Party, the centrist Brazilian Democratic Movement, and the right-wing Brazilian Progressive Party. Many of Cardoso's signature initiatives, from the (belated) signing of the Nuclear Non-Proliferation Treaty to the shift toward a more assertive South America policy, actually originated in *Itamaraty*.[26]

Even during the Lula presidency (2003–2010), characterized by a large number of initiatives coming from the Planalto Palace (housing the presidency), President Lula relied heavily on his experienced foreign minister, Celso Amorim.[27] Indeed, most of these initiatives came out of *Itamaraty*, whose role in policy making was actually strengthened under Lula. In his memoirs, Amorim describes in great detail *Itamaraty's* role and his personal diplomacy leading up to the 2010 Tehran Declaration, in which Brazil and Turkey sought to broker a negotiated resolution to the Iranian nuclear program. In this episode as in others covered in his book, Amorim shows how a presidential initiative was shaped, adjusted, and implemented by professional diplomats under the authority of President Lula and in constant interaction with him and his staff.[28]

Brazil has no body analogous to the US National Security Council to coordinate policy among the foreign policy agencies, relying instead on a foreign affairs advisor, normally a senior diplomat, within the office of the president, along with diplomats in liaison positions in other key ministries. The military plays a key role in the National Defense Council (NDC), but that body's responsibilities are limited to advising the president on declarations of war and peace and other defense matters. (There had been a National Security Council—with the same restricted mandate—until 1988, when the new Constitution renamed it the NDC.) The NDC has no jurisdiction on broader matters of foreign policy, and since the end of the *ditadura* Brazil's military has generally played a low-key role in foreign policy and other matters of national policy. This is changing with the election in 2018 of retired military officer Jair Bolsonaro as president and his early moves to install army officers in key ministerial positions. As of this writing, the military's growing role seems to be focused more on domestic law and order than on external affairs, and the basic contours of Brazilian foreign policy seem like to persist, aside from a shift away from what Bolsonaro decries as the "globalism" of the Lula yeas. Certainly, there are no external threats on the near horizon that would thrust the armed forces into a more prominent foreign policy role.

Even before the latest election, several trends had eroded *Itamaraty's* privileged place in foreign policy making. As in other countries covered in this volume, globalization has produced new foreign policy agents and actors who often take the lead, or at least share power, in foreign policy making. The Ministry of Finance and Ministry of Planning have long played important roles in economic and commercial policy, and many other ministries with predominantly domestic mandates also exert influence on foreign policy issues related to health, education, environment, agriculture, and culture. Civil society likewise exerts influence through Congressional standing committees as well as through powerful trade union associations such as the Federation of Industries of the State of São Paulo (FIESP, in its Portuguese acronym).[29] As the Brazilian scholars Carlos Milani and Leticia Pinheiro have put it:

> Until recently, it was common to refer to Brazilian foreign policy as a state policy relatively immune to changes and to the interference of governmental agencies, business, media, and civil society. This is in part due to the professionalism and negotiation capacities of *Itamaraty* and its relative autonomy in defining Brazilian foreign policy agendas… [but] several events illustrate a loss of this alleged and somehow cult-like belief in the autonomy of *Itamaraty*.[30]

Nonetheless, with a longstanding and deeply rooted national tradition that favors international law, multilateralism, non-interference, and negotiation, Brazil's foreign policy is particularly well-suited to diplomacy. As has been noted, its borders were secured not by conquest but by negotiation. As a middle power with few external threats, Brazil continues to rely on diplomatic virtuosity rather than military or economic power for its security. In short, Brazil has developed and maintained an effective diplomatic corps because it needs one.

Preparations for the Future

Henry Kissinger once characterized Germany as being "too big for Europe, too small for the world." Allowing for certain crucial differences—the absence of militarism in Brazil's case and the much larger disparity in size in their respective regions—the same might be said of Brazil in its region: "too big for South America, too small for the world." As former foreign minister Celso Amorim put it, "Even if Brazil is big, it's not big enough to face the big blocs like the United States, which is a bloc in itself, China, which is a bloc in itself, or the European Union."[31] Just as Germany found it necessary to play its global role mainly in the context of the EU, Brazil has seen regional leadership through "consensual hegemony" as a vehicle to greater global influence.[32]

Driven by regional rivalry with Argentina as well as a desire to offset US dominance in the hemisphere, Brazil has seen sub-regional integration in the "southern cone" as a vehicle for regional leadership and ultimately for a stronger global role. Brazil played a key role in the creation of MERCOSUR (the Common Market of the South) and UNASUR (Union of South American Nations), as well as in leading the UN Stabilization Mission in Haiti from 2004–2017 and in mediating regional conflicts between its neighbors.[33] It also negotiated with Argentina a series of agreements to regulate nuclear technology and ban its use for military purposes, leading to their joint ratification of the Treaty of Tlatelolco, providing for a nuclear-weapons-free zone in Latin America.[34]

Under the presidency of Luiz Inácio Lula de Silva (2003–2011), Brazil aspired more openly to a global role. This it did by "acting globally" (to use the title of a book by Lula's foreign minister Celso Amorim) in tactical collaboration with other rising economic powers in an alphabet soup of loose groupings: the BRICS (Brazil, Russia, India, China, and South Africa), BASIC (Brazil, South Africa, India, and China), and IBSA (India, Brazil, and South Africa). Brazil also has been an active proponent of the Group of 20 (G-20), which it saw as a more representative and relevant grouping than the longstanding G-7 and a vehicle for Brazil to exercise greater influence a de facto spokesman for the Global South. Despite the absence of deep shared interests or a coherent policy agenda, the BRICS, in particular, have been successful in presenting a common front and forcing change in Western-dominated international institutions. Among the joint initiatives—some successful, some not—undertaken by the BRICS countries were their opposition to restrictions on Russian participation in the 2014 G20 summit, launching of a New Development Bank, and efforts to transform the emerging global norm of "Responsibility to Protect" (R2P), which they saw as giving Western countries too much license to intervene in the affairs of other states. In its place, then-Brazilian Foreign Minister Antonio Patriota advanced the norm of "Responsibility While Protecting," intended to raise the moral standard regarding possible interventions.[35]

Brazil has been among the most active proponents of multilateralism and global governance, from its early support of the League of Nations and its ongoing active role in the United Nations. At the same time, it has been a harsh critic of US dominance of and in international institutions, which former foreign minister Celso Amorim called "multilateralism placed in the service of unipolarity."[36] The complaint is underscored by Brazil's active "Let Us In" campaign, waged since the 1990s, to join the UN Security Council as a permanent member.[37] Another former foreign minister, Antonio Patriota, made a similar complaint: "What do we want? A multilateral system in which everyone is subject to the same rules."[38]

It is worth underscoring how many of the foreign policy priorities and challenges listed above relate to diplomacy rather than power projection, in contrast to the overwhelming security focus of US foreign policy or the strong commercial focus of German or Japanese foreign policy. Of course, the *ends* of Brazilian policy are the political, economic, and social objectives set out in Article 3 of the 1988 Constitution: "I. to build a free, just and unified society; II. to guarantee national development; III. to eradicate poverty…and reduce social and regional inequalities; IV. to promote the well-being of all…." Major foreign policy decisions, as is the case with every other country covered in this book, are made by the senior political leadership and with the growing involvement of other ministries and actors. Within those parameters, however, the role of the Brazilian foreign ministry has been perhaps the strongest and least contested of any of the world's largest diplomatic services.

Itamaraty has been hard hit in the last several years. Lula's successor, Dilma Rousseff, evinced little interest in foreign policy, and her administration soon became mired in corruption scandals that ultimately led to her impeachment in 2016. Political turmoil coupled with the worst recession in the country's history led to sharp budget and staffing cuts in the ministry and freezes on new hiring. Following the rapid expansion of the diplomatic corps under Lula, these new constraints were particularly disruptive.[39] Lack of investment in new technology and inadequate preparation for the information revolution have further hampered *Itamaraty's* adaptation.

The election of President Jair Bolsonaro and his appointment of Ernesto Araújo as foreign minister marked a sharp departure in Brazilian diplomacy—and a dramatic reversal of the globally focused foreign policy of Lula. Fifty-one years old and having only recently risen to ambassadorial rank, Araújo promised "to liberate Brazilian foreign policy" through a religious-based nationalism.[40] Where this orientation will lead and how long it will last are open questions. Certainly, the Brazilian Foreign Service faces a challenging period ahead. Yet one suspects that Celso Amorim is right that "Brazil is too important to stay out of global issues,"[41] and that the enduring historical and geopolitical factors that contributed to *Itamaraty's* historic role will, sooner or later, reassert themselves. Current Brazilian diplomats may take comfort in the words of former minister Rubens Ricúpero: "The values that Rio Branco espoused—peace, moderation, trust in international law, non-intervention and what would now be called the pursuit of soft power—became integral to Brazil's idea of itself."[42]

Acknowledgment *The authors wish to thank the following diplomats and scholars who were consulted in researching and writing this chapter:* Larissa Schneider Calza, Jean Karydakis, Franklin Neto, Jose Estanislau do Amaral Souza Neto, Carla Silva-Muhammad, Antonio de Aguiar Patriota, Paulo Sotero, and Chandler Stolp.

NOTES

1. The original *Itamaraty* Palace, built in the mid-nineteenth century, housed the Foreign Ministry in Rio de Janeiro from 1899 to 1970; the new one, designed by the architect Oscar Niemeyer and given the same name, has housed the ministry in Brasilia since 1970.
2. Celso Amorim, *Acting Globally: Memoirs of Brazil's Assertive Foreign Policy* (New York: Rowman & Littlefield, 2017).
3. Sean W. Burges and Fabrício H. Chagas Bastos, "The Importance of Presidential Leadership for Brazilian Foreign Policy," *Policy Studies* vol. 38, no. 3, 278–9.
4. "French Republic," http://www.itamaraty.gov.br/en/ficha-pais/6080-french-republic. Accessed February 11, 2019.
5. See, e.g., the interview with Eumano Silva, author of "The Death of a Diplomat." in *Gazeta Online*, January 15, 2017: https://www.gazetaonline.com.br/noticias/politica/2017/11/itamaraty-tinha-rede-clandestina-de-espionagem-e-perseguia-adversarios-no-exterior-1014109418.html. Accessed February 4, 2019. See also Fabiano Post, "CIEX: Itamaraty and the Military Dictatorship," Revista Opera, October 24, 2018: http://diplomatizzando.blogspot.com/2018/10/ciex-o-itamaraty-e-ditadura-militar.html. Accessed February 4, 2019; and a doctoral dissertation on the *Itamaraty's* role during the *ditadura*, published in 2010 by the Federal University of Pernambuco: *Habitus Diplomático: Um Estudo do Itamaraty em Tempos de Regime Militar (1964–1985)* (Diplomatic Structures: A Study of the Itamaraty Under Military Rule (1964–1985)), https://repositorio.ufpe.br/handle/123456789/9199. Accessed February 4, 2019.
6. Carlos R. S. Milani and Leticia Pinheiro, "The Politics of Brazilian Foreign Policy and Its Analytical Challenges," *Foreign Policy Analysis* vol. 13, no. 2 (2017): 13, 281.
7. José Vicente de Sá Pimentel, ed., *Brazilian Diplomatic Thought—Policymakers and Agents of Foreign Policy (1750–1964)* (Brasilia: *Fundação Alexandre de Gusmão*, 2016), 3.

8. Ibid., 19.
9. Interview with Ambassador José Estanislau do Amaral Souza Neto, Director of the Rio Branco Institute.
10. *Parecer Preliminar: Projeto de Lei Orcamentaria para 2015, Portal Orcamento Orcamento (Preliminary Opinion: Draft Budget Law for 2015)*. (*Congreso Nacional, Comissão Mista de Planos, Orcamentos Publicos e Fiscalizacao*, 2014), 25; Oliver Stuenkel, "Brazilian Foreign Policy: Into the Dark." *Post-Western World*. 12 December 2014. https://www.postwesternworld.com/2014/12/12/brazilian-foreign-policy-into/. Accessed February 11, 2019.
11. There were nine under-secretariats up until the new Bolsonaro administration, which reduced the number to seven.
12. The organizational structure of the Foreign Ministry has been changed under the new administration of President Jair Bolsonaro in 2019, but the scope of these changes was not clear at the time of this writing.
13. "*Itamaraty* and the Foreign Service Careers." *Ministry of Foreign Affairs*. http://www.itamaraty.gov.br/en/perguntas-frequentes-artigos/19384-itamaraty-and-the-foreign-service-careers#I9. Accessed February 10, 2019.
14. Ibid.
15. Interview with Ambassador José Estanislau do Amaral Souza Neto, Director of the Rio Branco Institute.
16. "Concurso De Admissao a Carreira Diplomatica." http://www.institutoriobranco.itamaraty.gov.br/concurso-de-admissao-a-carreira-de-diplomata. Accessed February 11, 2019.
17. See, for example, Lucia Garcia-Navarro, "For Affirmative Action, Brazil Sets up Controversial Board to Determine Race." National Public Radio. 29 September 2016. http://www.npr.org/sections/parallels/2016/09/29/495665329/for-affirmative-action-brazil-sets-up-controversial-boards-to-determine-race; Cleuci de Oliveira, "Brazil's New Problem With Blackness," *Foreign Policy*, April 5, 2017, https://foreignpolicy.com/2017/04/05/brazils-new-problem-with-blackness-affirmative-action/. Accessed February 11, 2019; and Edward E. Telles, *Another America: The Significance of Skin Color in Brazil* (Princeton: Princeton University Press, 2004).
18. Carlos Aurélio Pimenta De Faria, Dawisson Belém Lopes, and Guilherme Casarões, "*Itamaraty* on the Move: Institutional and Political Change in Brazilian Foreign Service under Lula Da Silva's Presidency (2003–2010)," *Bulletin of Latin American Research* vol. 32, no. 4 (2013): 468–82. https://doi.org/10.1111/blar.12067.
19. "Instituto Rio Branco." The International Forum on Diplomatic Training. 14 March 2010.
    http://forum.diplomacy.edu/profile/instituto-rio-branco. Accessed February 11, 2019.

20. Ministry of Foreign Affairs, "The Ministry." http://www.itamaraty.gov.br/en/the-ministry. Accessed February 11, 2019.
21. "Itamaraty and Foreign Service Careers."
22. These insights are based on discussions with current Brazilian diplomats, Washington, D.C., August 2, 2018.
23. Ibid.
24. Carlos Aurélio Pimenta De Faria, Dawisson Belém Lopes, and Guilherme Casarões, "*Itamaraty* on the Move: Institutional and Political Change in Brazilian Foreign Service under Lula Da Silva's Presidency (2003–2010)," *Bulletin of Latin American Research* vol. 32, no. 4 (2013): 468–82. https://doi.org/10.1111/blar.12067.
25. Milani and Pinheiro, "The Politics of Brazilian Foreign Policy," 278–9.
26. Sean W. Burges and Fabrício H. Chagas Bastos, "The importance of presidential leadership for Brazilian foreign policy," *Policy Studies* vol. 38, no. 3, 283.
27. Ibid., 284–5.
28. Amorim, *Acting Globally*.
29. Ibid., 289–90.
30. Milani and Pinheiro, "The Politics of Brazilian Foreign Policy," 281. See also Oliver Stuenkel, "The domestic politics of Brazilian foreign policy," *Post-Western World*, May 1, 2017 https://www.postwesternworld.com/2017/05/01/domestic-politics-brazilian/. Accessed February 3, 2019.
31. "The Wholesale Attack on Brazilian Sovereignty: An Interview with Former Foreign Minister Celso Amorim, *Truthdig*, May 23, 2018. https://www.truthdig.com/articles/the-wholesale-attack-on-brazilian-sovereignty-an-interview-with-former-foreign-minister-celso-amorim/. Accessed February 3, 2019.
32. Oliver Stuenkel and Matthew M. Taylor, "Brazil on the Global Stage: Origins and Consequences of Brazil's Challenge to the Global Liberal Order," in Oliver Stuenkel and Matthew M. Taylor, eds. *Brazil on the Global Stage: Power, Ideas, and the Liberal International Order* (New York: Palgrave Macmillan, 2015), p. 3.
33. Ibid., 2–4; and Arlene B. Tickner, "Rising Brazil and South America," in Steve Smith, Amelia Hadfield, and Tim Dunne, eds., *Foreign Policy: Theories, Actors, Cases* (Oxford, UK: Oxford University Press, 2nd edition, 2012), 368, 373, and 375–80.
34. Tickner, "Rising Brazil," 376; and Rodrigo Mallea, Matias Spektor, and Nicholas J. Wheeler, eds., *The Origins of Nuclear Cooperation: A Critical Oral History Between Argentina and Brazil* (Washington, D.C.: Woodrow Wilson International Center for Scholars, 2012): https://www.wilsoncenter.org/publication/the-origins-nuclear-cooperation. Accessed February 9, 2019.

35. These cases are all examined in Oliver Stuenkel, *The BRICS and the Future of Global Order* (New York: Lexington Books, 2015). See also Stuenkel and Taylor, "Brazil on the Global Stage," 4–10.
36. Cited in Stuenkel and Taylor, "Brazil on the Global Stage," 12.
37. Celso Amorim, "Let Us In: Why Barack Obama must support Brazil's drive for a permanent seat on the U.N. Security Council," *Foreign Policy*, March 11, 2014. See also Eugênio Vargas Garcia, Maria Clara de Paula Tusco, and Sérgio Eduardo Moreira Lima, eds., *A Security Council for the 21st Century: Challenges and Prospects* (Brasilia: Fundação Alexandre de Gusmão, 2017).
38. Cited in Stuenkel and Taylor, "Brazil on the Global Stage, 12.
39. Caio Pizetta Torres, "What (not) to Expect from Brazilian Diplomacy." *Plus55: Brazil Opinion*. February 19, 2016. http://plus55.com/opinion/2016/02/what-not-to-expect-from-brazilian-diplomacy.
40. "The contradictions of Brazil's new foreign policy," *The Economist*, January 12, 2019, 30.
41. "'Brazil is too important to stay out of global issues', says Celso Amorim." http://www.institutolula.org/en/brazil-is-too-important-to-stay-out-of-global-issues-says-celso-amorim. Accessed February 9, 2019.
42. Cited in "Open or closed? The contradictions of Brazil's new foreign policy," *The Economist*, January 12, 2019, 30.

References

Amorim, C. 2014, March 11. Let Us In: Why Barack Obama Must Support Brazil's Drive for a Permanent Seat on the U.N. Security Council. *Foreign Policy*, March 11, 2014.

———. 2017. *Acting Globally: Memoirs of Brazil's Assertive Foreign Policy*. New York: Rowman & Littlefield.

Batista, D.N. 2010. *Habitus diplomático: um estudo do Itamaraty em tempos de regime militar (1964–1985)*. Federal University of Pernambuco. https://repositorio.ufpe.br/handle/123456789/9199. Accessed February 4, 2019.

'Brazil Is Too Important to Stay Out of Global Issues,' Says Celso Amorim. *Instituto Lula*. http://www.institutolula.org/en/brazil-is-too-important-to-stay-out-of-global-issues-says-celso-amorim. Accessed February 9, 2019.

Burges, S.W., and F.H. Chagas Bastos. 2017. The Importance of Presidential Leadership for Brazilian Foreign Policy. *Policy Studies* 38 (3): 277–290.

Concurso de admissao a carreira diplomatica. 2017. *Instituto Rio Banco*. http://www.institutoriobranco.itamaraty.gov.br/concurso-de-admissao-a-carreira-de-diplomata. Accessed February 11, 2019.

de Faria, C.A.P., D.B. Lopes, and G. Casarões. 2013. Itamaraty on the Move: Institutional and Political Change in Brazilian Foreign Service Under Lula Da Silva's Presidency (2003–2010). *Bulletin of Latin American Research* 32 (4): 468–482. https://doi.org/10.1111/blar.12067.

French Republic. n.d. *Ministry of Foreign Affairs.* http://www.itamaraty.gov.br/en/ficha-pais/6080-french-republic. Accessed February 11, 2019.

Garcia, E.V., M.C.P. Tusco, and S.E. Moreira Lima, eds. 2017. *A Security Council for the 21st Century: Challenges and Prospects.* Brasilia: Fundação Alexandre de Gusmão.

Garcia-Navarro, L. 2016, September 29. For Affirmative Action, Brazil Sets up Controversial Board to Determine Race. *National Public Radio.* http://www.npr.org/sections/parallels/2016/09/29/495665329/for-affirmative-action-brazil-sets-up-controversial-boards-to-determine-race. Accessed February 11, 2019.

Instituto Rio Branco. 2010. *The International Forum on Diplomatic Training.* http://forum.diplomacy.edu/profile/instituto-rio-branco.

Itamaraty and the Foreign Service Careers. n.d.. http://www.itamaraty.gov.br/en/perguntas-frequentes-artigos/19384-itamaraty-and-the-foreign-service-careers#I11. Accessed February 11, 2019.

Mallea, R., M. Spektor, and N.J. Wheeler, eds. 2012. *The Origins of Nuclear Cooperation: A Critical Oral History Between Argentina and Brazil.* Washington, DC: Woodrow Wilson International Center for Scholars. https://www.wilsoncenter.org/publication/the-origins-nuclear-cooperation. Accessed February 9, 2019.

Milani, C.R.S., and L. Pinheiro. 2017. The Politics of Brazilian Foreign Policy and Its Analytical Challenges. *Foreign Policy Analysis* (2017): 278–296.

Ministry of Foreign Affairs. n.d. *Itamaraty.* http://www.itamaraty.gov.br/en/the-ministry http://www.itamaraty.gov.br/en/faq#I1. Accessed February 11, 2019.

de Oliveira, C. 2017, April 5. Brazil's New Problem with Blackness. *Foreign Policy.* https://foreignpolicy.com/2017/04/05/brazils-new-problem-with-blackness-affirmative-action/. Accessed February 11, 2019.

Open or Closed? The Contradictions of Brazil's New Foreign Policy. 2019, January 12. *The Economist,* 30.

Parecer preliminar: Projeto de lei orcamentaria para 2015 (Preliminary opinion: Draft budget law for 2015). 2014. *Congreso Nacional, Comissão Mista de Planos, Orcamentos Publicos e Fiscalizacao.* https://www12.senado.leg.br/orcamento/documentos/loa/2015/elaboracao/parecer-preliminar/relatorio-preliminar. Accessed February 11, 2019.

Pimentel, J.V.S., ed. 2016. *Brazilian Diplomatic Thought—Policymakers and Agents of Foreign Policy (1750–1964).* Brasilia: Fundação Alexandre de Gusmão.

Post, F. 2018, October 24. CIEX: *Itamaraty* and the Military Dictatorship. *Revista Opera.* http://diplomatizzando.blogspot.com/2018/10/ciex-o-itamaraty-e-ditadura-militar.html. Accessed February 4, 2019.

Silva, E. 2017, January 15. The Death of a Diplomat. *Gazeta Online.* https://www.gazetaonline.com.br/noticias/politica/2017/11/itamaraty-tinha-rede-clandestina-de-espionagem-e-perseguia-adversarios-no-exterior-1014109418.html. Accessed February 4, 2019.

Stuenkel, O. 2014, December 12. Brazilian Foreign Policy: Into the Dark. *Post-Western World*. http://www.postwesternworld.com/2014/12/12/brazilian-foreign-policy-into/.

———. 2015. *The BRICS and the Future of Global Order*. New York: Lexington Books.

———. 2017, May 1. The Domestic Politics of Brazilian Foreign Policy. *Post-Western World*. https://www.postwesternworld.com/2017/05/01/domestic-politics-brazilian/. Accessed February 3, 2019.

Stuenkel, O., and M.M. Taylor. 2015. Brazil on the Global Stage: Origins and Consequences of Brazil's Challenge to the Global Liberal Order. In *Brazil on the Global Stage: Power, Ideas, and the Liberal International Order*, ed. O. Stuenkel and M.M. Taylor. New York: Palgrave Macmillan.

Telles, E.E. 2014. *Another America: The Significance of Skin Color in Brazil*. Princeton: Princeton University Press.

The Wholesale Attack on Brazilian Sovereignty: An Interview with Former Foreign Minister Celso Amorim. 2018, May 23. *Truthdig*. https://www.truthdig.com/articles/the-wholesale-attack-on-brazilian-sovereignty-an-interview-with-former-foreign-minister-celso-amorim/. Accessed February 3, 2019.

Tickner, A.B. 2012. Rising Brazil and South America. In *Foreign Policy: Theories, Actors, Cases*, ed. S. Smith, A. Hadfield, and T. Dunne, 2nd ed. Oxford: Oxford University Press.

CHAPTER 2

China

Michael Deegan, Joel Keralis, and Robert Hutchings

Executive Summary

The Ministry of Foreign Affairs of China (MFA) is the Chinese government agency charged with matters of diplomacy and foreign affairs. Although China's history of relations with other countries and peoples is an ancient one, the development of a modern diplomatic service came much later than for other countries surveyed in this book. It was not until the early twentieth century that China established a fully functioning Ministry of Foreign Affairs, whose development was subsequently stifled by the Chinese civil war from 1928 to 1949 and then by the early period of domestic consolidation under Communist rule. The full "professionalization" of the service came only after the death of Mao

---

M. Deegan
2018 Master of Arts Degrees, Global Policy Studies and Russian, East European, and Eurasian Studies, The University of Texas at Austin, Austin, TX, USA

J. Keralis
2017 Master of Arts Degrees, Global Policy Studies and Asian Studies, The University of Texas at Austin, Austin, TX, USA

R. Hutchings (✉)
Lyndon B. Johnson School of Public Affairs, The University of Texas at Austin, Austin, TX, USA
e-mail: rhutchings@austin.utexas.edu

© The Author(s) 2020
R. Hutchings, J. Suri (eds.), *Modern Diplomacy in Practice*,
https://doi.org/10.1007/978-3-030-26933-3_2

Zedong in 1976 and China's opening to the outside world beginning in the 1980s.

Chinese diplomats are known for their exceptional discipline as well as for their linguistic and regional expertise. For many years, recruitment into the diplomatic service came almost exclusively from the Beijing Foreign Language University (*Beiwai*), leading to internal criticism that "translator diplomacy" had come at the expense of a fully prepared diplomatic corps. This is changing, however, as the new generation of Chinese diplomats has been recruited from a wider variety of international relations and public policy schools, with skill sets that match those of other leading diplomatic services. Professional training is identified as a weakness, however, particularly in that the MFA has sharply curtailed the opportunities for study abroad that earlier generations had. One distinctive feature of China's diplomatic service, similar to Russia's and because of the premium placed on loyalty, is that ambassadors to key posts serve an average of six years in the same position.

Authority over foreign policy decision making rests with the senior levels of the Communist Party, particularly the Politburo Standing Committee and its associated coordinating bodies like the National Security Commission. The Ministry of Foreign Affairs nonetheless plays a number of key roles. Through the practice of interlocking memberships, key diplomatic officials also occupy senior positions in the Communist Party, and many are important decision makers in their own rights. The MFA also is the principal executor of a foreign policy decision, and its missions abroad are the primary interface and day-to-day negotiators with foreign governments and international organizations. Through its reports and analyses, as well as participation by its staff in key coordinating bodies, the MFA also informs, shapes, and frames foreign policy decisions for the seniormost political leadership.

Looking forward, the Ministry faces a number of challenges related to party and state leader Xi Jinping's much more ambitious foreign policy. As China interacts in more complex ways with the rest of the world, coordination among the various foreign policy "actors"—military, economic, diplomatic, and other—becomes more difficult, leading also to a growing centralization of decision-making at the top. Pursuing Xi's ambitious "Belt and Road Initiative" calls for a skilled, strategically-minded, and empowered diplomatic corps, which will in turn call for a dramatic shift in the MFA's rigid and hierarchical diplomatic culture.

History and Culture

Chinese diplomacy is marked both by the "great divide" of 1949, with the victory of the Chinese Communists in the Chinese civil war, and by the deep and enduring legacies of the world's oldest civilization. The "Middle Kingdom" (*Zhongguo*, the Chinese word for China) was seen as the cultural center of the universe. It was, as John King Fairbank observed, "the great holdover, the one ancient empire that largely because of its isolation in the Far East, survived into the twentieth century."[1] Although repeatedly overrun by barbarians—which instilled a deep-seated sense of vulnerability and insecurity—Chinese civilization endured and with it an essential continuity of tradition, interests, and habits of thought and action.

Contemporary Chinese diplomats often invoke Zhang Qian and Su Wu, emissaries of the Han dynasty in the first and second centuries B.C., both of whom are household names in China today. Zhang Qian, a military officer sent by the emperor to the "Western regions," is honored for his role in opening China to the world of commercial trade and the establishment of what would later be called the Silk Road, an opening that presaged by more than two millennia China's contemporary Belt and Road Initiative. Su Wu is remembered less for his accomplishments than for his courage and loyalty despite torture and hardship during 19 years of exile. His steadfastness is echoed in the motto of the China Foreign Affairs University (CFAU), through which many current Chinese diplomats have passed: "Unswerving Loyalty, Mastery of Policies, Professional Competency, Observance of Discipline."

Historical legacies go back even further, to the fifth century B.C. and to two rough contemporaries: Confucius and Sun Tzu (Sun Zi).[2] Confucius was regularly invoked by Chinese party leader Hu Jintao (2002–2012), who found the emphasis on harmonious development in Confucian thought a useful source of support for Hu's invocation of "peaceful rise" while China focused on domestic modernization. Current Party leader Xi Jinping actively promotes Confucianism under the banner of "great power diplomacy with Chinese characteristics," meant to reassure other countries that China's ambitious foreign policy has only peaceful intentions.[3] Of course, Chinese history is as replete with militarism as that of any other great power, but the principles of peaceful coexistence and noninterference are deeply ingrained in the way Chinese diplomats portray themselves internationally.

Similarly, Sun Tzu was avidly studied and applied by Mao Zedong during the Chinese civil war, along with the even more ancient Chinese board game of *Weiqi* (or *Wei-Ch'i*, known as *Go* in Japanese and *Baduk* in Korean), on which his own revolutionary strategy was partially based. Quite different from the frontal assault and decisive battlefield victory favored by later European military strategists such as Napoleon and Clausewitz, Sun Tzu and *Weiqi* counseled indirection, patience, retreat, and encirclement.[4] Chinese diplomats play much the same game.

These historical influences are still felt, not as historical artifacts or mere diplomatic "talking points" but because the historical and geopolitical realities that gave rise to them are present today, albeit in modified form. Confucianism, apart from its guidance for personal morality, responded to the reality of an empire that was vulnerable both internally and externally and hence required a hierarchical social order domestically and a foreign policy of compromise and adjustment.[5] Similarly, Sun Tzu's *Art of War* offered guidance appropriate to China's exposed geographic position and history of invasions from "Inner Asia" through borders that were easier to penetrate than to defend. Like *Weiqi* logic, Sun Tzu's counsel responded to geostrategic circumstances that favored insurgency and "stratagems (*ji*) designed to win battles against superior forces."[6]

If the tradition of Chinese relations with other countries is an ancient one, that of a foreign office and diplomatic corps is not. It was not until the latter half of the nineteenth century that China established its first real diplomatic corps with the creation, in 1861, of an Office for the Management of all Foreign Countries, known in China as the *Zongli Yamen*,[7] and not until the early twentieth century that the office was converted to a fully functioning Ministry of Foreign Affairs. Both these developments were direct responses to foreign interventions, the allied occupation of Beijing in 1860 and the Boxer Rebellion of 1898–1901.[8] Thus, China's modern diplomacy had anti-imperialism baked in, long before the Communist takeover in 1949. China's "foreign policy" in those days reflected an insularity and defensiveness, with its encounters abroad seen not as active engagement with the rest of the world but as defending against outside incursions. China's world-view thus reflected the modern memories of humiliation and subjugation under the "unequal treaties" with Western powers, imparting a sense of victimization and national self-righteousness.

During the Republican period, 1912–1949, China was rendered additionally vulnerable by the long civil war between the Nationalist-led government and Communist insurgents that began in 1928. The task of defending the country's essentially indefensible borders—and indeed of reclaiming this vast territory as "Chinese"—fell mainly to diplomacy.[9] It was actually toward the latter years of the civil war that contemporary Chinese foreign policy was forged, as the Chinese Communist Party (CCP) led by Mao Zedong, from its wartime capital in Yan'an (Yen'an), first opened relations with the great powers. Out of this period came several enduring legacies: the fusion of foreign policy and domestic policy, the primacy of the Communist Party in foreign policy decision making, and—as a consequence of Russia's failure to provide support during the civil war—the principle of self-reliance in developing policy both at home and abroad.[10]

Thus, the "great divide" of 1949 and the creation of a distinctive Chinese Communist foreign policy had strong elements of continuity as well. The new Ministry of Foreign Affairs, created in 1949 with Premier Zhou Enlai serving concurrently as Foreign Minister, was staffed from three sources: civilian veterans of Yan'an's quasi-diplomacy, military officers from the People's Liberation Army, and foreign language students from universities.[11] The priority in the early years was, of course, on consolidating power, establishing the legitimacy of Communist and Maoist ideology, and gaining international recognition, all while postponing an active international role until the domestic rule was more secure. Subsequent years saw the development of a more pragmatic and less ideological foreign policy after Mao's death in 1976, the expansion of China's contacts with the outside world under Deng Xiaoping in the 1980s and in the 2000s under Hu Jintao, and the growing professionalism of the Chinese diplomatic service.[12]

Profile

The Ministry of Foreign Affairs of China does not publish data on the size of its diplomatic corps, but estimates from a few years ago put the number at approximately 7500 people. Around 4500 of these diplomats worked in missions abroad, making it the world's second largest diplomatic service, after the United States.[13] Those numbers likely have increased significantly in the last few years, along with an increase in the overall foreign affairs budget from $5.2 billion in 2012 to $8 billion in 2017. The budget presented by the government in March 2018 called for a further increase to $9.5 billion. This dramatic increase, based on published accounts of China's National Bureau of Statistics, is more the result of overall Chinese economic growth than of the priority accorded the MFA, whose growth rate was lower than overall government spending growth. China's foreign affairs spending remains below 1% of Gross Domestic Product, lower than that for the United States and much lower than for France or Germany. In absolute terms, China's foreign affairs budget is roughly half that of Germany's ($16.2 billion) and a quarter that of the United States ($31.3 billion).[14]

Additionally, the overall number of Chinese diplomats is somewhat misleading, in that China, out of security concerns, employs far fewer local hires at its missions abroad than is the case for most other countries. The result is that many of the lower level functions that would be performed by local hires in other services are done by regular Chinese diplomats. In terms of gender breakdown, 30.7% of MFA diplomats are women, but this percentage shrinks considerably at the senior-most ranks, with 30.4%, 24.4%, and only 7.9% women at the ranks of a counselor, consul, and ambassador, respectively.[15]

Those who work for the MFA do not choose a specific "cone" as in the United States and instead are a part of a non-differentiated service with relatively few technical experts. Unlike the British Foreign Office, which prizes generalists over specialists, the Chinese MFA puts a premium on language skills and regional expertise. Up until the late 1990s, new Chinese diplomats were drawn almost exclusively from the Beijing Foreign Language University (*Beiwai*), many serving as interpreters and translators before being entrusted with diplomatic responsibilities.[16] Officers typically spend an entire career in the same region, sometimes in the same country, earning Chinese diplomats—like their Russian counterparts—a reputation for language and regional expertise.[17] However, even as new diplomats come in with broader backgrounds and are encouraged to gain experience outside their region of primary interest, the Chinese diplomatic service continues to draw mainly from the Foreign Language University, and has been criticized for "translation diplomacy" and for lacking the diplomatic skills and "international strategic literacy" that other services instill in their rising diplomats.[18] The focus on language ability and regional expertise fits in with this general picture of China's diplomatic culture dating back long before the Communist period: Chinese diplomats are trained to report on foreign countries and represent the official position as dictated from Beijing. With the exception of a relatively few well-connected senior diplomats, they are not expected to engage directly in international negotiation or provide input to strategic decision-making to the extent that say, a Brazilian or French diplomat would routinely do.

Chinese diplomats work in China or at one of the 258 missions around the world. This number includes 163 embassies, 87 consulates, and 8 permanent missions.[19] Top officials in the MFA include the Minister of Foreign Affairs, six Vice Ministers, four Assistant Ministers, one Chief Inspector, and 28 Director Generals. The Vice Ministers have both region-specific and general administrative responsibilities. For example, the current Vice Minister in charge of Latin American affairs also has the administrative duty of overseeing "translation and interpretation." Director Generals, however, are heads of the 28 departments of the MFA. The Director General for Latin America, for example, is the point-person for Chinese foreign affairs in Latin America, and he reports to the Vice Minister.

Like most of the services surveyed in this volume, the Chinese Ministry of Foreign Affairs is organized both regionally and functionally. The regional departments of the MFA include Asia, Western Asia and North Africa, sub-Saharan Africa, the European and Central Asian Region, the European Region, North America and Oceania, and Latin America. There is one special regional department, the Department of Hong Kong, Macao, and Taiwan Affairs. There are also six non-regional, functional departments including the Department of Arms Control and the Department of Party-Related Affairs. Each functional department leads a specific function or activity necessary for the day-to-day operations of the ministry. The Department of Finance, for example, develops the budget for the MFA and coordinates the financial regulations of Chinese missions abroad. Likewise, the Consular Affairs department guides the consular operation of the Chinese MFA. These offices, along with each regional office, provide the structure within the MFA to allow the organization of information, ensuring that it flows in a hierarchical fashion.

Recruitment and Selection

Civil service positions have historically been held in high esteem in Chinese culture and are still viewed in a favorable light by the general public. As noted above, recruitment into the MFA traditionally came almost exclusively from language programs, particularly the Foreign Language University in Beijing, but the MFA increasingly looks to graduates in the humanities and international relations programs from among China's prestigious international studies and public policy schools. Typically, around 30% of new entrants are graduates of the China Foreign Affairs University (CFAU), founded in 1955 under the direction of then-Premier Zhou Enlai and affiliated with the

Ministry of Foreign Affairs. CFAU's motto, as previously observed, is "Unswerving Loyalty, Mastery of Policies, Professional Competency, Observance of Discipline." The two bookends of loyalty and discipline are noteworthy.

While the Chinese Ministry of Foreign Affairs does not enjoy the level of prestige of many of the counterpart institutions in other countries covered in this book, it nonetheless attracts a wide talent pool for potential recruitment. Applicants must clear two hurdles: the public service examination required for all government officials, and the MFA's own entrance exam, consisting of a written portion and interviews to test language ability, comprehensive skills, and knowledge of global issues. Only those from specified disciplines (usually international affairs, political science/public policy, and languages) are allowed to apply.[20] Owing to growing security concerns, the MFA reportedly imposed a rule that no new recruits may have studied overseas. All applicants must have some English language competency, and the ministry actively recruits students with a wide variety of language backgrounds, including English. An advanced degree is valued but not required, with only 30% of officers holding an advanced degree in a field related to diplomacy. Applicants join the ministry at a relatively young age with a maximum age of entry at 45. The annual intake of new officers has been between 100 and 300 each year, but that intake is believed to have increased significantly under the Xi Jinping "surge."

New hires are expected to spend their first three-year assignment at MFA headquarters in Beijing, and are not actually considered full diplomats until their first international posting. This three-year initial posting is reduced to one year for those who possess an advanced degree in a related field. In either case, the first year is considered provisional, although it is rare for new recruits to be dismissed during this period. The first year of service at the ministry is unique in that new hires work under different departments, rotating every three months, a practice that helps the candidate and MFA determine the best fit for future placement. Additionally, this structure demonstrates the lengths taken by the MFA to ensure that diplomats have been indoctrinated with a holistic understanding of their service before beginning their first assignments abroad. The initial assignment process has been described as "interactive," as the MFA and the new officer work to match knowledge, skills, and abilities to the positions available in the service. Still, all officers must be cleared for worldwide posting and might not be placed into their preferred job upon entry. Senior officers have more negotiating power when future assignments are made. Officers are expected to alternate between Beijing and overseas missions with each new posting. This rule likely exists to prevent Chinese diplomats from "going native" or becoming too dissociated from life in China and developments in Beijing. Also, it could exist in order to foster a closer ideological integration between the Communist Party and the Ministry of Foreign Affairs. Assignments, both foreign and domestic, usually last between two and four years, depending on the needs of the ministry and available vacancies.[21]

Professional Development and Training

Immediately after selection, new hires complete a six-month training course designed to familiarize them with the MFA and the Chinese diplomatic system. This training has been held at the China Foreign Affairs University, an institution that also offers mid-career officials the opportunity to pursue graduate education while stationed at MFA headquarters in Beijing. The new China Diplomatic Academy, which officially opened in March 2016, was intended to take over training courses for MFA diplomats allowing for more direct involvement of the Minister and ministry's senior ranks. Graduates of the China Foreign Affairs University are exempted from this training, but it is not known if there will be any exemptions for future training after, as is planned, the programs are transferred to the China Diplomatic Academy.[22] There is an additional one-month training with the People's Liberation Army where recruits participate in military drills and physical training, but there is no published information on the size and scope of this optional training.

Junior officers are required to participate in a certain number of training modules or classes in order to be eligible for promotion. There are both long-term courses that can last up to two years and short-term courses that span only a few days or weeks. These training sessions are available regularly and cover a variety of different subject material relating to professional development, job skills, and job knowledge. Officers choose when they want to take courses and gain credits for passing them, and a certain number of training credits are necessary for junior officers to be promoted. This incentive-based training system demonstrates that the Chinese MFA promotes a culture of continuous professional development. MFA employees have a clear understanding of how to move up through the ranks and are given the tools necessary to do so. Occasionally, officers are asked to help lead these professional development initiatives in addition to their usual duties.[23]

Until recently, approximately 140 officers were sent to major national and international universities each year to complete a full year of graduate-level academic study, but this practice evidently has been stopped or greatly curtailed.[24] Selection for this additional academic training was a strong indicator of future promotion to leadership ranks and officers of all levels are eligible to apply. Promotion to senior ranks begins after ten years of service, and is accompanied by a comprehensive, 360-degree review process which involves the participation of both superiors and subordinates. Lower ranking officers uninterested in or unable to achieve promotion to senior ranks are able to stay at their current rank until retirement, and all MFA employees face a mandatory retirement age of 55 for women and 65 for men, although the Chinese government intends to slowly increase the mandatory retirement age over the next several years.[25]

According to currently serving Chinese diplomats, the strengths of the MFA's professional development—and of China's diplomatic corps more generally—are discipline, professionalism, language ability, and regional expertise. Training is seen as a weakness, as is the small number of current diplomats who were educated abroad.[26] US diplomats and scholars who have worked closely with Chinese counterparts report a lack of initiative and capacity for independent judgment, though this is said to be changing with younger Chinese diplomats, who are more confident in dealing with foreigners and can be more demanding, pushy, and sometimes arrogant.[27] As will be discussed later in the chapter, this evolution roughly coincides with the evolution of China's strategy and style from "peaceful rise" to "great power diplomacy with Chinese characteristics."

LEADERSHIP

An institutionalized promotion system emerged after Mao's death in 1976, as the MFA (and the Chinese government generally) move "away from charismatic to legal-rational modes of legitimation."[28] The ministry does not publish its promotion criteria, but according to interviews conducted by former Indian Ambassador Kishan Rana, promotions at lower levels are based on a combination of years of service, a written examination, interviews, and recommendations from the immediate supervisor and the next higher-level official for final review by the Director General heading the division. Training is mandatory for major promotions, such as to Division Chief, and the most important training programs are run by the Communist Party.[29] Virtually senior officials, and the vast majority of junior ones as well, are Communist Party members.[30] As is the case with other diplomatic services surveyed in this volume, current and former Chinese diplomats complain that the slow sequencing of promotions and the preference given for seniority, while delays in filling key diplomatic posts make it hard for the emerging generation of diplomats to rise to the highest levels.[31]

An interesting feature of the Chinese diplomatic service is that all those selected for ambassadorships must spend three months attending a course run by the China Foreign Affairs University that includes extensive travel around the country, much as Indian and Brazilian diplomats do earlier in their professional training. Additionally, the most senior officials appointed to the rank of Vice Minister must first successfully pass through a six-month program at the Communist Party Central Party School.[32]

Ambassadors are appointed in three ranks based on the importance of the post to which they are assigned: Vice Minister, Director General, and Deputy Director General. Some Chinese ambassadors are appointed in their 40s, but those at the more senior levels are typically much older. The average time in post for ambassadors is 3.5 years, but those at the most critical posts—that is, those at the level of Vice Minister—remain in post an average of six years, and two thirds of them are near the mandatory retirement age of 65. Beijing has left trusted ambassadors at high priority embassies such as Washington, Moscow, or London in their posts for as many as nine years. For example, China's current (2019) ambassador to the United States, Cui Tiankai, has been in his post for six years already. In this regard, the Chinese MFA is an outlier, along with its Russian and Soviet counterparts, and for the same reasons of proven loyalty, reliability, and deep knowledge of the country to which they are posted.[33]

Some insight into what it takes to advance to the senior-most ranks can be gained by looking at the official biographies of various top Chinese diplomats. From a sample of ten of the most senior Chinese diplomats in 2016–2017,[34] all joined the ministry in 1989 or before, and most had completed between 9 and 12 assignments over their 30 to 40-year careers. Several had experience in interpretation or had studied languages in their formal education before joining MFA. It was not uncommon for senior diplomats to take a short absence from MFA for education or to take some other leadership role within the Communist Party structure, but the majority of their career was occupied within the MFA. Especially at junior ranks, they tended to follow the standard rotations between postings abroad and postings in Beijing, but interestingly several of the senior diplomats were sent abroad immediately after joining the ministry, something that would be highly unusual today. Many of the diplomats served at the rank of Assistant Minister or Vice Minister before their promotion to Ambassador. Generally speaking, these profiles suggest a "typical" senior Chinese diplomat: male, Han Chinese, university educated (often with some graduate education), active within the Communist Party, a regular progression through the MFA ranks, and with significant experience in a single region or discipline. However, there are the occasional outliers. Vice Minister (at the time of our survey) Wang Chao, despite serving in several embassies over the early portion of his government career, was actually not directly affiliated with MFA until his appointment as Assistant Minister in 2006. He had previously been a member of the Ministry of Commerce, working in foreign trade and economic cooperation for 20 years.

Role in Foreign Policy Making

Foreign policy decision-making authority resides with the top leadership of the Chinese Communist Party: the CCP Politburo and its Standing Committee, the Foreign Affairs Commission (formerly the Foreign Affairs Leading Small Group), the National Security Leading Small Group, the Central Military Commission, and other key bodies.[35] As those bodies meet relatively infrequently, the Foreign Affairs Office (FAO) of the Central Committee oversees foreign policy for the top party leadership on a day-to-day basis. The FAO has a small staff—reportedly around two dozen people, considerably smaller than the US National Security Council staff—and so relies on the Ministry of Foreign Affairs, which supplies much of its staff, for analysis and input. This is one of the many ways the MFA plays a role in foreign policy decision making.

The MFA is the lead organization in international negotiations, including critical ones like the handover of Hong Kong from the British, the six-party talks on North Korea, and the establishment of the Shanghai Cooperation Organization.[36] Through China's missions abroad, the MFA is also the key interface and negotiator with foreign governments, albeit on instruction from Beijing, and through its reports, analyses, and policy recommendations it informs, frames, and shapes decisions at the highest level.

The principle of interlocking memberships, whereby senior government officials are also senior party members, means that the leading role of the Communist Party in foreign policy making does not mean diminished influence for the MFA. The current Minister of Foreign is also one of 25 senior-most Party officials serving on the Politburo, while the Director of the Foreign Affairs Commission and its Foreign Affairs Office (FAO), Yang Jiechi, is also a Politburo member. Yang is a career diplomat, having served as Ambassador to the United States, Foreign Minister, and State Councilor in charge of foreign affairs. Additionally, many ambassadors to key posts hold vice-ministerial rank and, of course, are senior members of the CCP, so they exercise personal authority on foreign policy matters.

At the same time, as is the case with most other countries, foreign policy making in China is increasingly shared with other key ministries and agencies, including the Ministry of Commerce, Ministry of Foreign Trade, China International Development Cooperation Agency (one of at least 33 agencies involved in foreign aid), and the Ministry of Information Industry Technology, among many others. The advent of these new foreign policy "actors" in turn places a premium on coordination among them from the policy making center through the Foreign Affairs Commission, Foreign Office of the Central Committee and other bodies. This is the same combination of policy fragmentation and centralization that we see in other countries.

The role of the People's Liberation Army (PLA) has been eclipsed somewhat in recent years: it is still powerful within its own sphere, and PLA personnel participate together with MFA personnel in "strategic dialogues" with foreign countries. It is less influential on matters of national policy, however, particularly under Xi's sweeping military reforms of 2015–2016 and his assertion of Party authority and his own personal authority over foreign policy.[37] The International Department of the Central Committee plays an important role in forging relationships with political parties and politicians all over the world, giving Chinese foreign policy an additional point of access and leverage with other countries.[38] There is considerable interaction between the International Department and the MFA: MFA personnel frequently are seconded to the International Department, and occasionally vice versa, and officers from both institutions serve as staff members to the Foreign Affairs Office.

One of the characteristics of Chinese foreign policy decision-making is the cumbersome process of bureaucratic bargaining that precedes and often impedes major decisions. Described some years ago by Richard Solomon,[39] this pattern was manifest during the April 2001 downing of a

US EP-3 spy plane by a Chinese fighter jet, as China's response evolved over a two-week period. In the wake of that incident, President Jiang Zemin reportedly tried to create a US-style National Security Council but was opposed on grounds that it would dilute the authority of the Politburo Standing Committee.[40]

The difficulties of coordination have only gotten worse since that time, as is evidenced by the frequent shifts in organizational structures and recurrent critiques in the Chinese press, particularly by Xi himself. The Foreign Affairs Leading Small Group was elevated to a Commission in 2018, and its head elected to the Politburo. Meanwhile, the National Security Leading Small Group, created in 1999 and elevated to Commission in 2013, has the same membership as the Foreign Affairs Commission, the difference seeming to be that crisis management is the purview of the National Security Commission.[41] These overlapping and duplicative structures seem to be a symptom of the problem rather than its solution. Speaking at the first meeting of the Foreign Affairs Commission in May 2018, Xi Jinping issued a strong call for "enhancing the centralized and unified leadership of the CPC Central Committee over foreign affairs and opening up new prospects for major-country diplomacy with Chinese characteristics."[42]

Some have seen Xi's centralization of control over foreign policy as coming "at the expense of the Foreign Ministry."[43] This is by no means clear, however. The elevation of key figures in the Foreign Ministry and Foreign Affairs Office to the Politburo serve to strengthen the connections between Party and Ministry, even as Xi's expansive foreign policy thrusts the MFA into a more prominent role. There are also the questions of whether Xi's span of control is too broad to be effective and whether his amassing of no fewer than 12 senior leadership posts is a sign of strength or of overreach.[44] For now at least, the MFA's importance seems to be on the rise, and one can be certain that the latest organizational and personnel changes will not be the last.

Preparations for the Future

The Chinese diplomatic service faces two major challenges going forward. One is to help manage a vastly more ambitious and complicated foreign policy than China has ever had in its long history. In imperial times and even into the twentieth century, Chinese leaders sent envoys and emissaries to distant lands, but did not have an active strategy of engagement and influence with those leaders and peoples. Even as Communist China opened up to the outside world, starting in the 1980s and accelerating in this century, its approach until recently was to keep a low profile of reassurance to preserve a nonconfrontational international profile while giving primacy to domestic economic development. Now, as "peaceful rise" gives way to "great power diplomacy with Chinese characteristics," China has adopted a far-reaching and multi-level campaign that would radically extend China's reach and influence.[45]

Chinese leaders portray the "Belt and Road" initiative as a non-threatening development and investment project. This highly intrusive set of projects extending primarily through Asia and into Europe but also overseas to Oceania to the east and Africa to the west, will, however, have huge consequences and high risks for China. Chinese diplomats claim to see no danger of China's becoming overextended or embroiled unwittingly in local conflicts, but there is little sign that the senior leadership has fully thought through the implications of this unprecedented leap into great-power diplomacy. A complicating factor is that China's diplomatic projection of reassurance and commitment to a "harmonious world order" is increasingly at odds with China's rapid military expansion and the aggressive actions of China's rapidly expanding naval forces (PLA-N) in the South China Sea.[46]

It is for these reasons that influential Chinese thinkers such as Wang Jisi and Li Xue have called for a grand strategy commensurate with the magnitude of the undertaking and for more modern and dynamic mechanisms for foreign policy decision-making.[47] To some extent, the organizational steps taken in the past few years are a response to those concerns, but China has a long way to go. Xi's amassing and consolidation of personal power is beyond the scope of this chapter; for our purposes, suffice it to say that Xi's standing at home will depend to a large extent on the success or failure of the Belt and Road Initiative.[48] The stakes are high.

The second major challenge is to adapt and modernize China's diplomatic service, which did not become fully professional until the 1980s, in the aftermath of the Cultural Revolution, Mao's death, and China's opening to the outside world.[49] The strengths of the service—discipline, loyalty, language, and regional competencies—have served China reasonably well up until now, but its weaknesses are increasing liabilities when it comes to meeting twenty-first century challenges. In particular, entering Chinese diplomats have only in the past few years equaled those of other services surveyed in this book in terms of social science, diplomatic, and strategy preparation, and they are rarely empowered to take independent initiative without waiting for approval from Beijing. As other diplomatic services have discovered, hierarchical systems do not work well in a networked world and digital age. Similarly, the security concerns that led to reduced opportunities for education abroad have both stifled professional development and reduced the appeal of a diplomatic career for younger officers who see opportunities elsewhere in the Chinese economy.

The budget and staff increases of recent years will help, but in this new era, with growing Chinese global interests and the information requirements of the digital age, deeper cultural shifts are needed to recruit, train, and empower a new generation of skilled Chinese diplomats. Just as Chinese economists learned that intensive development via inputs of capital and labor were insufficient for the new phase of extensive development, Chinese statesmen will need invest in and commit to a new diplomatic model that is equal to the ambitions China has set for itself.

Acknowledgment *The authors wish to thank the following diplomats and scholars who were consulted in researching and writing this chapter:* Richard Bush, Iris Ma Eisenman, Joshua Eisenman, Zhu Haiquan, J. Stapleton Roy, David Shambaugh, Andrew Scobell, Jun Wang, and Lanxin Xiang.

Notes

1. John K. Fairbank, "China's Foreign Policy in Historical Perspective," *Foreign Affairs* 47, no. 3 (1969): 449–63.
2. Generally, we have used the *Pinyin* system of romanization of Chinese words, with the Wades-Giles system that was common up until 1979 placed in parentheses, but for a familiar name like Sun Tzu, we have reversed the order.
3. A frequently cited quote of Confucius—"To have friends coming from afar, isn't that a joy?"—is used by the state to indicate that the Chinese have always been a hospitable people. For insight to the recent debate, see Dengdeng Chen, "Chinese Foreign Policy Needs Major Reform: *Tao Guang Yang Hui* or *Fen Fa You Wei?*" *The Diplomat*, August 21, 2014.
4. Scott A. Boorman, *The Protracted Game: A Wei-Ch'i Interpretation of Maoist Revolutionary Strategy* (Oxford: Oxford University Press, 1971); Scott A. Boorman, "Mao Tse-tung and the Art of War," *Journal of Asian Studies* 24 no. 1 (November 1964): 129–35 (Review of *Sun Tzu: The Art of War*, translated with an Introduction by Samuel B. Griffith, with a foreword by B.H. Liddell Hart. Oxford: Clarendon Press, 1963).

5. See, e.g., Fairbank, "China's Foreign Policy in Historical Perspective"; David Shambaugh, *China Goes Global: The Partial Power* (Oxford: Oxford University Press, 2013), 53–67; and Andrew J. Nathan and Andrew Scobell, *China's Search for Security* (New York: Columbia University Press, 2012), 3–36.
6. Nathan and Scobell, *China's Search for Security*, 24–25.
7. Its full name was *Zongli geguo shiwu yamen*, literally "office in charge of affairs with all countries."
8. Jonathan D. Spence, *The Search for Modern China* (New York: W.W. Norton & Company, 1990), 199, 235.
9. William C. Kirby, "The Internationalization of China: Foreign Relations at Home and Abroad in the Republican Era," *The China Quarterly*, No. 150, Special Issue (June 1997), 433–58.
10. James Reardon-Anderson, *Yenan and the Great Powers: The Origins of Chinese Communist Foreign Policy, 1944–46* (New York: Columbia University Press, 1980), 1–4, 163–72.
11. Xiaohong Liu, *Chinese Ambassadors: The Rise of Diplomatic Professionalism Since 1949* (Seattle and London: University of Washington Press, 2001), 14.
12. The Ministry of Foreign Affairs was known to follow the principle of *Taoguang yanghui* (to keep a low profile) under Deng, and the precept of "peaceful rise" under Hu Jintao, but has been gradually shifting to a different principle that emphasizes *Fenfa youwei* (striving for achievement) since Xi Jinping took office.
13. Kishan S. Rana, "Diplomacy Systems and Processes: Comparing India and China," *China Report* 50, no. 4 (2014): 297–323. Rana's estimates for 2003 put personnel numbers at 2000 at the ministry and 2500 abroad. See Kishan S. Rana, "The Structure and Operation of China's Diplomatic System," *China Report* 41, no. 3 (2005): 224.
14. Markus Herrmann and Sabine Mokry, "China Races to Catch Up on Foreign Affairs Spending," *The Diplomat*, August 9, 2018.
15. This figure was calculated for the year 2015. 中新社, "中国妇女发展白皮书:中国有 1695 名女外交官," 中国新 闻网, http://www.chinanews.com/gn/2015/09-22/7537560.shtml. Accessed October 25, 2016.
16. Liu, *Chinese Ambassadors*, esp. 203.
17. Sabine Mokry, "Chinese Experts Challenge Western Generalists in Diplomacy," *Diplomat*, August 15, 2018.
18. Hou Feng, "'Translator Diplomacy' Distorted Chinese Diplomacy." September 29, 2012.
https://web.archive.org/web/20160520055556/http://www.21ccom.net/articles/qqsw/zlwj/article_2012092968634.html. Accessed March 2, 2019. See also Qiu Zhibo, "China's Outdated Foreign Service Needs Rebooting for the Age of Trump," *Foreign Policy*, January 23,

2017, which describes China's diplomatic corps as "silent, passive, (and) isolated."
19. China ranked second globally in the 2017 Global Diplomacy Index, a metric designed to compare diplomatic networks. "Lowy Global Diplomacy Index," https://globaldiplomacyindex.lowyinstitute.org/country_rank.html. Accessed March 12, 2019. See also Rana, "The Structure and Operation of China's Diplomatic System," 223–24.
20. Rana, "The Structure and Operation and China's Diplomatic System," 227–28.
21. This paragraph is based largely on interviews with currently serving Chinese diplomats. See also Rana, "The Structure and Operation of China's Diplomatic System," 228–29.
22. Kishan S. Rana, "Diplomatic Training: New Trends," *Foreign Service Journal* 93, no. 7 (2016): 41–43.
23. Rana, "The Structure and Operation of China's Diplomatic System," 228.
24. Interviews with currently serving Chinese diplomats, Washington, D.C., August 24, 2018.
25. The PRC employs a mandatory national retirement age of 50 (male)/60 (female) for blue collar workers, and 55/65 for white collar workers. A detailed plan for increasing the mandatory retirement age has yet to be completed, and may not begin until 2022. Owen Haacke, "China's Mandatory Retirement Age Changes: Impact for Foreign Companies," *The US-China Business Council*, April 1, 2015, https://www.uschina.org/china's-mandatory-retirement-age-changes-impact-foreign-companies. Accessed March 3, 2017.
26. Interviews in Washington, D.C., August 24, 2018. See also Liu, *Chinese Ambassadors*, 204.
27. Interviews in Washington, D.C., July 16–17, 2018. See also Qiu Zhibo, "China's Outdated Foreign Service Needs Rebooting."
28. Liu, *Chinese Ambassadors*, xv.
29. Rana, "The Structure and Operation of China's Diplomatic System," 228–29.
30. Ibid., 224. Rana reports that as of 2005, when his article was published, Party membership was no longer mandatory for MFA officials, but this seems to be the case for lower-level administrative staff, not for the diplomatic corps.
31. Mokry, "Chinese Experts Challenge Western Generalists."
32. Rana, "The Structure and Operation of China's Diplomatic Service," 228–29.
33. Ibid., 228–32, and Mokry, "Chinese Experts Challenge Western Generalist."
34. The officials surveyed were the Chinese Minister of Foreign Affairs, the Permanent Representative to the United Nations, and ambassadors to

Brazil, France, Germany, India, Russia, Turkey, the United Kingdom, and the United States. For brief profiles of these officials, see Robert Hutchings and Jeremi Suri, eds., *Developing Diplomats: Comparing Form and Culture Across Diplomatic Services* (Austin, TX: The University of Texas, 2017), 53–58.

35. For good overview analyses, see David Shambaugh, *China Goes Global: The Partial Power* (Oxford: Oxford University Press, 2013), 60–72; Marc Lanteigne, *Chinese Foreign Policy: An Introduction* (London: Routledge, third edition, 2016), 23–46; and Robert Sutter, *Foreign Relations of the PRC: The Legacies and Constraints of China's International Politics since 1949* (Lanham, MD: Rowman & Littlefield Publishers, Inc., 2013), 119–47.
36. Rana, "The Structure and Operation of China's Diplomatic System," 221–22.
37. Li, *Chinese Politics in the Xi Jinping Era*, 10–13.
38. See Julia G. Bowie, "International Liaison Work for the New Era: Generating Global Consensus?" *Party Watch Annual Report 2018* (October 18, 2018), 41–49: https://docs.wixstatic.com/ugd/183fcc_687cd757272e4618850 69b3e3365f46d.pdf; and: The International Department of the Chinese Communist Party," *China: An International Journal*, Vol. 5, No. 1 (March 2007): 26–52.
39. Richard H. Solomon, *Chinese Negotiating Behavior* (Washington, D.C.: U.S. Institute of Peace Press, second edition, 1999).
40. Richard C. Bush, *The Perils of Proximity: China-Japan Security Relations* (Washington, DC: Brookings Institution Press, 2010), 129–30. See also David M. Lampton, "Xi Jinping and the National Security Commission: Policy Coordination and Political Power," *Journal of Contemporary China* 24, no. 95 (2015): 759–77.
41. Ibid., 129.
42. "Xi Stresses Centralized, Unified Leadership of CPC Central Committee over Foreign Affairs." *Xinhua*, May 15, 2018.
43. Thomas Eder, "Chinas New Foreign Policy Setup" *The Diplomat*, August 1, 2018. https://thediplomat.com/2018/08/chinas-new-foreign-policy-setup/. Accessed March 12, 2019.
44. Lampton, "Xi Jinping and the National Security Commission," and Cheng Li, *Chinese Politics in the Xi Jinping Era: Reassessing Collective Leadership* (Washington, DC: Brookings Institution, 2016), 17.
45. Bonnie S. Glaser and Evan S. Medeiros, "The Changing Ecology of Foreign Policy-Making in China: The Ascension and Demise of the Theory of 'Peaceful Rise'," *China Quarterly*, no. 190 (June 2007): 291–310.
46. Robert Sutter, *Chinese Foreign Relations: Power and Policy Since the Cold War* (Rowman & Littlefield, 2016), 101–23.

47. Wang Jisi, "China's Search for a Grand Strategy: A Rising Great Power Finds Its Way," *Foreign Affairs* 90, no. 2 (March/April 2011): 68–79; and Li Xue, "China's Foreign Policy Decision-Making Mechanism and 'One Belt One Road' Strategy," *Journal of Contemporary East Asia Studies* 5, no. 2 (2016): 23–35.
48. Li, *Chinese Politics in the Xi Jinping Era*, 8–26.
49. Liu, *Chinese Ambassadors*, 200–209.

References

Boorman, S.A. 1964. Mao Tse-Tung and the Art of War. *Journal of Asian Studies* 24 (1): 129–137.

———. 1971. *The Protracted Game: A Wei-ch'i Interpretation of Maoist Revolutionary Strategy*. Oxford: Oxford University Press.

Bush, R.C. 2010. *The Perils of Proximity: China-Japan Security Relations*. Washington, DC: Brookings Institution Press.

Chen, D. 2014, August 21. Chinese Foreign Policy Needs Major Reform: *Tao guang yang hui* or *fen fa you wei*? *Diplomat*.

Eder, T. 2018, August 1. China's New Foreign Policy Setup. *Diplomat*. https://thediplomat.com/2018/08/chinas-new-foreign-policy-setup/. Accessed March 12, 2019.

Fairbank, J.K. 1969. China's Foreign Policy in Historical Perspective. *Foreign Affairs* 47 (3): 449–463.

Feng, H. 2012, September 29. *Translator Diplomacy's Distorted Chinese Diplomacy*. https://web.archive.org/web/20160520055556/http://www.21ccom.net/articles/qqsw/zlwj/article_2012092968634.html. Accessed March 2, 2019.

Gao, K. 2015, September 22. 中新社, "中国妇女发展白皮书:中国有 1695 名女外交官," 中国新闻网. http://www.chinanews.com/gn/2015/09-22/7537560.shtml. Accessed March 13, 2019.

Glaser, B.S., and E.S. Medeiros. 2007, June. The Changing Ecology of Foreign Policy-Making in China: The Ascension and Demise of the Theory of "peaceful Rise". *China Quarterly* (190): 291–310.

Global Diplomacy Index: 2017 Country Ranking. 2017. Lowy Institute. https://globaldiplomacyindex.lowyinstitute.org/country_rank.html. Accessed March 12, 2019.

Haacke, O. 2017, March 3. *China's Mandatory Retirement Age Changes: Impact for Foreign Companies*. The US-China Business Council. https://www.uschina.org/china's-mandatory-retirement-age-changes-impact-foreign-companies. Accessed March 3, 2017.

Herrmann, M., and S. Sabine Mokry. 2018, August 9. China Races to Catch Up on Foreign Affairs Spending. *Diplomat*.

Jisi, W. 2011. China's Search for a Grand Strategy: A Rising Great Power Finds Its Way. *Foreign Affairs* 90 (2): 68–79.
Kirby, W.C. 1997. The Internationalization of China: Foreign Relations at Home and Abroad in the Republican Era. *The China Quarterly* 150: 433–458.
Lampton, D.M. 2015. Xi Jinping and the National Security Commission: Policy Coordination and Political Power. *Journal of Contemporary China* 24 (95): 759–777.
Lanteigne, M. 2016. *Chinese Foreign Policy: An Introduction*. London: Routledge.
Li, C. 2016. *Chinese Politics in the Xi Jinping Era: Reassessing Collective Leadership*. Washington, DC: Brookings Institution.
Liu, X. 2001. *Chinese Ambassadors: The Rise of Diplomatic Professionalism Since 1949*. Seattle and London: University of Washington Press.
Mokry, S. 2018, August 15. Chinese Experts Challenge Western Generalists in Diplomacy. *Diplomat*.
Nathan, A.J., and A. Scobell. 2012. *China's Search for Security*. New York: Columbia University Press.
Rana, K.S. 2005. The Structure and Operation of China's Diplomatic System. *China Report* 41 (3): 215–236.
———. 2014. Diplomacy Systems and Processes: Comparing India and China. *China Report* 50 (4): 297–323.
———. 2016. Diplomatic Training: New Trends. *Foreign Service Journal* 93 (7): 41–43.
Reardon-Anderson, J. 1980. *Yenan and the Great Powers: The Origins of Chinese Communist Foreign Policy, 1944–46*. New York: Columbia University Press.
Shambaugh, D. 2013. *China Goes Global: The Partial Power*. Oxford: Oxford University Press.
Solomon, R.H. 1999. *Chinese Negotiating Behavior*. Washington, DC: U.S. Institute of Peace Press.
Spence, J.D. 1990. *The Search for Modern China*. New York: W.W. Norton & Company.
Sutter, R.G. 2013. *Foreign Relations of the PRC: The Legacies and Constraints of China's International Politics Since 1949*. Lanham, MD: Rowman & Littlefield Publishers, Inc.
———. 2016. *Chinese Foreign Relations: Power and Policy Since the Cold War*. Rowman & Littlefield.
Tzu, Sun. 1963. *The Art of War*. Trans. B.H.L. Hart. Oxford: Clarendon Press.
Xi Stresses Centralized, Unified Leadership of CPC Central Committee over Foreign Affairs. 2018, May 15. *Xinhua*.
Xue, L. 2016. China's Foreign Policy Decision-Making Mechanism and "One Belt One Road" Strategy. *Journal of Contemporary East Asia Studies* 5 (2): 23–35.
Zhibo, Q. 2017, January 23. China's Outdated Foreign Service Needs Rebooting for the Age of Trump. *Foreign Policy*.

CHAPTER 3

France

Bryce Block, Catherine Cousar, and Jeremi Suri

EXECUTIVE SUMMARY

French diplomats maintain a very high *esprit de corps*. They see themselves as exponents for their nation's revolutionary ideals of liberty, equality, and fraternity. They operate with a wide range of independent decision-making authority, especially concerning daily relationships and policy implementation. The open two-way consultation between Paris and its embassies and missions appears to be unique to French diplomacy. While largely a top-down organization, the French Foreign Ministry cultivates diplomats with significant autonomy and responsibility in their daily work. For its historical performance, the French Foreign Ministry is generally held in high regard among its citizens and employees. Recruitment is highly competitive and selective, requiring various separate entrance exams, and the system depends on a robust public educational system to prepare the best prospective employees. The requirements for entry into the French service are very rigorous, including working knowledge of French, English,

B. Block • C. Cousar
2017 Master of Arts Degree, Global Policy Studies, The University of Texas at Austin, Austin, TX, USA

J. Suri (✉)
Lyndon B. Johnson School of Public Affairs, The University of Texas at Austin, Austin, TX, USA
e-mail: suri@austin.utexas.edu

and a third European language. The Foreign Ministry focuses on strengthening the managerial skills and leadership capacities of diplomats, as well as deepening their knowledge in the priority areas of international action (especially economic diplomacy, soft diplomacy, security and defense, European affairs, and climate change). Promotion within the ministry is based upon initial classifications when entering as a junior member. Promotion is highly formalized and built upon early training and examinations. It is rare, but occasionally diplomats from the consular level are able to cross over to diplomatic roles. The most elite diplomats follow very similar career paths; deviations are not common. The greatest challenge for contemporary French diplomacy is maintaining its very high standards and historical focus in a time of turmoil within the European Union and transatlantic relations. France's goals are typically global in focus, but the ministry might need to redefine geographical and issue priorities in coming years.

History and Culture

French diplomats believe that they invented modern diplomacy in the sixteenth century, and perhaps they did. The Bourbon kings hosted the most impressive European diplomatic court, and their representatives set the standard throughout the continent and the New World. Until the early twentieth century, French was the international language of diplomacy, and it remains one of the six official United Nations languages today. Historically, French diplomats have come from the landed and intellectual aristocracy, they have assumed a highly respected status in French politics, and they have retained their status despite various regime changes. Charles Maurice de Talleyrand-Périgord most famously served as a leading French diplomat before and after the French Revolution.

The legacy of the French Revolution continues to influence all aspects of French society, particularly diplomacy. The French see themselves as missionaries for their revolutionary ideals of liberty, equality, and fraternity. Their diplomats seek not only to secure the interests of the French state, but also to promote these ideals through public diplomacy and other forms of "soft power." The French Empire expanded across the world over four centuries to enrich French society and spread what the French have called their "*mission civilisatrice.*" The French clung to the last pieces of their empire through the early Cold War, and they continue to maintain deep influence in former colonial territories in Africa and the Caribbean.

The 2013 French intervention in Mali attested to Paris' continued influence in former colonial lands.

The Second World War and the Algerian War marked the end of the French colonial empire, replaced by the Fifth Republic with Charles de Gaulle's popular coup in 1958. De Gaulle created a presidential system, with a directly elected national leader who oversees all foreign policy, including the professional diplomatic corps. The French president has historically defended France's continued status as a leading global power, a promoter of European integration, and a sponsor of economic development in the developing world. France has been a close American ally on major strategic issues during the last half-century, but French leaders have also asserted flagrant independence from Washington at key moments, most recently opposing the Iraq War. French diplomats are deeply integrated in the Western alliance, and they remain strongly nationalistic at the same time.

From 1791–2007 the official title for the French Foreign Ministry was the "Ministry of Foreign Affairs" (*Ministère des affaires étrangères*). In 2007, leaders in Paris changed the name to the "Ministry for Foreign and European Affairs" (*Ministère de l'Europe et des affaires étrangères*) indicating a renewed focus on Europe.

Profile

The foreign ministry of France is the second-largest diplomatic service in the world.[1] After moving many times during prior centuries, the current physical location of the foreign ministry was established in the mid-twentieth century on the left bank of the River Seine at number 37, *Quai D'Orsay*.[2] The budget for the entire foreign ministry was €5029 million in 2012 ($7.305 billion in 2016 dollars), which represents just over 1% of the total 2012 French federal budget.[3] Missions abroad include 163 embassies, 4 diplomatic branch offices, 92 consulates general and consulates, and 135 embassy consular sections and other missions. In addition to its 163 bilateral missions, French Ambassadors represent France within multilateral organizations as 16 permanent representatives and 25 dedicated ambassadors. France also designates nearly 500 honorary consuls in countries without a consular post, but where they deem it important to have a local point of contact.[4]

The foreign ministry has approximately 14,798 personnel supporting offices in Paris and the network of embassies, consulates, and missions abroad. There are 5503 staff recruited under local laws, 3099 tenured and open-ended contractual agents in the central administration, 2905 tenured and open-ended contractual agents abroad, 3017 fixed-term contractual agents (including international volunteers and temporary staff), and 724 Military Staff (not from the Defense budget).[5] The total of these separate divisions makes up the heart of the French foreign service.

It is divided into three categories or cadres, each of which is selected through a separate exam process.[6] "*Catégorie A*" is considered the top level, which places employees on tracks to reach the most senior diplomatic officers (from 1st secretary of the embassy to ambassador and counselor and *secretaire* of the ministry in Paris). Next in line is "*Catégorie B*," which is made up of primarily consular, management, and administrative officers (including some who may also pass by exam into the A cadre). The final level is "*Catégorie C*," containing primarily support personnel, such as clerks, personal assistants (secretaries), administrative, and security and communications technicians.[7]

As professional prospects for talented and well-educated French citizens have improved in the private sector, the foreign ministry has faced pressures to adjust how it recruits and promotes. The general makeup of the ministry has also become more diverse, as it seeks to reflect a more diverse French citizenry. The ministry has varying levels of gender representation, depending on the cadre of service. In total, 53% of civil servants are women, including 30% of Category A agents, 43% of Category B agents, and 68% of Category C agents.[8] In January of 2013, 25 of the 180 ambassadors abroad were women, which shows a rise to 14% from 10% in 2006.[9]

Recruitment and Selection

The French foreign ministry continues to maintain great prestige among French citizens. Serving in the ministry is considered an honor and positions are coveted. Recruitment is highly competitive and selective.[10] The basis of recruitment is founded in the two-tiered French education system. Universities are free for all, but students must pass the *baccalauréat* examination in order to enroll. On this pathway, the student must hold an additional masters-level degree, or a diploma level II recognized as equivalent by the ministry of foreign affairs. The individuals must apply and succeed in four separate exams in order to be allowed into the A cadre.[11] The second pathway is the *Grandes Écoles*, first established by Charles de Gaulle after the Second World War. This pathway is much harder to pursue because seats are limited and it requires two years of preparation for the entrance exam. It does, however, offer more specific preparation for access to a position within the ministry.

Upon completion of a degree at either the *École Polytechnique* (IRA) or the *École Nationale d'Administration* (ENA), students are ranked, and carry that ranking for the rest of their careers. Graduates can join the *grand corps* (civil service) and leading ENA graduates can get a public sector assignment in the foreign ministry. This would be a direct assignment into the A cadre.[12] Only those who have graduated from ENA are able to achieve A+ status.[13] Not all diplomats in the foreign ministry come from the *Grandes Écoles* or universities. There are also *ad hoc* examinations offered, from time to time, for specialized needs within the organization. A program known as "*Concours d'Orient*," for example, allows ministers to recruit individuals who have specific language skills and area specializations. These individuals are often graduates from the *Institut des Langues Orientales*.[14]

In addition to passing the various exams, all foreign ministry entrants must have mastery of English and a second foreign language, in addition to French. A third foreign language is recommended in order to enter the A cadre. In the French system, mastery of the culture and history of a foreign language area is also required and considered as important as speaking the language itself. In the early 2010s, German was specifically added as a "hard language," not because of the decline of its popularity in France, but because of its need in maintaining a "balanced" Franco-German partnership. Language facility is periodically tested and rated in recognition that without adequate practice, fluency changes, and old ratings are meaningless.[15]

The routes to positions within the B and C Categories are different. The B cadre requires a diploma level IV prior to taking the first examination. Successful completion of the exam opens up positions as chancery secretaries as well as information systems and communications secretaries.[16] *Cadre C* requirements do not require a diploma. Upon admittance in this function, the roles are secretarial or administrative, and they support the other two cadres.[17]

Upon entry into the ministry, new officers are expected to be highly and professionally educated for diplomatic service. All A cadre staff members are required to enroll in an internal education service, the *École Diplomatique* (School of Diplomacy); they are tested on a rigorous six month curriculum. The internal training school is staffed by retired diplomats, highly regarded practitioners, respected journalists, and academics. In addition to A cadre, long-standing training for B and C cadre personnel has been folded into the *École's* responsibilities. The stated purpose of the *École* is to "assure an initial formation of all diplomats entering the *Quai d'Orsay*," and "provide an ongoing formation to acquire competencies in line with requirements."[18]

Another path to enter the French Foreign Ministry is open specifically to individuals who have five to ten years of experience in the private sector, such as former company managers and experts. Entrance requires a different exam and interview process.[19] The connection to the private sector is first established with the students of the *Grande Écoles* during their rotations. They engage in a multitude of ministries as well as various private and governmentally run corporations.[20] Since the group of graduates is all intermingled, some individuals may be well connected across the different organizations. This route is intended to bring in former students who have institutional knowledge at a non-governmental entity but maintain a background from their high level of education. The ministry consistently promotes economic relationships for its private-sector corporations abroad, and diplomats with private-sector experience are especially valuable for this work.

In discussions with diplomats, we noted that the caliber of education and pedigree required to be a top-level diplomat is still highly pursued during the recruitment process.[21] There are various levels and opportunities to become a *Catégorie A* diplomat, but a vast majority follow the traditional route of the *Grande École*. France's ministry has worked to allow entrance in a more egalitarian way, but on a whole, it values the sophistication and preeminence of the traditional route over all others. Due to this preference, the traditional elite French diplomatic profile remains dominant.

Finally, in the area of diversity, France has come a long way in employing a better balance of men and women, at least at the lower levels and among new recruits. The ministry also runs programs to train and hire hard languages. The ministry's success in the area of ethnic and religious diversity however, is less clear. France does not record the ethnicity of staff in government positions. A survey of staff profiles, however, suggests that they still have some way to go.

Professional Development and Training

The French foreign service does not have a "cone" or "track" system for career development, and it allows its employees to self-select positions based upon personal interests. While assignments are not commonly refused, the officers are allowed to create points of focus within each role they take, building a professional profile. Within *cadre A*, officers self-select into various career paths or streams such as, "representation," "negotiation," "search for information," "protection of French interests," "promotion of bilateral relations," and "communication on the ground."[22] They are encouraged to focus their roles in these specific areas and apply to positions that promote the streams. In response to a White Paper[23] prepared in 2007, a new program of training was started with the creation of the *Institut diplomatique et consulaire* (IDC).[24] The IDC addresses the dual issues of insufficient training for first-term diplomats, as well as experienced diplomats prior to reaching senior management posts.

An academic-focused competition is utilized to hire staff; as a result, the initial training sessions are essentially focused on practice, skills, and the sharing of experience. The initial training program was created in 2010 and lasts 14 weeks. It requires a participatory teaching approach and makes wide use of peer training. On completion of their initial program, trainees should possess basic knowledge of their administrative environment and of the missions and values of the ministry. The IDC offers modules with a variety of content: the organization and functioning of the ministry (working tools, diplomatic drafting, security, and deontology), the range of functions at the *Quai d'Orsay* (negotiation, budget management and accounting, communication, and crisis management), and public outreach. There are also thematic training modules: European and legal dimensions, multilateral matters, global issues, Franco-German and Franco-British relations, and public speaking, among others. The initial training program also allows trainees to participate actively through simulation exercises and practical workshops in subgroups. Coursework emphasizes the need for openness and has a major Franco–German component involving two trips jointly with the Germany Foreign Service Academy, as well as a joint program with the British Foreign and Commonwealth Office.[25]

Later in a diplomat's career, at approximately 15 years of service, the ministry offers mid-career course training. The first session of mid-career training was launched in October 2011. This course is aimed at staff who will return to central administration for the first time in roles such as deputy director, heads of department, or head of unit. The goal of the formalized program is to create a pool of officers who will exercise upper management roles within the Ministry. The training aims, in particular, to strengthen the managerial skills and leadership capacities of diplomats, as well as to deepen their knowledge in the priority areas of international action (including economic diplomacy, soft power, security and defense, European affairs, and climate change). France hopes that its diplomats will lead the international community in directing the future of many of these actions. Training, therefore, focuses on building foundational knowledge in specific areas of importance. The personalized dimension also involves language training, with assessment of language skills and the design of individual training programs. This training is also a major event for diplomats themselves who, in addition to a first personal assessment, will enjoy assistance and support for their later careers postings with growing responsibilities.[26]

Leadership

Recent promotion procedures within the French foreign ministry have shed a spotlight on historical inequities between men and women. In the past ten years, the ministry has worked to promote more women within higher levels, not just the historical lower cadres (B and C). The recent details regarding this transition have been widely publicized as the French work to reform gender inequality within the entire government.[27] Despite these significant efforts, current evidence points to a steep divide within the higher levels of the ministry. As evidenced by the diplomatic profiles of France, nine out of ten of the highest level diplomats are still men, as of 2013.

French ambassadors are appointed directly by the President of the Republic in a meeting of the Council of Ministers, following the suggestions of the Minister of Foreign Affairs in a formal process. The ambassadorial position is regarded as one of the highest within the government, but by law, the President is able to appoint whomever he or she chooses. While other ambassadors change within administrations, similar to the United States, France's ambassadors rarely change over. Diplomats are appointed based upon merit within the profession, and historically, must reach the grade of envoy prior to the promotion.[28] Although transcripts of the meetings between the president and minister of foreign affairs are not published, the president has almost never rejected the recommendations of the minister. There is a historical precedent prior to the founding of the fifth Republic to maintain a professional service whose members are largely not influenced by partisan politics. This precedent is maintained by allowing the foreign minister to make appropriate suggestions for ambassadorial posts, and not replacing them with each new president. Interviews within the service have confirmed that this relationship is highly supported and is a key to the high morale of the ministry.[29]

The president has the power and authority to act as his or her own foreign minister, if desired. Charles de Gaulle set this precedent. In contrast, some presidents have relied wholly on the work of the minister of foreign affairs. In recent elections within France, a key issue has been engagement with the United Nations and the rest of the world, suggesting that presidents will pursue more internationalist policies, possibly relying more heavily on the leadership of the foreign ministry.

The ministry remains a highly centralized organization, with a clear policy line issuing from Paris. Most French diplomats holding senior positions entered the ministry through examinations and worked their way up, serving both in Paris and abroad in positions of increasing responsibility. The majority attended either *Sciences Po ÉNA* in Paris or *École nationale d'administration*, or both, and have spent their entire career in the French Ministry of Foreign Affairs.

The majority of ambassadors are still men in early middle age, although in recent years there have been increases in diversity, including more women in powerful positions. Sylvie Bermann, French Ambassador to the United Kingdom, is a good example. In her prior role, when she served as ambassador to China, she was the first Frenchwoman to be an ambassador to a country on the UN Security Council.

Role in Foreign Policy Making

The French foreign ministry is largely a top-down organization, but not inflexible. Embassies and consulates receive direct and detailed instructions from Paris. In practice, however, the relationship between a mission and headquarters is more of a dialogue. One of the greatest strengths of the French foreign ministry is its mix of central authority and flexible support for ministers in the field. Nearly all interviews conducted with service members affirmed a consensus: although central policy comes from Paris, officers still feel empowered (and protected) to question their superiors and act according to their best local judgment. If a mission receives instructions from Paris that do not make sense or are impractical, French officials are permitted to seek adjustments, and even a reversal of instructions. Officers are expected to share their opinions with headquarters and pursue the best approach in any given situation. Of course, when there is a difference of viewpoint on priority issues between a mission and headquarters, headquarters will choose the approach to be taken.[30] For many issues, however, headquarters will cede leadership to local, respected representatives.

France has exhibited consistent success leading conversations and directing dialogue around multilateral issues, including climate change and economic development. In interviews, we learned that the French diplomats are empowered to take stances that are consistent with the message of the organization without returning to base at every juncture. The freedom of local representatives is a great strength for adapting to regional needs and pressures. This flexibility has allowed diplomats to act as international agenda-setters, rather than merely react to the positions of others.

A recent example of this dynamic has been France's leading role in European discussions about Russian aggression in Ukraine, and negotiations with Russia through the Minsk process. France pushed for a reinstatement of the Minsk Protocol ceasefire, and an opening for aid to alleviate the suffering of the people in the conflict-ridden Donbass region of Ukraine. France's role was pivotal in bringing about this limited but significant agreement.

There is a strong culture in France of retiring diplomats sharing their experiences and wisdom with successors. A multitude of memoirs, diaries, and other documents are available from various sources that provide an internal perspective on French diplomacy. The culture of the foreign ministry is maintained as a highly intellectual practice. Being a diplomat is a respected, lifetime achievement, and it follows as only natural to document those experiences. New or hopeful diplomats draw upon these works as manuals for their future roles. As a result of this process, a culture of learning and historical rigor animates the ministry and is recreated with each new generation of diplomats.

PREPARATIONS FOR THE FUTURE

Over the last decade, the French foreign service has shifted much of its focus to specific areas of interest, including Africa, the Middle East, and Asia. Ukraine has risen as an area of interest due to its profound recent effect on France's relationship with Russia.[31] Africa, due to France's colonial ties, remains a major area of interest and involvement.[32]

One of the most significant new trends is a focus on economic diplomacy. The French foreign service would like to do better but still struggles with economic influence. While France has turned its focus towards economic diplomacy, the foreign ministry is still in the process of hiring talent with deeper economic background, and supporting appropriate training. The ministry has some of the best educated diplomats possible, but they do not always focus on key areas they might need, possibly due to personal preferences. Exams for the foreign service have shifted appropriately, changing one section of the exam that was previously focused on public finance and economics, to cover economics more exclusively.[33]

In 2007 a white paper was prepared to investigate France's role in Europe and the world. A number of ideas were developed within the document, and changes previously mentioned came directly from the research conducted. In the second part of the White Paper five priorities for external action are underlined, including[34]:

1. Ensure the security of France and the French people, defend and promote their interests.
2. Build a strong, democratic, and efficient Europe with our partners.
3. Intervene in the world for peace, security, and human rights.
4. Help to organize a process of globalization that can ensure the sustainable and well-balanced development of the planet.
5. Make French ideas, French language, and French culture visible, while following the principle of cultural diversity.

These five measures represent the traditional and now modernized external face of France as it navigates a tumultuous contemporary world. They are inherited ideas updated for the emerging challenges identified by the ministry: "New World Balances, A Different Europe, New Peace and Security Dimensions, Growing Economic and Environmental Interdependencies, the Global Competition of Ideas, and the Challenge of Democracy."

Each of these emerging challenges will test the highly successful traditions of French diplomacy. Each of these challenges will define the future of French diplomacy. The French foreign ministry has a distinguished pedigree, and it is building on that institutional history with careful thought and energetic determination in the twenty-first century.

Acknowledgment *The authors wish to thank the following diplomats and scholars who were consulted in researching and writing this chapter:* Frédéric Bozo and Bernard Tuche.

Notes

1. Archis Mohan, "Indian Diplomacy Fails Numbers Test," *StratPost*, October 1, 2013, http://www.stratpost.com/indian-diplomacy-fails-numbers-test. Accessed February 28, 2019.
2. Paul Gordon Lauren, *Diplomats and Bureaucrats: The First Institutional Responses to Twentieth-Century Diplomacy in France and Germany* (Stanford, Calif: Hoover Institution Press, 1976).
3. "Expenditures and Receipts of General Government in 2016," *Institut National de la Statistique et des Études Économiques* (National Institute of Statistics and Economic Studies) http://www.insee.fr/en/themes/comptes-nationaux/tableau.asp?sous_theme=3.2&xml=t_3201. Accessed February 28, 2019; "Euros (EUR) to US Dollars (USD) Rates for 12/31/2012—Exchange Rates," http://www.exchange-rates.org/Rate/EUR/USD/12-31-2012. Accessed February 28, 2019; "US Inflation Calculator," *US Inflation Calculator*. http://www.usinflationcalculator.com/. Accessed February 28, 2019. Note—The foreign ministry budget was converted from December 31, 2012 Euros to October 26, 2016 US Dollars, accounting for historical exchange rates and inflation. The federal budget excludes Social Security, local & regional government, and quasi government body spending.
4. Ministry for Europe and Foreign Affairs, "The Ministry and its Network." *France Diplomatie*, 2017. https://www.diplomatie.gouv.fr/en/the-ministry-and-its-network/. Accessed March 2, 2019.
5. Ibid.
6. Ministère des l'Europe et des Affaires Étrangères, "*Concours*," *France Diplomatie*. January 14, 2019. http://www.diplomatie.gouv.fr/fr/emplois-stages-concours/concours/. Accessed February 28, 2019.
7. Ibid.
8. Ministry for Europe and Foreign Affairs, "Gender Equality at the Ministry for Europe and Foreign Affairs," *France diplomatie*. January 2014. http://www.diplomatie.gouv.fr/en/the-ministry-of-foreign-affairs/gender-equality-at-the-french-foreign-ministry/. Accessed February 28, 2019.
9. Ibid.
10. Authors' interview of career French diplomat, November 4, 2016.
11. Ministère des l'Europe et des Affaires Étrangères, "*Les Métiers Du Ministère des Affaires Étrangère*" (Jobs in the Foreign Ministry), October 25, 2018. https://www.diplomatie.gouv.fr/fr/photos-videos-publications-infographies/publications/brochures-institutionnelles/article/les-metiers-du-ministere-de-l-europe-et-des-affaires-etrangeres. Accessed February 28, 2019.

12. Ibid.
13. Authors' interview of career French diplomat, November 4, 2016.
14. Charles Cogan, *French Negotiating Behavior: Dealing with La Grande Nation* (Washington, DC: United States Institute of Peace Press, 2003).
15. Stephanie Kinney, "AFSA Benchmarking Exercise: Brazil, China, UK, Germany, France, Canada, Mexico, India Selection and Entry Level Training," (Washington, DC: American Foreign Service Association, n.d.).
16. Ministère de l'Europe et des Affaires Étrangères, "Les Métiers Du Ministère des Affaires Étrangères."
17. Ibid.
18. Kinney, "AFSA Benchmarking Exercise."
19. You must have five or ten years of experience in the private sector in a role similar to a company manager and there is a different exam process. Authors' interview of career French diplomat, November 4, 2016.
20. Authors' interview of career French diplomat, December 15, 2016.
21. Ibid.
22. Kinney, "AFSA Benchmarking Exercise."
23. *Le President de la Républic Francaise*, Le Livre blanc: Defense et Sécurité Nationale/White Paper on Defense and Security, 2013. http://www.livreblancdefenseetsecurite.gouv.fr. Accessed February 28, 2019.
24. Ministry for Europe and Foreign Affairs, "The Diplomatic and Consular Institute (IDC)," *France Diplomatie*, January 2014. http://www.diplomatie.gouv.fr/en/the-ministry-of-foreign-affairs/training-of-diplomats-and-personnel/article/the-diplomatic-and-consular. Accessed February 28, 2019.
25. Ibid.
26. Ministry for Europe and Foreign Affairs, "Training of Diplomats and Personnel."
27. Ministry for Europe and Foreign Affairs, "Gender Equality."
28. Ministry for Europe and Foreign Affairs, "The Ambassador," *France Diplomatie*. https://www.diplomatie.gouv.fr/en/the-ministry-and-its-network/missions-and-structure/what-diplomats-do/article/the-ambassador. Accessed February 28, 2019.
29. Ibid.
30. Interview of career French diplomat by authors. November 4, 2016.
31. "Russia is Negotiating with Germany and France over Ukraine," *Economist*. October 22, 2017. http://www.economist.com/news/europe/21709066-while-foreign-powers-argue-about-its-future-ukrainians-struggle-take-their-destiny. Accessed March 11, 2017.
32. Authors' interview of career French diplomat, November 4, 2016.
33. Ibid.
34. "Le livre blanc/White Paper."

References

Cogan, C. 2003. *French Negotiating Behavior: Dealing with La Grande Nation.* Washington, DC: U.S. Institute of Peace.

Concours. 2019. France Diplomatie: Ministère des l'Europe et des Affaires étrangères. http://www.diplomatie.gouv.fr/fr/emplois-stages-concours/concours/. Accessed February 28, 2019.

Diplomatic and Consular Institute (IDC). 2019. France Diplomatie: Ministry for Europe and Foreign Affairs. http://www.diplomatie.gouv.fr/en/the-ministry-of-foreign-affairs/training-of-diplomats-and-personnel/article/the-diplomatic-and-consular. Accessed February 28, 2019.

Evans-Pritchard, A. 2017, February 15. France's Marine Le Pen Explains How She Aims to Smash the European Order. *The Telegraph.* http://www.telegraph.co.uk/business/2017/02/15/frances-marine-le-pen-explains-aims-smash-european-order/.

Expenditures and Receipts of General Government in 2016. 2017, March 27. Institut national de la statistique et des études économiques (National Institute of Statistics and Economic Studies). http://www.insee.fr/en/themes/comptes-nationaux/tableau.asp?sous_theme=3.2&xml=t_3201. Accessed February 28, 2019.

Gender Equality at the Ministry for Europe and Foreign Affairs. 2014, January. France Diplomatie: Ministère des l'Europe et des Affaires étrangères. http://www.diplomatie.gouv.fr/en/the-ministry-of-foreign-affairs/gender-equality-at-the-french-foreign-ministry/. Accessed February 28, 2019.

Kinney, S. n.d. *AFSA Benchmarking Exercise: Brazil, China, UK, Germany, France, Canada, Mexico, India: Selection and Entry Level Training.* Washington, DC: American Foreign Service Association.

Lauren, P.G. 1976. *Diplomats and Bureaucrats: The First Institutional Responses to Twentieth-Century Diplomacy in France and Germany.* Stanford, CA: Hoover Institution Press.

Le livre blanc: Defense et sécurité nationale/White Paper on Defense and Security. 2013. *Le President de la Républic Francaise.* http://www.livreblancdefenseetsecurite.gouv.fr. Accessed February 28, 2019.

Lequesne, C., and J. Heilbronn. 2012. Senior Diplomats in the French Ministry of Foreign Affairs: When an Entrance Exam Still Determines the Career. *Hague Journal of Diplomacy* 7: 269–285.

Les métiers du ministère de l'Europe et des Affaires étrangères. 2018, October 25. Ministère des l'Europe et des Affaires étrangères. https://www.diplomatie.gouv.fr/fr/photos-videos-publications-infographies/publications/brochures-institutionnelles/article/les-metiers-du-ministere-de-l-europe-et-des-affaires-etrangeres. Accessed February 28, 2019.

Macron, E. 2017, August 29. *For a Global French Diplomacy*. Permanent Mission of France to the United Nations in New York. https://onu.delegfrance.org/Speech-by-President-E-Macron-for-a-global-french-diplomacy. Accessed March 4, 2019.

Mak, D.S. 2003. The Nature of French Diplomacy: Reflections of American Diplomats. *American Diplomacy*. http://americandiplomacy.web.unc.edu/2003/09/the-nature-of-french-diplomacy-reflections-of-american-diplomats/. Accessed March 4, 2019.

Mohan, A. 2013, October 1. Indian Diplomacy Fails Numbers Test. *StratPost*. http://www.stratpost.com/indian-diplomacy-fails-numbers-test. Accessed February 28, 2019.

Russia Is Negotiating with Germany and France over Ukraine. 2016, October 22. *The Economist*. http://www.economist.com/news/europe/21709066-while-foreign-powers-argue-about-its-future-ukrainians-struggle-take-their-destiny. Accessed March 11, 2017.

Training of Diplomats and Personnel. 2019. France Diplomatie: Ministry for Europe and Foreign Affairs. http://www.diplomatie.gouv.fr/en/the-ministry-of-foreign-affairs/training-of-diplomats-and-personnel/. Accessed February 28, 2019.

What Diplomats Do: The Ambassador. 2019. France Diplomatie: Ministry for Europe and Foreign Affairs. https://www.diplomatie.gouv.fr/en/the-ministry-and-its-network/missions-and-structure/what-diplomats-do/article/the-ambassador. Accessed February 28, 2019.

CHAPTER 4

Germany

Marne Sutten, Catherine Cousar, and Robert Hutchings

EXECUTIVE SUMMARY

The German diplomatic service is an elite, professional diplomatic corps with a highly centralized organizational culture.[1] As in other countries surveyed in this volume, globalization and the growing number of bureaucratic "actors" in foreign policy making, particularly on EU (European Union) issues, have led to the simultaneous fragmentation and centralization of foreign policy. With more ministries involved in certain aspects of external relations, there has been a growing tendency toward centralization of policy making in the office of the Chancellor. The foreign office continues to play a key role, but the locus of activity has shifted to the Chancellor's office, to which many professional diplomats have been seconded.

M. Sutten
US Army Fellow, 2016–2017, The University of Texas at Austin, Austin, TX, USA

C. Cousar
2017 Master of Arts Degree, Global Policy Studies, The University of Texas at Austin, Austin, TX, USA

R. Hutchings (✉)
Lyndon B. Johnson School of Public Affairs, The University of Texas at Austin, Austin, TX, USA
e-mail: rhutchings@austin.utexas.edu

© The Author(s) 2020
R. Hutchings, J. Suri (eds.), *Modern Diplomacy in Practice*,
https://doi.org/10.1007/978-3-030-26933-3_4

The German Foreign Service selects and trains a diverse diplomatic corps that is well-socialized into a cohesive diplomatic culture, which makes for disciplined and coherent foreign policy messaging, sometimes at the cost of flexibility and autonomy. The selection process and early training are among the most rigorous in the world and include a battery of written and oral examinations followed by 14 months to 3 years of training at the Diplomatic Academy. This training period includes an internship and final examination before new officers are assigned to their first posting. Language skills are highly valued and candidates must speak English and French or a second UN language to apply. Diplomats receive additional training mid-career to include classes on leadership, resiliency, team building, and management for continued promotion.

Germany's longstanding preference for a low-key foreign policy conducted mainly through multilateral institutions has served the country well, but may no longer be feasible in today's fragmented global system. German leaders acknowledge the need for Germany to take a more active role in the world, as was evident in several speeches at the 2014 Munich security conference, but the needed steps will be unsettling. The combination of new challenges—the refugee crisis, Brexit, harder-line Russian policies, and others—and the weakening of multilateral institutions including NATO (North Atlantic Treaty Organization), the UN (United Nations), the World Trade Organization, and even the EU, make Germany's instinctive preference for multilateralism increasingly hard to maintain. Foreign Minister Heiko Maas's call for an "alliance of multilateralists" during his 2018 visit to Japan so far has not been translated into consistent policy. The resignation of Angela Merkel as Christian Democratic Union (CDU) party leader in 2018 and her announcement that she will not seek another term as chancellor add to the uncertainties ahead.

HISTORY AND CULTURE

German diplomatic culture derives from the combined legacies of geography, history, tradition, and philosophy. Although Germany achieved statehood and national unity only in 1871, it has a long history and a rich diplomatic tradition that long predate unification. Its diplomacy is strongly influenced by geography: situated in the middle of the continent with no natural protective boundaries, Germany of necessity has adopted a foreign policy of adjustment and maneuver. As a trading state whose economic well-being is heavily export-led, Germany inherited from its preunification past a strong tradition of economic diplomacy.[2] This dimension was, of course, accentuated by the deep aversion to military force that came out of the searing national trauma of the Nazi period.

Contemporary German diplomacy reflects the competing traditions of Metternich and Bismarck—or, to put it more precisely, those two nineteenth century statesmen reflected some of the same geopolitical realities that continue to shape German policy today. The tradition of Austrian foreign minister Klemens von Metternich was characterized by the maneuver and compromise required to hold together the multi-ethnic Austro–Hungarian Empire, whereas the tradition of Prussian Chancellor Otto von Bismarck was that of the *Machtpolitik* (power politics) employed to unite Germany's disparate principalities into a modern nation-state. As the website of the German foreign office notes, "The name '*Auswärtiges Amt*' dates back to the eponymous institution of the North German Confederation in 1879 and the German Empire from 1871... During Bismarck's time, the *Auswärtiges Amt* had only two directorates: a Political Directorate and a second Directorate responsible for foreign trade and other issues as well as legal and consular affairs." It retains the name "office" (*Amt*) from Bismarck's time, whereas other federal departments are called ministries, and the titles of senior officers (e.g. *Staatsminister*) are also carried over from the Bismarckian era. Some 90% of the diplomatic corps in those days was drawn from the nobility. The service was opened to those outside the nobility in 1918, but it was not until the 1950s, and particularly the 1971 Herwarth Report commissioned by Chancellor Willy Brandt, that it was converted into a modern merit-based service.

Trained as a diplomat himself, serving as ambassador to Russia and later to France, Bismarck created the professional diplomatic corps and left behind a tradition of urbane and well-prepared diplomats. The foreign office at *Wilhelmstrasse 76* was also a highly centralized and rigid operation, organized along military lines and tightly controlled by the Chancellor,[3] who once declared that "if an ambassador can obey, more is not required."[4] Yet Bismarck's Realpolitik and his diplomatic style demanded tactical flexibility and skill; it was opposed to the Romanticism and over-militarization to which his twentieth century successors succumbed.[5]

The record of the *Auswärtiges Amt* during the Third Reich was thoroughly (if belatedly) examined in a nearly 900-page report commissioned in 2005 by Foreign Minister Joschka Fischer.[6] Its role during the Nazi era, neither better nor worse than that of most other German institutions, contributed to the decline of professionalism and prestige of the diplomatic corps well into the post-war period, particularly in that the service continued of necessity to rely on officers who had served during the Nazi regime.[7] With the findings and recommendations of the Herwarth Commission, however, the Foreign Office began to rebuild its strong professional culture. The report's analysis of global trends stands up well half a century later, and its key recommendations—decentralization of decision making and strengthening of Germany's economic diplomacy—have served Germany well.[8] By the 1970s and 1980s, the ministry had reestablished itself as the most important government office after the Chancellery and among the most popular employers in the country. German unification in 1990 caused hardly a ripple in the work of the service in that not a single senior officer of the former East Germany (German Democratic Republic) was added to the ministry.[9]

German diplomacy is also shaped by a philosophical tradition that is so deeply internalized that it is often unrecognized even by the diplomats themselves. (The same could be said of most other political cultures, of course. It took de Tocqueville to explain American political culture to Americans.) The German intellectual tradition was not shaped by seminal political philosophies comparable to those of Locke and Mill in Britain or Montesquieu and Rousseau for France, but it is revealed in the thinking of Leibniz, Kant, and Fichte, stressing abstract thought over empiricism, as well as the distinctive dialectical method of Hegel, which enables German diplomats to hold opposing, even contradictory ideas together in an overarching *Gesamtkonzept*.[10] The German intellectual style is guided by *Gedankennotwendigkeit*: "if one has accepted the premises and certain rules of inference, then the conclusion follows."[11] It is quite different from the Anglo-Saxon style of inductive reasoning via discourse and debate, a philosophical disjuncture that can create difficulties in negotiation quite apart from the substantive issues on the table. The German style is closer to the Cartesian rationality of the French, though in the Gallic style the conclusion is achieved not through rigorous deduction but rather by means of elegant synthesis.[12]

Profile

The Foreign Office budget is 5.2 billion euros (approximately $5.9 million) and accounts for roughly 1.5% of the total federal budget. Of the entire budget, approximately 1.3 billion euros is spent by the Federal Ministry to include staffing and administrative costs to support the ministry headquarters and 227 missions worldwide. Additionally, 923 million euros is spent on cultural relations and education policy, 215 million euros is spent on bilateral cooperation and fostering internal relations, and 32.7 million euros is spent to support the German Archaeological Institute. The Federal Foreign budget also account for approximately 2.7 billion euros spent on safeguarding peace and stability, which includes contributions to the United Nations, humanitarian aid, and crisis prevention.[13] Missions abroad include 153 embassies, 61 consulates, and 12 permanent missions. Several ambassadors represent Germany in more than one country, as Germany has diplomatic relations with 195 countries. Germany also designates approximately 350 honorary consuls in countries without a consular post, but where they deem it important to have a local point of contact.

The German Federal Foreign Office (*Auswärtiges Amt*) is fairly modestly staffed compared to the US, British, and French services, with 6030 personnel, not counting the 5622 locally-employed staff.[14] The Foreign Service has five personnel categories, including secretarial staff, ordinary service, intermediate service, higher intermediate (administrative) service, and higher (executive) service. Of these categories, the intermediate, administrative, and executive services are considered career Foreign Service professional and require training and examinations.[15] The intermediate service includes 1348 vocational degreed technicians including consular, administrative, and information technology specialists. The administrative service category includes 1813 Foreign Service professionals including consular cadre, ministry desk officers, and Chancery as First Secretaries in small embassies. The executive category includes 1692 Foreign Service Officers. The executive and administrative service accounts for the 3505 career diplomats. The secretarial category includes 849 staff members, and the ordinary service category includes 397 non-degreed drivers, technicians, and laborers. The missions abroad also employ an additional 5731 German and local national employees to support embassies and consulates.[16]

Organizationally, the ministry is divided into regional Directorates General (DGs) for EU foreign policy and North America (DG-2), Europe (E), Asia and the Pacific (AP), and the Middle East, Africa and Latin America (DG-3), as well as functional DGs for stabilization operations and crisis prevention (S) and International Order (IO).[17] The addition of E in 1998, and AP and S more recently reflects the changing global environment and Germany's shifting priorities. As is the case with other EU member countries, European policy (E) overlaps to a large extent with domestically focused ministries—in what former German foreign minister Hans-Dietrich Genscher called the "internationalization of domestic policy."

Germany's diplomatic service, once the preserve of the nobility, was transformed substantially after World War II and especially in the 1970s into a meritocratic service drawing on well-educated university graduates with diverse backgrounds. The current "Charter of Diversity" expresses the Foreign Ministry's commitment to a diverse workforce according to which employees are hired regardless of gender, nationality, ethnic origin, religion or belief, disability, age, sexual orientation, and identify appreciation. Like other foreign ministries, the Federal Foreign office is struggling to achieve gender diversity.[18] Women actually account for more than half of the total work force, but they are predominantly in the secretarial staff (where women account for 94% of the total), intermediate service (62%), and administrative service (57%). Women comprise just 33% of the executive service, though this represents a significant increase in recent years.[19]

RECRUITMENT AND SELECTION

For career diplomats, the German Foreign Service selection process is rigorous and demanding. Under Article 116 of German law, all applicants must be German nationals and affirm their commitment to a free and democratic Germany. Once they pass initial screening through an on-line examination, applicants for the executive service are given a written examination at the German Diplomatic Academy on Lake Tegel in Berlin that includes German history, economics, law, and general knowledge, as well as separate examinations in English and another foreign language. This is followed by a series of oral examinations, designed to test general grounding in foreign policy as well as ability to work in a team. It includes questioning before a panel that includes a psychologist as well as professional diplomats, a five-minute extemporaneous speech on a policy issue (from a choice of two topics) with 15 minutes to prepare, a group discussion to judge interaction with other applicants, and a role-playing situation on a diplomatic or personnel issue with professional actors.[20] Language skills are highly valued in the German Foreign Service, and officer candidates must speak English and French or a second UN language to apply. The best Foreign Service Officers are expected to acquire at least one "hard language" in addition to English and French.

An officer serving in the intermediate service must have a secondary education degree or vocational training before applying to the Federal Foreign Service. Approximately, 60 people a year will be selected into the intermediate category and will attend two years at the academy, which works in conjunction with administrative colleges for training. During the two years, intermediate service candidates will complete a five-month internship at the Foreign Office headquarters and approximately eight months at a mission abroad. At headquarters, personnel in intermediate services will handle procurement, equipment, and vehicles and transportation. At missions, they work in legal, consular services, and registry administration. The candidates will take an examination at the end of the two years to become certified as an intermediate Foreign Service employee.[21]

An administrative service officer must have a college or technical college degree before applying to the Federal Foreign Service. Approximately, 40 are selected each year to attend three years at the academy, including a six-month internship at the headquarters and another six to eight months at a mission abroad. Administrative service officials are "in charge of routine tasks in legal and consular services and administration, trade promotion, development and economic co-operation, cultural affairs, public diplomacy and protocol." These officials spend approximately two-thirds of their time at missions abroad and are entrusted with executive positions including Chief of Administration, Deputy Head of Mission, and Head of Legal or Consular Department. The variety of responsibilities and positions for administrative service officials require that they are generalists and can handle a multitude of topics. Administrative services personnel will take an examination at the completion of their training and internship.[22]

All officers in the executive service have a university degree before attending the Foreign Service academy. The training at the academy involves a 12- to 14-month program that includes courses in history, German law, international law, political science, communications, language, and economics.[23] The Federal Foreign Service states that "intellectual flexibility, and understanding of political contexts and the ability to think strategically and a high degree of intercultural and social competence" are traits valued for executive service,[24] though some have likened the socialization process as being akin to a military academy. Approximately, 35 officers a year will be selected for the executive service out of 1700–2000 applicants.[25] The average age of personnel selected into the executive branch is 30, and most have a master's degree.

Historically, lawyers were disproportionately represented in the German foreign office, as is the case throughout the German federal government. Lawyers used to account for between 40% and 50% of the diplomatic corps, but this has changed in recent years, as the foreign office has spread its recruiting net more widely among graduates in political science, economics, regional studies, and hard languages, with the result that the foreign office is now has fewer lawyers than is the case in most other federal ministries.[26]

The German Foreign Service is extremely supportive of families and the concept of *"Audit berufundfamilie"* or "work-life balance," which has won four awards since 2005.[27] This includes opportunities for flexible and part-time work arrangements and the possibility of telecommuting. Daycare is provided to 70 children at a facility located in close proximity to the Berlin headquarters. The Foreign Office tries to mitigate the challenges associated with job placement for partners of officers stationed in foreign countries. The service attempts to identify appropriate jobs for partners at foreign missions and offer advanced training courses to help partners find jobs while stationed abroad. The Foreign Office also established reciprocal agreements with 30 countries to allow partners of Foreign Service Officers the opportunity to work abroad, and is currently in consultation with another 30 countries for additional agreements. Language training is also offered to families of Foreign Service Officers before they are stationed abroad.[28] *Audit berufundfamilie*, extends to when an officer must be away from family for a hardship posting. In high-risk postings, such as Baghdad, every position is assigned twice. This allows staff to serve six to eight weeks in country and then take six to eight weeks off at home. They receive up to 72 holiday days in a year while serving in hardship postings. This makes these positions quite attractive and allows officers to maintain family bonds even during such posting.[29]

Professional Development and Training

The German Foreign Service does not have cones or a track system like many countries, and it follows the *Generalistenprinzip* (generalist principle), whereby all officers are considered generalists until they reach the counselor level.[30] Foreign Service Officers typically change postings every three to four years depending on the needs of the organization, normally serving two tours abroad followed by one at the headquarters. Personnel are transferred from missions to headquarters or to another mission abroad without returning to headquarters, but officers normally return to the headquarters for their fourth assignment to focus on a specialization.[31]

The Foreign Service's diplomatic academy conducts training courses for its personnel throughout their career. Once the initial training is completed, new diplomats receive a combination of on the job training in conjunction with one- and two-week mandatory courses provided by the academy. Course topics include leadership training, legal instruction, self-management, time management, and foreign language courses. In the last three to four years, the service also shifted to focus on management skills. Attending these courses is required for promotion; the courses are approximately four days long. Longer-term mid-career training is rare, as the German Foreign Service does not budget for extended training or attendance at civilian institutions. Language training, especially in "hard languages," is viewed as another shortfall, compared, for example, to the Russian diplomatic corps.[32] Additionally, every year over 300 international diplomats attend one of the 15 courses offered by the academy.[33] In this way, the Foreign Service aims to use its "soft power" to build cohesive relationships between Germans and diplomats worldwide.

The German Diplomatic Service also supports opportunities for officers to serve on rotation in positions outside the Federal Foreign Office. The Foreign Office provides staff to the European External Action Service and also sends officers to serve for brief periods in the foreign ministries of other countries, including Poland, France, the Netherlands, the United States, Norway, and Italy. There are also service exchanges with the Association of German Industry as well as corporations such as Siemens. These opportunities are limited, however, in that there is not a sufficient personnel overhead to cover all required positions.[34]

The Federal Foreign Office has a top-down management style. The socialization diplomats receive early in their career, the slow and ordered pace of promotion, and the centralization of decision making in Berlin all combine to make for a disciplined and predictable approach to foreign policy. These features are consistent with a culture favoring multilateralism and self-restraint; indeed, multilateralism is a key element of the initial training diplomats receive at the Foreign Service Academy. As the 2014 Steinmeier Report observed, however, these same factors can inhibit innovation, autonomy, and the habits of strategic thinking.[35]

German diplomats at embassies and consulates report that they have influence and opportunities to make recommendations about policy, but they also clearly understand the position of Berlin and rarely deviate from the official position. In major posts and on major issues, especially those of high importance or subject to public scrutiny, guidance comes directly from Berlin; in regions that are not in the headlines, there is more room for diplomats to exercise discretion. These patterns are similar to those in other diplomatic services, one difference being that Germany's tradition of coalition governments means that arduously negotiated foreign policy positions leave somewhat less room for flexibility and interpretation by missions abroad. Although there is no official "dissent channel," as there is in the US State Department, the diplomats that we interviewed felt empowered to provide feedback to their superiors without fear of retribution and believed that the leadership heard their thoughts.

Leadership

The administrative regulations that outline the requirements for promotions are listed in the Federal Officials Act (FOA, *Bundesbeamtengesetz*), in combination with the Federal Ordinance on Careers and Promotion of Civil Servants (FOCPCS, *Beamtenrechtsrahmengesetz*). These prerequisites are common to all civil servants in the German Government. Officers in the executive service will "be promoted four times during a career of some 35 years, with the retirement age set at 65 years."[36] Early in their career, most officers will be promoted after spending one to three years in a position, and generally will be promoted two or three times in this fashion. Thereafter, in this pyramidal hierarchy, officials will generally not be promoted for another ten years. Only a small percentage will receive a fifth promotion to the remuneration grade of B6 or a sixth promotion to the remuneration grade of B9. In 2004, there were 51 grade B6 positions, 18 grade B9 positions, and only 2 B11 positions.[37] Promotions are not directly connected to specific positions, but, as a general rule, personnel at the headquarters are promoted at a faster rate to fill the top positions. All staff receive performance appraisals that help determine promotions (Table 4.1).

Table 4.1   Grade and rank classifications for German Foreign Service

Remuneration grade	Title
Preparatory training	Attaché
Probationary period	Second Secretary/Vice Consul
Entry grade A13	Desk Officer/Second Secretary/Consul
Remuneration grade A14	Desk Officer/First Secretary/Consul
Remuneration grade A15	Desk Officer/Counselor, Minister, Consul, General/Deputy Consul General, Ambassador
Remuneration grade A16	Head of Division/First Counselor/Minister Counselor, Counsel/Consul General, Ambassador
Remuneration grade B3	Head of Division/First Counselor, Minister, Consul General/Deputy Consul General, Ambassador
Remuneration grade B6	Director, Minister, Consul General/Deputy Consul General, Ambassador
Remuneration grade B9	Director General, Minister, Ambassador
Remuneration grade B11	State Secretary

Source: Anke Freibert, "Classifications and Career Development in the German Foreign Service," SIGMA, Organization for Economic Cooperation and Development, December 2004

Most German diplomats holding senior positions below the level of minister have gradually progressed through their careers beginning as basic officers and moving up, usually serving as a deputy head of mission before becoming a full ambassador. Most have had a career balance between serving in Berlin and abroad, and while some have regional specialties, not all do. Many have German doctoral degrees, and some have also served as professors or assistant professors prior to entering the service or during sabbaticals. Peter Wittig, former German Ambassador to the United States, taught as assistant professor at the University of Freiburg, and Harald Braun, former State Secretary and Permanent Representative of Germany to the UN, was a Research Professor for Global Studies and Diplomacy at the State University of New York at Stony Brook. They tend, on average, to be older than their counterparts in France or Britain. Almost all ambassadors are career Foreign Service Officers rather than political appointees. In recent years, only a very few in relatively minor posts such as Latvia or the Vatican were not career diplomats.[38]

The position of foreign minister has specific characteristics in the German case. Because Germany has been governed by multi-party coalitions for virtually its entire post-war existence, German foreign ministers tend to be senior politicians from political parties different from the Chancellor's. They typically have had senior positions in other ministries at the federal or state (*Land*) level. Former foreign minister Sigmar Gabriel, who served from 2017 to 2018, had been Vice Chancellor from 2013 to 2018 and leader of the Social Democratic Party (SPD) from 2009 to 2017. He had served earlier as Federal Minister of the Environment and Federal Minister of Economic Affairs and Energy and as Prime Minister of the state of Lower Saxony. His successor, Heiko Maas, served as Federal Minister of Justice and Consumer Protection and earlier in a series of Land-level political positions in the Saarland. Gabriel's predecessor as foreign minister, Frank-Walter Steinmeier (2013–2017), who was elected President of Germany in 2017, had a career mostly at the federal level and largely focused on foreign affairs and thus had an unusual level of foreign policy experience compared to other recent foreign ministers.

Role in Foreign Policy Making

The political system of the Federal Republic of Germany (FRG), established under the Basic Law (*Grundgesetz*) of 1949, was specifically designed to prevent the concentration of political power that occurred under the Nazi regime. The Basic Law does not clearly stipulate the definitive authorities in foreign policy making between ministerial authority (*Ressortprinzip*) and chancellor authority (*Kanzlerprinzip*).[39] In practice, ministers are accorded wide latitude on matters internal to the ministry. Only rarely would a chancellor interfere on an issue within a minister's purview, and only on issues where the most basic German interests were involved.[40] Foreign policy making is another matter, however, and the nature of German political system both strengthens and weakens the role of the Foreign Office in foreign policy making. On one hand, the electoral system of mixed-member proportional representation has produced coalition governments for almost the entirety of the FRG's existence, most often with the Foreign Minister coming from a political party other than the Chancellor's, and serving concurrently as Vice Chancellor and party chairman. Thus, as has been noted, German foreign ministers typically are powerful figures with independent political bases, whose partisan political responsibilities sometimes set them apart from the professional diplomatic corps. Some, like Willy Brandt, Hans-Dietrich Genscher, and Joschka Fischer, have rivaled their chancellors in terms of power and prestige. Of course, coalition governments impose constraints on foreign ministers as well as on chancellors, particularly when they are grand coalitions like the *GroKo's* (*Grosse Koalitions*) that prevailed for most of the chancellorship of Angela Merkel.

Additionally, the federal system accords considerable power to Germany's 16 states (*Länder*) via the upper house (*Bundesrat*) of the bicameral legislature as well as directly through the Minister-President of each *Land*.[41] Some, notably Bavaria's legendary Minister-President Franz-Josef Strauss, have been independent foreign policy actors in their own rights, particularly on matters of foreign commercial policy.

For all these reasons, as is the case with other countries analyzed in this book, Germany manifests a simultaneous fragmentation and centralization of foreign policy decision making, with a concomitant relative decline of influence of the foreign office. Foreign ministers and chancellors alike, even long-serving ones, have to build and maintain consensus among coalition partners as well as with rivals in their own party. A case point is the role played in the late 1990s by Defense Minister Volker Rühe in shaping the policy of NATO enlargement to include the new democracies of East Central Europe over the objections of the Foreign Office, which wanted to defer NATO enlargement until after EU enlargement had been accomplished.[42] Cultivating the support of the German military and of pro-NATO enlargement circles in Washington, Rühe engaged in a rare public dispute with Foreign Minister Klaus Kinkel, prompting an angry outburst from Chancellor Helmut Kohl against this open airing of grievances. Kohl was ultimately brought around to a policy that EU and NATO enlargement should be linked, that the NATO process should come first owing to the inherently time-consuming procedures for EU accession, and that NATO should simultaneously pursue a partnership with Russia. In this case, the Defense Ministry played an unusually assertive role in outmaneuvering the Foreign Office, led by a relatively inexperienced minister who succeeded the long-serving Hans-Dietrich Genscher. A more common feature has been the dominant role of the foreign affairs division of the Chancellery, particularly on matters of high importance and visibility.

An equally important trend is the growing role of ministries with a predominantly domestic focus in the conduct of foreign policy, particularly on matters of European Union affairs. This has been variously termed the "fragmentation of foreign policy" or the "internationalization of domestic policy," and has led to a distinction between foreign policy (*Aussenpolitik*), where the foreign office continues to play a strong role, and external relations (*Aussenbeziehungen*), where many other ministries have powerful roles that often eclipse that of the foreign office.[43] In such cases, the Foreign Office, particularly "E" (the Directorate-General for

European Affairs), becomes, at best, the manager or coordinator of policy rather than the lead ministry. As von Ploetz has put it, "as a result of the increasing interdependence of policy areas and simultaneous fragmentation of both actors and fora, co-ordination has as such become a prime task for the Foreign Service."[44]

Given all these cross-pressures, it is no surprise the policy coordination across government is a major challenge. On operational matters, the interagency process is said to work reasonably well. Five key ministries meet regularly to coordinate, with ministers joined by different members of their senior staff depending on the issues under discussion.[45] Strategic coordination is another matter, however, and there is no regular structure akin to the US National Security Council to set priorities, clarify interests, and referee interagency differences. Cases in point include the clash between the Foreign Office and the Ministry for Economic Cooperation on development assistance to Middle Eastern countries after the Gulf War of 1991, and with the Ministry of Education over cooperation with Russia on supplies of highly enriched uranium.[46] More recent examples include conflicts over handling of the Greek debt crisis, immigration policy, and the Nord Stream 2 natural gas pipeline from Russia. The growing number and complexity of such challenges have led to calls for German foreign policy to become more strategic and better coordinated.

Preparations for the Future

In 2014, then-German Foreign Minister Frank-Walter Steinmeier, concerned that the ministry had an "outdated West-German culture of passivity, lack of strategy, and adversity to a more exposed role for Germany in the world,"[47] commissioned an extensive, year-long evaluation of German foreign policy. The key focus of the Steinmeier Report, or "Review 2014," was how the Federal Foreign Office might be better prepared to respond to the challenges of unexpected events and encourage discourse about Germany's role in the world.[48] There was also a recognition that the Foreign Office had not kept pace with rapid technological change. In Germany as elsewhere, "cyberdiplomacy" has broken down the barriers between the Foreign Office and missions abroad, as diplomats overseas create new networks with desk officers in Berlin and indeed with counterparts in other countries, bypassing traditional lines of authority. Simply put, "network structures do not correspond well to hierarchical structures."[49] Politically, Minister Steinmeier knew that the review would make a public statement about the foreign ministry's desire for more funding and increased staff, and enable his Social Democratic Party (SPD) to offset the growing dominance, including over foreign policy, of Chancellor Angela Merkel.[50] The process was as important as the result, and Steinmeier called for an "open, wide and nuanced debate on German foreign policy."[51]

Under the banner of "Crisis Order Europe," Review 2014 did produce some organizational changes, described above, and led to significant new funding for reconstruction, development, and crisis response in the new "S" directorate. Crisis response is by definition reactive, however, and "Review 2014" was criticized for failing to articulate core German interests or lay out a comprehensive strategy in the new global environment. As a former member of the Foreign Office's planning staff put in a report for a Study Committee for Franco–German Relations, "In view of Germany's new economic and political weight, the country faces greater responsibilities [but] remains ill-prepared for this role, both conceptually and strategically." With particular reference to "Review 2014," she added, "Not only is the idea of a policy expressing the national interest taboo for most of the German political class, but receives limited support in the context of discussions between experts."[52] It is not that Germany does not act on the basis of core national interests but rather that for understandable historical reasons, is loath to admit to having them. There are, however, deeply rooted guiding principles in German foreign policy—principles that have held up for many decades but which face new challenges in a radically shifting global environment.

No tenet of post-war German foreign policy is more deeply held that that of multilateralism. Because of the Nazi past, German political leaders were wary of "going it alone" (*Alleingang*), and because of Germany's post-war division, its most ardent national goal—the unification of the country—could only be achieved in partnership with its European and transatlantic allies. That situation changed objectively with the achievement of unity on October 3, 1990, yet Germany's "instinctive preference for multilateralism" and "strict avoidance of *nationale Alleingänge*" persisted.[53] This multilateralist orientation is sincerely held, yet it can also be a cover for a German foreign policy that is no less driven by national interests than is the case for other countries. Beverly Crawford labeled this phenomenon "embedded hegemony" and examined three cases in which Germany acted unilaterally but within a multilateral framework, including its premature recognition of Slovenia and Croatia in 1991.[54] Acting—or professing to act—"in Europe's name"[55] (to use Timothy Garton Ash's description of the same phenomenon) has served Germany well, but it is an orientation that is harder to sustain in light of new global challenges, growing populism at home, and eroding multilateral institutions.

The 2018 resignation of Angela Merkel as party leader of the CDU (Christian Democratic Union) and her announcement that she would not seek reelection as chancellor create new uncertainties, not only for Germany's domestic politics, but also for its foreign policy orientation. The flux in the global environment adds to these uncertainties. Britain's decision to leave the European Union, along with a growing north–south divide in the EU, will make it harder to forge coherent and effective European policies, and harder for Germany to pursue its interests via this multilateral structure. The "America first" policies of the Trump Administration have seriously damaged both German–US relations and NATO solidarity, two other pillars of post-war German foreign policy. In this context of eroding multilateral institutions, managing relations with a newly revanchist Russia threatens to upset Germany's longstanding foreign policy consensus. It is a future that calls for skilled diplomacy on the part of Germany's highly regarded diplomatic corps, but it also demands facing up to new and unwelcome challenges.

Acknowledgment *The authors wish to thank the following diplomats and scholars who were consulted in researching and writing this chapter:* Philipp Ackermann, Helga Barthe, Harald Braun, Anke Freibert, Maria Gosse, Helge Holleck, John Kornblum, Wolfgang Seibert, Klaus Scharioth, and Stephen Szabo.

Notes

1. Over-centralization was a key finding of the 2014 Steinmeier report, discussed below.
2. W.R. Smyser, *How Germans Negotiate: Logical Goals, Practical Solutions* (Washington: U.S. Institute of Peace Press, 2003), pp. 11–26. In today's Germany, "economic diplomacy" is led mainly be the Council for Investment and Trade (a public/private partnership) and the Ministry of Economics, with the Foreign Office in a support role.
3. Lamar Cecil, *The German Diplomatic Service, 1871–1914* (Princeton, NJ: Princeton University Press, 1976), pp. 104–5 and 226–56.
4. From the diary of Friedrich von Holstein, one of Bismarck's counselors, as cited in ibid., p. 236.
5. Henry Kissinger, *Diplomacy* (New York: Simon & Schuster, 1994), pp. 121–31.

6. Eckart Conze, Norbert Frei, Peter Hayes, and Moseh Zimmermann, *Das Amt und die Vergangensheit: Deutsche Diplomaten im Dritten Reich und in der Bundesrepublik* (Munich: Karl Blessing Verlag, 2011). See also Norbert Frei and Peter Hayes, "The German Foreign Office and the Past," *Bulletin of the German Historical Institute* 49 (Fall 2011).
7. Daniel Lewin, "The Decline of Tradition in the German Foreign Service," *The Western Political Science Quarterly*, Vol. 19, No. 4 (December 1966): 653–62.
8. D.C. Watt, "The Reform of the German Foreign Service: The Herwarth and Duncan Reports Compared," *The World Today*, Vol. 26, No. 8 (August 1970): 352–58.
9. Ralf Neukirch, "German Foreign Ministry Fights to Stay Relevant," *Spiegel Online*, May 4, 2012.
10. Ibid., pp. 22–25.
11. Johan Galtung, "Structure, Culture, and Intellectual Style: An Essay Comparing Saxonic, Teutonic, Gallic and Nipponic Approaches," *Social Science Information*, 20, 6 (1981): 829.
12. Ibid., 830–32.
13. *The Federal Foreign Office: Facts and Figures* (Berlin: Federal Foreign Office, 2018).
14. Ibid.
15. Anke Freibert, "Classifications and Career Development in the German Foreign Service," SIGMA (Support for Improvement in Governance and Management), Organization for Economic Cooperation and Development, December 2004.
16. *The Federal Foreign Office*.
17. Additional DGs focus on budget and personnel, economic affairs, international law, cultural diplomacy and protocol.
18. Interview with the Foreign Office Director-General for Central Services, Berlin, November 1, 2018.
19. *The Federal Foreign Office*.
20. Interview with a senior German diplomat, recently retired, who served as an oral examination panelist, Berlin, November 2, 2018.
21. Freibert, "Classifications and Career Development in the German Foreign Service."
22. Ibid.
23. Interviews at the Federal Foreign Office, Berlin, November 1–2, 2018, and at the German Embassy in Washington, November 9, 2018.
24. "AFSA Benchmarking Exercise: Brazil, China, UK, Germany, France, Canada, Mexico, India Selection and Entry Level Training" American Foreign Service Association, Washington, DC, June 14, 2010.

25. Freibert, "Classifications and Career Development in the German Foreign Service."
26. Interviews with senior German diplomats at the Federal Foreign Office, Berlin, November 1 and 2, 2018.
27. "Foreign Office: Questions and Answers on the Selection of Higher Service." https://www.auswaertiges-amt.de/de/karriere/auswaertiges-amt/hoeherer-dienst/faq/-/214498, accessed January 12, 2019.
28. Ibid.
29. Interview with First Secretary, Permanent Representation of Germany to the EU, Brussels, October 27, 2016.
30. Lisette Andreae and Karl Kaiser, "The 'Foreign Policies' of Specialized Ministries," in *Germany's New Foreign Policy*, p. 40.
31. Freibert, "Classifications and Career Development in the German Foreign Service."
32. Interview with the Director-General for Central Services, Berlin, November 1, 2018.
33. *Training for International Diplomats: Yearbook 2015*: https://www.auswaertiges-amt.de/blob/1586126/4dbcd121dac8c9e8cc7e9ecc70b90ee1/jahresheft-2015-data.pdf.
34. Interviews at the German Embassy in Washington, December 2016 and November 9, 2018.
35. Jan Techau, "The Steinmeier Review of German Foreign Policy," *Carnegie Europe*, March 19, 2015. http://carnegieeurope.eu/strategiceurope/?fa=59422.
36. Freibert, "Classifications and Career Development in the German Foreign Service."
37. Ibid.
38. Email from Anke Freibert, October 25, 2016.
39. Interview with senior German diplomat, Berlin, November 2, 2018. For a thorough discussion, see Judith Siwert-Probst, "Traditional Institutions of Foreign Policy," in *Germany's New Foreign Policy*, pp. 19–21.
40. Interview with senior German diplomat, Berlin, November 2, 2018.
41. Wolf-Dieter Eberwein and Karl Kaiser, "Academic Research and Foreign Policy-Making," in *Germany's New Foreign Policy*, pp. 4 and 11. See also Lisette Andreae and Karl Kaiser, "The 'Foreign Policies' of Specialized Ministries" in ibid., pp. 38–57.
42. Stephen F. Szabo, "Enlarging NATO: The German-American Design for a New Alliance," in *The Strategic Triangle: France, Germany, and the United States in the Shaping of the New Europe*, ed. Helga Haftendorn et al. (Washington and Baltimore: Wilson Center Press and The Johns Hopkins University Press, 2006), pp. 327–49, esp. pp. 330–42.
43. Andreae and Kaiser, "The 'Foreign Policies' of Specialized Ministries."

44. von Ploetz, "New Challenges for the Foreign Service," p. 75.
45. Andreae and Kaiser, "The 'Foreign Policies' of Specialized Ministries," p. 50; interview with a senior German diplomat who regularly attends these meetings on issues within his purview, Foreign Office, Berlin, November 2, 2018.
46. Andreae and Kaiser, "The 'Foreign Policies' of Specialized Ministries," pp. 43–45.
47. Techau, "The Steinmeier Review of German Foreign Policy."
48. Ibid.
49. von Ploetz, "New Challenges for the Foreign Service," pp. 82–83.
50. Techau, 'The Steinmeier Review."
51. "Closing Remarks by Foreign Minister Steinmeier at 'Review 2014' Conference," *Auswärtiges Amt*, accessed March 8, 2017, http://www.auswaertiges-amt.de/EN/Infoservice/Presse/Reden/2014/140520-BM_Review2014_Abschlussrede.html.
52. Annegret Bendiek, "The '2014 Review': Understanding the Pillars of German Foreign Policy and the Expectations of the Rest of the World," Working Paper RD EU/Europe, 2015/05, *Stiftung Wissenschaft und Politik*, May 2015. See also Katy A. Crossley-Frolick, "Revisiting and Reimagining the Notion of Responsibility in German Foreign Policy," *International Studies Perspectives* 18(4): 443–64, February 25, 2016.
53. Helga Haftendorn, *Coming of Age: German Foreign Policy since 1945* (New York: Rowman & Littlefield, 2006), pp. 3–4 and 6.
54. Beverly Crawford, *Power and German Foreign Policy: Embedded Hegemony in Europe* (London: Palgrave Macmillan, 2007).
55. Timothy Garton Ash, *In Europe's Name: Germany and the Divided Continent* (New York: Random House, 1993).

References

Andreae, L., and K. Kaiser. 2001. The 'Foreign Policies' of Specialized Ministries. In *Germany's New Foreign Policy*, ed. W. Eberwein and K. Kaiser, 38–57. Basingstoke, UK: Palgrave.

Ash, T.G. 1993. *In Europe's Name: Germany and the Divided Continent*. New York: Random House.

Bendiek, A. 2015. *The '2014 Review': Understanding the Pillars of German Foreign Policy and the Expectations of the Rest of the World*. Working Paper RD EU/Europe, 2015/05, *Stiftung Wissenschaft und Politik*, May 2015. https://www.swp-berlin.org/fileadmin/contents/products/arbeitspapiere/WP_IFRI_The_2014_Review.pdf. Accessed January 1, 2019.

Cecil, L. 1976. *The German Diplomatic Service, 1871–1914*. Princeton, NJ: Princeton University Press.

Conze, E., N. Frei, P. Hayes, and M. Zimmermann. 2011. *Das amt und die vergangensheit: Deutsche diplomaten im dritten reich und in der Bundesrepublik*. Munich: Karl Blessing Verlag.

Crawford, B. 2007. *Power and German Foreign Policy: Embedded Hegemony in Europe*. London: Palgrave Macmillan.

Crossley-Frolick, K.A. 2016. Revisiting and Reimagining the Notion of Responsibility in German Foreign Policy. *International Studies Perspectives* 18 (4): 443–464.

Eberwein, W., and K. Kaiser. 1998. Academic Research and Foreign Policy-Making. In *Germany's New Foreign Policy*, ed. W. Eberwein and K. Kaiser, 3–18. Basingstoke, UK: Palgrave.

———, eds. 2001. *Germany's New Foreign Policy: Decision-Making in an Interdependent World*. Basingstoke, UK: Palgrave.

Frei, N., and P. Hayes. 2011. The German Foreign Office and the Past. *Bulletin of the German Historical Institute* 49 (Fall 2011).

Freibert, A. 2004. Classifications and Career Development in the German Foreign Service. *SIGMA (Support for Improvement in Governance and Management), Organization for Economic Cooperation and Development*, December 2004. http://www.sigmaweb.org/publications/34874084.pdf. Accessed January 1, 2019.

Galtung, J. 1981. Structure, Culture, and Intellectual Style: An Essay Comparing Saxonic, Teutonic, Gallic and Nipponic Approaches. *Social Science Information* 20 (6): 817–856.

Haftendorn, H. 2006. *Coming of Age: German Foreign Policy Since 1945*. New York: Rowman & Littlefield.

Hellman, G. 2001. Precarious Power: Germany at the Dawn of the Twenty-First Century. In *Germany's New Foreign Policy*, ed. W. Eberwein and K. Kaiser, 293–311. Basingstoke, UK: Palgrave.

Kinney, S. n.d. *AFSA Benchmarking Exercise: Brazil, China, UK, Germany, France, Canada, Mexico, India Selection and Entry Level Training*. Washington, DC: American Foreign Service Association.

Kissinger, H. 1994. *Diplomacy*. New York: Simon & Schuster.

Lewin, D. 1966. The Decline of Tradition in the German Foreign Service. *The Western Political Science Quarterly* 19 (4): 653–662.

Neukirch, R. 2012. German Foreign Ministry Fights to Stay Relevant. *Spiegel Online*, May 4.

von Ploetz, H. 1998. New Challenges for the Foreign Service. In *Germany's New Foreign Policy*, ed. W. Eberwein and K. Kaiser, 70–86. Basingstoke, UK: Palgrave.

Siwert-Probst, J. 2001. Traditional Institutions of Foreign Policy. In *Germany's New Foreign Policy*, ed. W. Eberwein and K. Kaiser, 19–37. Basingstoke, UK: Palgrave.

Smyser, W.R. 2003. *How Germans Negotiate: Logical Goals, Practical Solutions.* Washington, DC: U.S. Institute of Peace Press.

Steinmeier, F. 2015. Closing Remarks by Foreign Minister Steinmeier at 'Review 2014' Conference. *Auswärtiges Amt.* https://www.auswaertiges-amt.de/en/newsroom/news/150225-bm-review-abschlussveranstaltung/269668. Accessed January 1, 2019.

Szabo, S.F. 2006. Enlarging NATO: The German-American Design for a New Alliance. In *The Strategic Triangle: France, Germany, and the United States in the Shaping of the New Europe*, ed. H. Haftendorn et al., 327–349. Washington and Baltimore: Wilson Center Press and The Johns Hopkins University Press.

Techau, J. 2015. The Steinmeier Review of German Foreign Policy. *Carnegie Europe*, March 19. http://carnegieeurope.eu/strategiceurope/?fa=59422. Accessed January 1, 2019.

The Federal Foreign Office: Facts and Figures. 2018. Berlin: Federal Foreign Office. https://www.auswaertiges-amt.de/blob/610638/c1978289a95db1b7b-ba7089078a22e9d/aa-ueberblick-data.pdf. Accessed January 1, 2018.

Watt, D.C. 1970. The Reform of the German Foreign Service: The Herwarth and Duncan Reports Compared. *The World Today* 26 (8): 352–358.

CHAPTER 5

India

Leena Warsi, Joshua Orme, and Jeremi Suri

EXECUTIVE SUMMARY

Established in 1947, the Indian Foreign Service (IFS) evolved from a fledgling service into one aspiring to regional and global leadership in a relatively short period of time. Considered one of the most prestigious government careers in India, the IFS takes pride in its commitment to promoting peaceful conflict resolution, economic freedom, and democratic values. The most striking feature of the organization is the small size of the corps—fewer than 1000 diplomatic officers. In the world's largest democracy, it should come as no surprise that ambition paired with limited positions translates into fierce internal competition.

Since the IFS funnels applicants through a common Civil Service Exam (CSE), the selection process not only involves screening for talent, drive,

---

L. Warsi
2018 Master of Arts Degrees, Global Policy Studies and Middle Eastern Studies, The University of Texas at Austin, Austin, TX, USA

J. Orme
2018 Master of Arts Degrees, Global Policy Studies and Asian Studies, The University of Texas at Austin, Austin, TX, USA

J. Suri (✉)
Lyndon B. Johnson School of Public Affairs, The University of Texas at Austin, Austin, TX, USA
e-mail: suri@austin.utexas.edu

and creativity but also rules out perfectly qualified candidates due to the high volume of applications. Accepted recruits undergo a period of initial training that typically lasts three years: about two years of domestic training followed by a foreign language tour with minimum durations ranging from less than one year to two years, depending on the language. The IFS has little to offer in the way of mid-career training; it relies on an informal culture of personal mentorship. Promotion within the service is handled on a seniority-as-merit basis. The advantages of a small cadre, according to many IFS officers, include a lean chain of command, which allows for increased independence. This independence is tempered by the guidance that comes from informal communications among a small group of officers. Many challenges remain for the IFS, including increasing the diversity of the workforce, managing often severe budget constraints, and promoting work-life balance for officers. The currently most pressing concern for the IFS, however, is insufficient diplomatic and support staff—a glaring disadvantage for a small cadre. As measures to increase staff size are under consideration and debate, diplomatic officers are unable to undergo formal mid-career training due to increased responsibilities in their current posts.

HISTORY AND CULTURE

Many national institutions claim long historical lineage, but the Indian Foreign Service (IFS) may have the deepest connections in the Indian past. Indian diplomats trace their tradition back to references in the great Indian epics, the *Ramayana* and the *Mahabharata*, of kings' envoys, including the Hindu deity Hanuman.[1] In addition to these legendary origins, the IFS has a direct lineage from within the Indian Civil Service (ICS) of the British Raj. As a part of the bureaucracy from the nineteenth century onward, the "Political Service" component of the ICS interacted with the numerous princely states within British India. The Political Service typically transferred officers from the ICS and the Army to fill its positions. Unlike those institutions, the Political Service was not open to actual Indians until the late 1930s.[2]

Following Indian independence in 1947, twenty Political Service officers and others from the Commerce and Finance ministries were quickly brought under the new Union (central) government of India as the IFS.[3] With this rather thin original bureaucracy, Jawaharlal Nehru, as the nation's first prime minister, directed Indian foreign policy and its diplomatic mechanisms personally as his own foreign secretary. Nehru's force of will largely shaped India's post-independence ideological posture, including non-alignment during the Cold War, restrictions on foreign investment in India, and camaraderie with other developing, particularly fellow Asian, countries.

As a prominent post-colonial state at independence, India has always aspired to global leadership, rather than limiting its resources to specific regions or targeted allies. In that process, India has taken upon itself a mantle of leadership, self-confidently claimed from the British, as not just the inherited regional power, but also a natural leader for other post-colonial countries and the world at large.[4] This culture and attitude have combined with an impressively professional corps of diplomats, however over-stretched and under-supported. Scholar Stephen Cohen considers the IFS a "persistent underachiever" on the global stage despite all its efforts and professionalism.[5] The IFS has been at the center of significant historical junctures within India's international experience—from the humiliating defeat in the Sino-Indian war of 1962, to the diplomatic height of defeating Pakistan and facilitating an independent Bangladesh in 1971, and to the dramatic economic reforms of 1991 following the dissolution of the Union of Soviet Socialist Republics. Through all of these moments, the IFS has been constant in its approach.[6] This consistency is especially noteworthy considering the dramatic impact of the end of the Cold War for India's global relevance as the Non-Aligned Movement's leader. The end of traditional East-West conflict after 1991 drained non-alignment of its meaning and influence.

The Indian Foreign Service has maintained a clear mission, consistently articulated by the nation's early leaders and thinkers. First, the religious leader Swami Vivekananda called on India to be "a messenger of peace...a catalyst for creating a just and moral world order," and second, Nehru envisioned world peace through an "active positive approach for international problems...leading first to the lessening of the present tension... and, then, to a growing cooperation between nations."[7] Displaying and sharing India's moral superiority with the world has involved a delicate balancing act due to the precedent of what Nehru called "a 'non-committal' and 'influential' stand on international issues."[8] The grand mission of Indian diplomacy has therefore become focused on, what Stephen Cohen calls, "getting to no" for anything that challenges Indian primacy. Indian negotiations are fraught with sensitivity about perceived slights, especially from large foreign powers.[9] Likewise, India's strategic culture has been described as ambivalent and restrained due to the heavy Nehruvian influences that balance one another.[10]

Profile

The IFS and the corresponding Ministry of External Affairs (MEA) seek to engage in global diplomacy with a widely recognized professional corps of diplomats.[11] Within this framework, the IFS is tightly constrained by the combination of a highly selective entrance process and limited resources. For 172 missions abroad, the IFS has a current cadre strength of only 770 officers.[12] Reported numbers from the MEA and IFS are often much higher, as the total Ministry employment is 4086, with 2700 considered "diplomatic" across multiple ministries. These additional individuals are not formal members of IFS and include support staff, translators, and "technical experts" from other governmental agencies. Another numerical discrepancy for the IFS is the term "sanctioned strength," which defines the IFS as 912 officers. This is merely the allowable number of officers, which to date has not been reached; but as IFS entering batches have increased in recent years, this total will likely be reached in the coming years.

The IFS also includes 212 "under-secretaries" identified as the B Cadre.[13] The B Cadre handles many administrative roles and consular responsibilities that typically fall to Foreign Service Officers in other national diplomatic corps. Although the B Cadre resides under the IFS umbrella, these staff members do not come through the IFS' exam or training pipeline, and are not eligible for promotions. While the IFS formally includes 770 officers as noted, numerical comparisons to other diplomatic services could reasonably include the B Cadre raising the IFS total to nearly 1000. It will be relevant for future study to determine if the additional "diplomatic officials" noted in recent Parliamentary committee meetings represent a less-trained class of diplomats carrying the burden of the IFS' staffing dilemma.

Entrance to the IFS is notoriously difficult, and it is in competition for recruits with the more popular Indian Administrative Service (IAS), as well as other Civil Service positions that share a unified examination process. The IFS has no designated cones or tracks, and its training structure is heavily tilted toward generalist skills with greater regional, rather than functional focus. Entering batches of IFS officers have diverse educational backgrounds from engineering and medicine to humanities and law.[14] In addition to a lack of cones, the IFS has no equivalent to a "fast-track" promotion system; rank promotions occur largely by "batch" of officers.[15] Batches are common across the All India Civil Service, and are functionally an identifier, like a graduation year.

Former diplomats criticize the organization of the IFS as overly hierarchical, with little in the way of ancillary services, such as human resources or career planning.[16] Funding for the MEA is small, with only 0.03% of GDP going to the MEA, versus over 2.3% to defense purposes.[17] The estimated 2016–2017 MEA budget approximately equals US $900 million after removing the budget allocations for technical and economic cooperation.

Since Jawaharlal Nehru's infamous description of the pre-Independence Indian Civil Service ("not Indian, not civil...not a service"[18]), the All India Civil Service, and especially the IFS, has struggled with appropriate representation of the Indian population. The Indian Constitution places importance on representation of the traditionally lower-caste groups of Indian society (designated as OBC, SC, or ST), which is why members of these groups receive certain advantages within the recruitment process and, in the last five years of IFS batches, have represented 46% of new officers.

Despite recent efforts, there remain several areas of representational concern. First, a significant gender imbalance persists within the IFS. Recent estimates suggest that less than 20% of the total diplomatic corps is female. However, IFS batches from 2010 to 2015 were 36% female including one year (2012) when more than 40% were women, the highest in IFS history. Second, the IFS, along with other Civil Service groups, faces domestic pressure to provide more opportunity for non-Hindi-speaking Indians and rural Indians.[19] Overall, there is a significant numerical advantage for urban Indian males with the native tongue of English or Hindi versus any other demographic.

Recruitment and Selection

To enter the IFS, candidates must apply through the Union Public Service Commission, which conducts the annual Civil Service Exam (CSE). The CSE covers many government positions within India, including the IAS, Indian Police Service, Indian Revenue Service, and the IFS.[20] There are three stages within the CSE—the preliminary exam, the main exam, and an interview—that occur over the course of a year from May to May annually. Recent years of the CSE have seen initial applications reach over 1 million. Due to a limit on the number of times an individual can sit for the exam, only about 50% of applicants typically appear for the preliminary exam. This means that more than 300,000 on average, and in recent years, closer to 500,000, still complete this first stage. Between the two examinations, a broad set of material is covered including several humanities subjects, Indian languages (a total of 20 official Indian languages, including English, are recognized for supplemental test subjects), English language proficiency, and an ethical aptitude case study.[21] In addition, optional sections cover a gamut of engineering, history, chemistry, and philosophy that can be used to demonstrate a specialized field of study. The Civil Services accept candidates from every academic background.

By the completion of the CSE, the final acceptance rate on average is less than 1% each year; most recently, narrowing down 1 million candidates to 1000 or so admitted equals only 0.1%.[22] This has been described by participants as more elimination process than selection process. Successful candidates have demonstrated commitment, perseverance, and ambition more than any other criteria.[23]

At their initial examination stage, candidates rank the Civil Service cadre they prefer most. This process has allowed for some periods of low IFS popularity vis-à-vis the other services. Many current IFS officers note that their first choice was initially the IAS based on their pre-existing knowledge and exposure to that institution.[24] Lulls in popularity have resulted in selection of new officers that are ranked relatively low on the annual merit list.[25] However, while that reality has caused concerns in some areas, especially parliamentary oversight committees, the exam process is so rigorous that some IFS officers believe that the quality of successful candidates is inconsequentially different from the "toppers" to the minimum qualifiers. More problematic for the MEA is its inability to include separate qualifications or testing requirements for IFS candidates because they have no independent legal mandate apart from the broader Civil Service mechanism.[26]

Our study has not uncovered any official mechanism for lateral transfers that by-pass the CSE; therefore, any of the very limited lateral transfers occurring would be from other Civil Service organizations that have already passed through the same evaluation. Of the small group accepted through the CSE process, currently, around 20 to 30 become IFS probationary officers. This level of intake has only been present for roughly a decade; historically, the average intake was only approximately a dozen new officers per year.[27]

Professional Development and Training

On the completion of the CSE and selection into the IFS, officers undergo three stages of induction training with future options for mid-career in-service courses. Induction training spans the first three years of service and consists of basic training at the Lal Bahadur Shastri National Academy of Administration (LBSNAA), professional training at the Foreign Service Institute (FSI) with attachments throughout the Indian government and MEA, and a Compulsory Foreign Language (CFL) training during the initial posting. After this, recruits are considered full-fledged officers. In-service training occurs after an officer has served for about 5–10 years or if he or she is being considered for senior-level promotions. Although there are various training institutes where officers of the All India Central Civil Services can matriculate, IFS recruits generally attend LBSNAA and FSI.

Lal Bahadur Shastri National Academy of Administration

Originally set up as a training school for the Indian Administrative Service (IAS), LBSNAA was chosen as a site for IFS induction training to promote "the ethos and values of higher civil services, especially the values of integrity, humanism, service, and professionalism."[28] By integrating IFS induction training with IAS foundational training, the MEA sought to instill a better understanding of domestic, especially rural, public affairs in IFS recruits. IFS officers are also linked by "batch" to a corresponding cadre of IAS officers.[29] The program lasts 15 weeks (3–4 months) during which recruits take courses on: public administration and social management, economics, law, political theory and the Indian constitution, Indian history and culture, Hindi or a regional language, and information and communications technology.[30]

In addition to attending classes, IFS recruits are required to participate in the Village Study Program. This consists of a 10-day trek in the Himalayas and a 12-day visit to a remote village.[31] The main objectives of this program are to cultivate better interpersonal relations, social awareness, and physical endurance. The Academy's Foundation Course is specifically intended to be "a transition from the academic world of colleges and universities to the structured system of government."[32] At the end of the induction training, IFS recruits take a final assessment in each of their courses. During this training, the IFS recruits are not distinguished from any other Civil Service trainee. Despite the military style of discipline and the lack of comforts, the experience is generally remembered with nostalgia. It is invaluable for instilling critical characteristics for long-term success in the IFS.[33]

Foreign Service Institute

In 1986, the Government of India realized that IFS officers needed more than general training at LBSNAA. The push for deeper expertise and skill preparation led to the creation of FSI. FSI provides professional training to IFS officers, MEA staff, and representatives and diplomats from foreign countries.[34] FSI also collaborates with foreign institutions, such as Harvard and Georgetown Universities, to conduct training and workshops for IFS officers abroad. IFS officers complete both their induction and in-service training at FSI.

After basic training at LBSNAA, IFS recruits undergo one year of professional training at FSI in New Delhi. The course consists of twenty-six modules including international relations, Indian foreign policy, and diplomatic practice and protocol, among others. FSI employs faculty from top Indian universities (such as Jawaharlal Nehru University and Banaras Hindu University), government think tanks (such as the Institute for Defense Studies and Analysis), and retired IFS officers. During this time, recruits also receive training as an attachment with the Armed Forces, Navy, and Air Force to study the structure of the Ministry of Defense.[35] Foreign language acquisition consists of learning basic French, one compulsory, and one optional foreign language. New recruits are also required to complete the *Bharat Darshan*, a tour of major cultural, commercial, and historic sites in India. The sites covered during the *Bharat Darshan* vary among the different batches of IFS recruits since the goal of the tour is for them to visit places they have not seen and will not see again during their diplomatic careers.[36]

It should be noted that the domestic tour of *Bharat Darshan* does not include the same level of social immersion as LBSNAA's Village Study Program and occurs only in preliminary training. However, this experience does provide the trainees with thorough exposure to all levels of state and local governance within India, as well as interaction with key stakeholders from non-governmental groups including leading Indian corporations.[37] This training has been identified as a highly unique feature of the IFS program in comparison to other diplomatic corps around the world.

FSI describes the year's phases as follows: five months for FSI Phase I, two months with MEA desks, three months of field attachment (i.e. district administration, army, etc.), one month for FSI Phase II, and one final month for pre-departure attachment with their assigned regional division. Over this year, the MEA hopes to instill a "strong sense of history, knowledge of diplomacy and international relations, and a grasp of general economic and political principles."[38] Upon completion of professional training at FSI, IFS recruits continue for another six months at the MEA to familiarize themselves with the functions of the Ministry and end their induction training with posting at an Indian Mission abroad chosen per their foreign language study.

The IFS' leadership chooses which languages are available for study at a particular time, and trainees indicate preferences based on rankings from the CSE results. English is never made available here, as a high level of proficiency in English is expected prior to the exam, and generally enhanced through the previous trainings. A trainee's language selection will determine his or her first placement abroad.

Each language has a minimum required study time ranging from less than one year for European languages to more than two years for such languages as Chinese and Arabic, which are considered more challenging. IFS trainees may take longer than the minimum time allotted if needed, but this is rare.[39] During the period of language study, the officer is considered a Third Secretary and is also expected to learn relevant diplomatic skills as well as demonstrate his or her ability to handle cross-cultural life. In addition to the training programs held within India, the final 1–2 years of training are considered crucial tests and development of the raw talent brought in through the examination process.[40] When the CFL exam is passed satisfactorily, the officer will be confirmed into the service as a Second Secretary. He or she may then begin applying for full IFS roles, which involve remaining in the current country or taking a new posting.[41]

In-Service Training

Following their first five years of service, IFS officers are required to undertake in-service training. The main objectives of this training are to increase efficiency, morale, and opportunities for advancement. Since the IFS promotes generalist training of its recruits, officers are not expected to choose specializations early in their career. In fact, one of the major complaints of IFS officers is that the MEA has yet to institute an effective career planning system. Not much has been changed or added to the career planning system since the Pillai Committee in 1965, which advised the MEA "to devise a broad framework of career growth within which the officer may be expected to develop."[42] Currently, IFS professional development is limited to geographical specialization—postings are assigned per the officers' region of interest. Two factors cited for the poor professional development system are (1) the small size of the IFS and (2) the unequal distribution of "comfortable" and "difficult" posts. Officers are generally assigned by geographic specialization, and some may therefore receive a larger share of "comfortable" posts, which fosters internal tension among IFS personnel.

The current in-service training opportunities at FSI are known as Mid-Career Training Programs. These programs are divided into three phases: Phase I is for officers returning after the first round of postings abroad. Training lasts four weeks and focuses on workshops and case studies regarding legislative and judicial institutions. Phase II is targeted toward officers returning after the second round of postings abroad. Training lasts three weeks at either FSI or another institution, and covers emergency foreign policy issues and domain specialization. Lastly, Phase III is for officers at the joint secretary level.[43]

Due to the small size of the IFS cadre and the growing number of missions, officers find it difficult to spare time to return for in-service training. As a result, the programs, especially Phase III, do not have a consistent curriculum and depend heavily on the particular batch of officers attending.

Leadership

IFS officers undergo yearly performance appraisals, known as Annual Confidential Reports (ACRs). These assessments focus on capability, achievement, and potential. IFS officers are reviewed in a "two-up" system that includes assessment by their immediate supervisor and one additional level above in seniority. Officers have identified the process as internally transparent in terms of criteria.[44] However, while the ACR provides the MEA with information on IFS officers, surveys show that officers rarely get feedback on their ACRs unless there are adverse assessments. Promotion in the IFS is largely based on seniority and is time-bound, for example, an attaché must serve for five years before rising to the rank of undersecretary. The highest posts of additional secretary and secretary are offered on the basis of merit, competence, and leadership.[45] In addition to rank-based promotions, IFS officers can infrequently rise quickly in terms of job description and responsibility due to pressing needs, allowing for a limited degree of meritocracy within the MEA.

The IFS has a minimal number of political appointees—traditionally, the prime minister appoints about ten ambassadors outside the IFS, though many are retired Indian diplomats returning to service. The early history of the IFS is, however, filled with personally connected, political appointments as newly independent India compensated for an extremely limited pool of candidates with diplomatic experience. Many of the first appointments to the IFS came from officers in the British Indian Army who had foreign experience and were members of the royal families from various princely states.[46]

Rising to the highest positions of influence and leadership within the contemporary IFS requires extensive experience throughout the MEA's apparatus and overseas postings. A review of top ambassadorial or high commissioner positions assigned to key countries and posts (including the United States, United Nations [UN], and other positions) illustrates some potential trends in the promotion process. Most current IFS leaders entered government service with high levels of education, beyond the mandatory minimum. Reaching the ambassadorial role at a critical post required career diplomats to serve 20–30 years in the IFS, and successfully complete an appointment as an ambassador in a smaller country. In general, these top leaders demonstrated the ability to have a regional area of focus, successfully served in a UN-related permanent mission or other multilateral organization. They have combined work experience abroad with managerial experience at the MEA headquarters in New Delhi.[47]

The profiles of the IFS leaders speak to flexibility within a hierarchical institution, as well as critical limitations on diversity. First, these diplomatic leaders entered the IFS in the late 1970s and early 1980s, and they found India's foreign policy dominated by a focus on Russia and likeminded Arab states. This is illustrated by an emphasis on Russian and Arabic language training. However, rather than exclusively focus on a regional expertise, these diplomats have had diverse opportunities to experience a wide range of countries and topical areas. In many cases, different points in a career have emphasized one skill set over another. For instance, the Indian Ambassador to Germany focused both on business and on Japan/East Asia, while the Indian Ambassador to France focused on Francophone relations and trade. At various times, they have used one or the other skillset.

Further flexibility is illustrated in relatively low rank IFS officers being assigned a high position of responsibility—such as Consul General or Head of Chancery at a relatively small mission or an external facing MEA post—where they can prove themselves on merit, despite a seniority focused promotion system.

Despite efforts to recruit for greater diversity, the top IFS positions remain populated overwhelmingly by men. And despite the IFS' pride in varied educational backgrounds for recruits, New Delhi's premier universities remain over-represented among IFS leaders. The IFS still has diversity challenges at the top of the organization.

Role in Foreign Policy Making

The influence of the IFS on India's foreign policy has diminished over time due, in part, to its links to Prime Minister Nehru. His personal prioritization of the IFS raised its national stature immensely. In recent years, Indian political leaders have rejected Nehru's legacy and the perceived elitism of the IFS. The government of Prime Minister Narendra Modi has increased the role of political appointees and private sector leaders in influencing Indian foreign policy.[48] This does not mean, however, that the IFS will necessarily see its position eroded in future, as the MEA is pushing to increase the prominence of the IFS and its recruitment quotas and lateral entry opportunities. The IFS continues to attract high-quality recruits; there is only a marginal difference between the traditionally selected "toppers" of the Civil Service Exam and those somewhat lower. The IFS and MEA remain a highly central and critical government body.

The IFS plays a unique and often contradictory policy role due to India's political and cultural history, illustrated perhaps most clearly by the strategies adopted in regards to UN Security Council Reforms. As previously noted, the fall of the Soviet Union and the end of the Cold War diminished the relevance of India's diplomatic position as the leader of the Non-Aligned Movement. In the "New World Order" and the UN's *Agenda for Peace*, India appeared poised for a new level of global leadership with a strong candidacy for a permanent UN Security Council seat.[49] India's diplomatic policy-making process is, in this context, consistently in tension between global leadership aspirations, urgent regional concerns, and the enduring impact of Gandhi's asymmetrical approach to power dynamics. Many within the IFS and MEA would see a Security Council seat as a major diplomatic success, but the diplomatic compromises required—particularly in relation to the Non-Proliferation Treaty and the conflict with Pakistan—could be untenable.[50] Echoing Stephen Cohen's observation about India's obsession with "getting to no," the IFS' efforts to acquire the Security Council seat were essentially self-sabotaged in its rejection of the purported rules of engagement created by the United States and other Western countries.[51] Thus, while the IFS can certainly drive India's foreign policy, the conflicting currents are a notable strain on a tight-knit corps of officers.

The IFS' effectiveness within the Indian government will continue to reflect broad cultural and historical realities, as well as the nuances of personal leadership. As the IFS grows, the concentration of bureaucratic authority under the foreign secretary will become logistically difficult. As India continues its self-proclaimed ascent to great power status, the trend of centralization of foreign policy within the Prime Minister's office will either invigorate the IFS as a key tool or sideline it, perhaps in favor of other ministries including Commerce, Defense, and Finance. These issues will deeply impact IFS' preparations for the future.

Preparations for the Future

When confronting the challenges of the future, there are several structural and bureaucratic issues facing the IFS. The small size of the IFS cadre remains the source of various complaints. In particular, mid-career training for IFS officers is often delayed because of short-staffing at missions. This, in turn, has created a system of promotion that is based more on seniority than merit. The MEA is currently considering offering Non-Resident Indians (NRIs) the opportunity to apply and work for the IFS. While the political logistics of allowing NRIs to take the Civil Service Exam appear difficult, Prime Minister Narendra Modi has publicly declared that working with the India diaspora community is a priority.[52]

Technologically, the current administration has been quick to implement an overhaul of the information systems within government ministries and establish a stronger digital presence.[53] The IFS is looking toward the extensive Indian diaspora community for new sources of engagement and collaboration within a broad "soft power" framework, in conjunction with bolstering economic ties through regional partnerships and development projects. India's ability to reconcile the disparate goals of its diplomatic agenda will depend on the capacity of the IFS' bureaucratic structure to support the weight of these expectations. It remains to be seen if the IFS' flexible and small nature will be an advantage or a burden.

In that light, it is critical to see the new priorities developing within the MEA. First, recent foreign ministers have expanded the role of public diplomacy. The integration of technology, especially social media, could potentially enhance the effectiveness of even a small officer corp. The relevance of global Indian business interests, as well as an increasing focus on the diaspora community, adds a significant and relatively new skillset needed for Indian diplomats, previously focused on gaining cultural competency abroad.

As the international landscape sees notable shifts in power, governance, and global objectives, will India's diplomats be able to respond? Will they thrive in a rapidly changing world system? These are the questions that the Indian diplomatic corps thinks most deeply about today. The IFS is highly skilled, but it needs more resources for future challenges and opportunities.

Acknowledgment *The authors wish to thank the diplomats and scholars who were consulted in researching and writing this chapter.*

Notes

1. J.N. Dixit, *Indian Foreign Service: History and Challenge* (New Delhi: Konark Publishers, 2005); Kishan S. Rana, *Asian Diplomacy: The Foreign Ministries of China, India, Japan, Singapore and Thailand* (Washington, DC: Woodrow Wilson Center Press, 2007).
2. Dixit, *Indian Foreign Service*, 9.
3. Ibid., 29.
4. Ibid., 13; Stephen Cohen, *India: Emerging Power* (Washington, DC: Brookings Institution Press, 2001), 84–89.
5. Cohen, *India: Emerging Power*, 72.
6. Rana, *Asian Diplomacy*, 48–50.
7. Dixit, *Indian Foreign Service*, 10.
8. Ibid., 14.
9. Cohen, *India: Emerging Power*, 87.
10. Mike Dyer, "Strategic Culture, National Strategy, and Policymaking in the Asia-Pacific: An Interview with Ashley J. Tellis," *The National Bureau of Asian Research*, published October 27, 2016, https://www.nbr.org/publication/strategic-culture-national-strategy-and-policymaking-in-the-asia-pacific/. Accessed March 25, 2019.
11. Cohen, *India: Emerging Power*, 72.

12. "Indian Foreign Service", *Ministry of External Affairs, Government of India*, April 22, 2015, http://www.mea.gov.in/indian-foreign-service.htm. Accessed March 25, 2019.
13. "If Shashi Tharoor's panel has its way, India's diplomatic corps could grow in quality and quantity," *FirstPost.com*, August 3, 2016, http://www.firstpost.com/world/india-is-strapped-for-diplomats-but-if-shashi-tharoors-panel-has-its-way-you-could-become-one-2931362.html. Accessed March 25, 2019.
14. "Training Programs: Officer Trainees," *Foreign Service Institute, Ministry of External Affairs, Government of India*, June 10, 2016, https://meafsi.gov.in/?5137?000. Accessed March 25, 2019.
15. Rana, *Asian Diplomacy*, 57.
16. Ibid.
17. Ibid., 53, "India Military Expenditure % of GDP," *World Bank*, 2016, http://data.worldbank.org/indicator/MS.MIL.XPND.GD.ZS?end=2015&locations=IN&start=1988&view=chart. Accessed March 25, 2019; "Union Budget at a Glance 2016–2017," *Ministry of Finance, Government of India*, no date, https://www.indiabudget.gov.in/glance.asp. Accessed March 25, 2019.
18. Jawaharlal Nehru, *Glimpses of World History* (London: Penguin Books, 1942), 94.
19. "Batch Profile," *Lal Bahadur Shastri National Academy of Administration*, http://www.lbsnaa.gov.in/batches, Accessed March 25, 2019; "Training Programs: Officer Trainees," *Foreign Service Institute, Ministry of External Affairs, Government of India*, June 10, 2016, https://meafsi.gov.in/?5137?000. Accessed March 25, 2019.
20. "Things you must know before you start preparing for UPSC civil services exam," *India Today*, June 2, 2016. http://indiatoday.intoday.in/education/story/upsc-civil-services-exam/1/683251.html. Accessed March 25, 2019.
21. "Question Papers," Union Public Service Commission, Government of India, September 15, 2016, http://www.upsc.gov.in/examinations/question-papers. Accessed March 25, 2019.
22. "Number of Candidates in Civil Services Exam," UPSC Syllabus, 2019, https://www.upscsyllabus.in/articles/number-of-candidates-in-upsc-scra-exam. Accessed March 25, 2019.
23. From interviews with IFS officers.
24. Ibid.
25. Rana, *Asian Diplomacy*, 52–53.
26. Ibid.
27. Rana, *Asian Diplomacy*, 58.

28. "Batch Profile FC93," *Lal Bahadur Shastri National Academy of Administration*, 2018, http://www.lbsnaa.gov.in/course/batch_profile. php?cid=97. Accessed March 25, 2019; Siran Mukerji, *Indian Foreign Service: Structure, Role, and Performance* (Jaipur: Aalekh Publishers, 2000), 123.
29. "Indian Foreign Service", *Ministry of External Affairs, Government of India*, April 22, 2015, http://www.mea.gov.in/indian-foreign-service.htm. Accessed March 25, 2019.
30. "Foundation Course," *Lal Bahadur Shastri National Academy of Administration*, 2019, http://www.lbsnaa.gov.in/course_listing.php?id=25. Accessed March 25, 2019.
31. Mukerji, *Indian Foreign Service*, 126.
32. "Batch Profile FC93."
33. From interviews with IFS Officers.
34. Mukerji, *Indian Foreign Service*, 95.
35. "Photo Features," *Ministry of External Affairs, Government of India*, May 1, 2016, https://www.mea.gov.in/photo-features-all.htm. Accessed March 25, 2019.
36. Mukerji, *Indian Foreign Service*, 136.
37. From interviews with IFS Officers.
38. "Training Programs: Officer Trainees."
39. From interviews with IFS Officers.
40. Ibid.
41. "Indian Foreign Service", *Ministry of External Affairs, Government of India*, April 22, 2015, http://www.mea.gov.in/indian-foreign-service.htm. Accessed March 25, 2019.
42. Mukerji, *Indian Foreign Service*, 185.
43. "MEA Training Framework 2013," *Foreign Service Institute, Ministry of External Affairs, Government of India*, February 4, 2015, https://meafsi.gov.in/?3558?000. Accessed March 25, 2019.
44. From interviews with IFS Officers.
45. Mukerji, *Indian Foreign Service*, 211.
46. Dixit, *Indian Foreign Service*, Chapter 2.
47. Biographical information found on Embassy websites for Indian Missions.
48. T.P. Sreenivasan, "Foreign Service Must Remain Elitist," *Hindu*, June 25, 2015, http://www.thehindu.com/opinion/op-ed/foreign-service-must-remain-elitist/article7350788.ece. Accessed March 25, 2019.
49. Mani Shankar Aiyar, *A Time of Transition: Rajiv Gandhi to the 21st Century* (New Delhi: Penguin, 2009), 258–261.
50. Strobe Talbot, *Engaging India: Diplomacy, Democracy and the Bomb* (Washington, DC: Brookings Institute Press, 2004), 228–230.
51. Aiyar, *Time of Transition*, 258–261.

52. "PM Modi hails Indian diaspora, says they are role models for other communities," *Economic Times*, January 2017, https://economictimes.indiatimes.com/nri/nris-in-news/pm-modi-hails-indian-diaspora-says-they-are-role-models-for-other-communities/articleshow/56400651.cms. Accessed March 25, 2019.
53. "Indian Diplomacy," Ministry of External Affairs, since July 2010, https://twitter.com/IndianDiplomacy?ref_src=twsrc%5Egoogle%7Ctwcamp%5Eserp%7Ctwgr%.5Eauthor. Accessed March 25, 2019.

References

Aiyar, M.S. 2009. *A Time of Transition: Rajiv Gandhi to the 21st Century*. New Delhi: Penguin.

Cohen, S. 2001. *India: Emerging Power*. Washington, DC: Brookings Institution Press.

Dixit, J.N. 2005. *Indian Foreign Service: History and Challenge*. New Delhi: Konark Publishers.

Dyer, M. 2016, October 27. Strategic Culture, National Strategy, and Policymaking in the Asia-Pacific: An Interview with Ashley J. Tellis. *The National Bureau of Asian Research*. https://www.nbr.org/publication/strategic-culture-national-strategy-and-policymaking-in-the-asia-pacific/. Accessed March 25, 2019.

If Shashi Tharoor's Panel Has Its Way, India's Diplomatic Corps Could Grow in Quality and Quantity. 2016, August 3. *FirstPost.com*. http://www.firstpost.com/world/india-is-strapped-for-diplomats-but-if-shashi-tharoors-panel-has-its-way-you-could-become-one-2931362.html. Accessed March 25, 2019.

Indian Foreign Service. 2018. *Ministry of External Affairs, Government of India*. https://www.mea.gov.in/indian-foreign-service.htm. Accessed March 25, 2019.

Jawaharlal Nehru, J. 1942. *Glimpses of World History*. London: Penguin Books.

Ministry of External Affairs. 2019. *Government of India*. https://www.mea.gov.in. Accessed March 15, 2019.

PM Modi Hails Indian Diaspora, Says They Are Role Models for Other Communities. 2017, January. *Economic Times*. https://economictimes.indiatimes.com/nri/nris-in-news/pm-modi-hails-indian-diaspora-says-they-are-role-models-for-other-communities/articleshow/56400651.cms. Accessed March 25, 2019.

Question Papers. 2016, September 15. *Union Public Service Commission, Government of India*, September 15. https://upsc.gov.in/examinations/previous-question-papers. Accessed March 25, 2019.

Rana, K.S. 2007. *Asian Diplomacy: The Foreign Ministries of China, India, Japan, Singapore and Thailand*. Washington, DC: Woodrow Wilson Center Press.

Sreenivasan, T.P. 2015, June 25. Foreign Service Must Remain Elitist. *Hindu.* http://www.thehindu.com/opinion/op-ed/foreign-service-must-remain-elitist/article7350788.ece. Accessed March 25, 2019.

Talbot, S. 2004. *Engaging India: Diplomacy, Democracy and the Bomb.* Washington, DC: Brookings Institute Press.

Things You Must Know Before You Start Preparing for UPSC Civil Services Exam. 2016, June 2. *India Today.* http://indiatoday.intoday.in/education/story/upsc-civil-services-exam/1/683251.html. Accessed March 25, 2019.

CHAPTER 6

Japan

Kazushi Minami

EXECUTIVE SUMMARY

Established in 1869, the Ministry of Foreign Affairs of Japan—*Gaimushō* in Japanese—serves Japanese diplomacy by assisting the political leadership in foreign policy decision-making and implementation. Historically, male graduates from the Faculty of Law at the University of Tokyo comprised a large portion of Japanese diplomats. In recent years, however, *Gaimushō* has been striving to diversify its workforce, hiring more women, science majors, and master's degree holders. Like other organizations in Japan, *Gaimushō* emphasizes on-the-job training and provides few professional development opportunities for mid-career diplomats who finished their initial language training. The so-called "American school"—a group of diplomats trained in the United States—has dominated leadership positions at *Gaimushō* since the *Meiji* era, a sign of the utmost importance it attaches to US–Japanese relations. Seasoned *Gaimushō* officials with experience as bureau or division directors usually become ambassadors to countries of strategic significance for Japan, including the United States,

K. Minami (✉)
Osaka School of International Public Policy, Osaka University, Osaka, Japan

Department of History, The University of Texas at Austin, Austin, TX, USA
e-mail: rhutchings@austin.utexas.edu

© The Author(s) 2020
R. Hutchings, J. Suri (eds.), *Modern Diplomacy in Practice*,
https://doi.org/10.1007/978-3-030-26933-3_6

but the Cabinet Office tries to appoint more ambassadors from non-career diplomats and individuals from industry and academe partly to fend off public criticism on the near monopoly of ambassador positions by career diplomats. While competing with the Ministry of Defense for influence on Japanese diplomacy, *Gaimushō* cooperates with other ministries, such as the Ministry of Economy, Trade, and Industry, to carry out a diverse array of foreign policy initiatives. Reflecting the primacy of economic diplomacy, about half of *Gaimushō's* budget is devoted to official development assistance (ODA) for developing countries in Asia and Africa, managed through the Japan International Cooperation Agency (JICA). Hoping to reinforce its diplomatic corps, *Gaimushō* is facing challenges in budget, staff size, and diversity.

History and Culture

The origins of Japan's global diplomacy date back to the Edo period (1603–1868). The Tokugawa shogunate managed limited interactions with Asian neighbors and Western merchants while restricting free trade and travel, a policy often misrepresented as a "closed country" (*sakoku*). The *sakoku* policy ended abruptly in 1853, when Commodore Matthew Perry's squadron, feared by the Japanese as "black ships," appeared in the Edo Bay and "opened" Japan for trade with Western countries. In 1869, a year after the fall of the Tokugawa shogunate, the new Meiji government established *Gaimushō* to conduct modern diplomacy based on international law.

Japanese diplomacy during the *Meiji* era (1868–1912) aimed at achieving an equal international status with Western powers. The *Meiji* government tried to do so by adopting Western political systems and legal practices. Most Japanese diplomats, therefore, were trained in Western countries, especially the United States and Great Britain, a tradition that continues to characterize *Gaimushō* today. Between 1871 and 1873, a large delegation of more than a hundred politicians and scholars, led by Foreign Minister Iwakura Tomomi, toured the United States and Europe, importing their legal, political, and industrial systems to modernize Japan. In the mid-1890s, Foreign Minister Mutsu Munemitsu succeeded in modifying the unequal treaties that the Tokugawa shogunate had reached with Western powers, restoring tariff rights and abolishing legal exemptions for Westerners in Japan. Following the Sino–Japanese War (1894–1895) and the Russo–Japanese War (1904–1905), Japan became a member of the major powers in the world, obtaining its own empire in Asia, such as Taiwan and Korea.

During the *Taishō* and the early *Shōwa* periods (1912–1926 and 1926–1989), *Gaimushō* found itself in constant struggle against the Army. In the 1920s Foreign Minister Shidehara Kijūrō cooperated with Western powers in arms control and nonintervention in China, while the Army sought to extend the empire into Manchuria. In 1928 the Kwantung Army, stationed in the Liaodong Peninsula, killed Zhang Zuolin, a powerful warlord in Northern China. The Kwantung Army then invaded Manchuria in 1931. Hirota Kōki, who served as the foreign minister and the prime minister in the mid-1930s, failed to contain the political power of the Army, especially after an attempted coup by young army officers in 1936. Following this incident, the Army restricted the ministers of war and navy to active duty officers, making it virtually impossible for a civilian cabinet to interfere in the selection of these positions. This policy enabled the Army to topple cabinets it opposed by refusing to appoint ministers of war and navy. Hirota also failed to keep the Kwangtung Army in control and allowed the Second Sino–Japanese War to expand in 1937, precipitating the infamous Nanjing Massacre. When the war with China stalled, the Army urged another war with the United States, a country that provided economic and military aid for China. In 1941 Foreign Minister Tōgō Shigenori negotiated with the United States to avoid war, but the army's insistence on the China issue frustrated the peace talks, precipitating the Japanese attack on Pearl Harbor.

Not all *Gaimushō* diplomats loathed the army, however. While mainstream Japanese diplomats preferred cooperation with the West, a group of *Gaimushō* officials called "reformists" embraced expansionism. Shiratori Toshio, a director of the intelligence department in the ministry and the leader of the reformists, established connections with army officers and endorsed their radical Asianist vision, where Japan replaced Western powers as a regional hegemon. Wary of Shiratori's influence, Vice Minister of Foreign Affairs Shigemitsu Mamoru named him an ambassador to Switzerland in 1933. When Shiratori returned to Japan in 1936, however, young reformist diplomats, including future Vice Minister Ushiba Nobuhiko, lobbied the ministry on numerous occasions, albeit unsuccessfully, to appoint Shiratori as vice minister, the highest position in *Gaimushō*. Expecting wars with the United States and the Soviet Union, Shiratori urged the Japanese government to establish an alliance with Germany and Italy, contributing to the Tripartite Pact of 1940. Historian Tobe Ryōichi argues that Shiratori and his reformist allies in *Gaimushō* hardly had direct impact on Japanese decision-making, but they maintained indirect influence in the 1930s and 1940s by creating pressure for expansionist foreign policy in the ministry.[1]

Japan's defeat in WWII transformed *Gaimushō* by eliminating army sympathizers in the ministry. Shiratori became a Class-A war criminal and died in prison. Although Shiratori's young followers remained in *Gaimushō*, they converted themselves into mainstream diplomats who supported Japan's new diplomatic strategy set by Prime Minister Yoshida Shigeru. In 1951, after six years of the US occupation, Yoshida signed the San Francisco Treaty, which restored Japan's sovereignty, and the US–Japan Security Treaty, the backbone of Japan's national security in the postwar era. His grand strategy—the so-called Yoshida Doctrine—consisted of two pillars: maintaining low military expenditures by relying on the US forces in Japan, and using available resources for economic development.[2] Yoshida rejected the US request for rearmament in the early 1950s as constitutionally illegal, although he agreed to establish the National Police Reserve, a predecessor for the Self-Defense Force (SDF).

Since the late 1960s, *Gaimushō* has focused much attention on providing foreign economic assistance for developing countries in Asia, cooperating with Japanese companies in infrastructure projects. Japan became the world's largest ODA provider throughout the 1990s. The limit of economic diplomacy, however, became apparent during the Gulf War of 1991, when Japan faced international criticism for only contributing financial assistance for the Allied Forces. Japan has since dispatched the SDF to areas it deemed noncombatant, including Cambodia, Iraq, and Sudan, but the overseas activities of the SDF, whose constitutional legitimacy remains unclear, aroused domestic controversies.

Historical legacies of the Japanese Empire continue to haunt *Gaimushō*. Japan normalized relations with neighboring countries that had not signed the San Francisco Treaty, including the Soviet Union in 1956, South Korea in 1965, and the People's Republic of China in 1972. Historical problems with these countries, however, have far from disappeared. South Korea and China, in particular, evince strong animosity toward Japanese cruelty during WWII, when the army exploited thousands of Korean women as "comfort women" and murdered hundreds of thousands of Chinese people during the Nanjing Massacre of 1937. These historical issues are further complicated by territorial disputes, including the Northern Territories/Kuril Islands dispute with Russia, the Takeshima/Dokdo dispute with South Korea, and the Senkaku/Diaoyu Islands dispute with China.

Today, *Gaimushō* is under growing pressure. With the expansion of Chinese power in Asia, Tokyo is trying to maintain Japanese influence in the region through political, economic, and military cooperation with its partners, including the Philippines, Vietnam, and India. Tokyo is struggling to keep itself relevant in disarmament negotiations on the Korean Peninsula, where Japan seems to have little control. Tokyo is hoping to develop economic cooperation with Russia, especially joint development in the Northern Territories/Kuril Islands, although Moscow's capricious attitude makes it difficult to proceed with the plan. Tokyo is concerned about President Donald Trump's vitriolic rhetoric on US–Japanese trade, as it understands that a closer alliance with the United States is essential in achieving other diplomatic objectives. *Gaimushō*, therefore, needs talented, well-trained diplomats who can address the new challenges facing Japan.

Profile

Budget

Gaimushō declassifies a detailed budget report and policy review each year, enabling outsiders to trace and evaluate its programs. The 2017 annual budget for *Gaimushō* was $8 billion (886.1 billion Japanese yen), and more than $3.9 billion (434.3 billion Japanese yen)—about half of the budget—was devoted to ODA. The proportion of ODA in *Gaimushō's* budget, however, has decreased significantly in recent years. Fifteen years ago, ODA comprised of more than 70 percent of the ministry's spending. ODA traditionally served Japan's economic diplomacy by assisting infrastructure projects in developing countries through Japanese corporations. In recent years, Japan bolstered the national security aspects of ODA. In 2013, for example, Prime Minister Abe Shinzō decided to spend $166.4 million ($18.7 billion Japanese yen) to provide ten Japan Coastal Guard patrol boats for the Philippine Coastal Guard, an initiative allegedly targeted against the expansion of Chinese naval power. The 2018 government budget plan maintains almost the same level of expenditures for *Gaimushō* as the previous years, promising to carry out a "Free and Open Indo-Pacific Strategy," aimed at maintaining freedom of navigation in the Pacific and the Indian Ocean to strengthen Japan's presence in Asia and Africa. The plan proposes four broad measures to achieve this goal: first, conducting strategic diplomacy to deal with the uncertainties in international politics ($3 billion);

second, protecting Japanese citizens at home and abroad from terrorism ($220 million); third, providing diplomatic assistance for the Japanese economy ($1.1 billion); and, finally, maintaining and strengthening public diplomacy ($650 million).[3]

Organizational Structure

The top figure in the *Gaimushō* bureaucracy is the vice minister for foreign affairs, who serves the political leadership, namely the minister for foreign affairs. A vice minister is supported by two deputy vice ministers; each specializing in politics and economics. *Gaimushō* consists of the ministry in Tokyo and Japanese representations overseas, including 223 embassies, consulates, and permanent missions in 150 countries. The ministry has numerous suborganizations as shown in Fig. 6.1.

The Minister's Secretariat is responsible for overall administration and coordination in *Gaimushō*. The Press Secretary and the Director-General for Cultural Affairs, placed under the Minister's Secretariat, oversee public diplomacy initiatives at home and abroad. The Foreign Policy Bureau administers policy planning and coordination, especially on national security matters. Other bureaus are divided into five regions (Asia and Oceania, North America, Latin America and the Caribbean, Europe, the Middle East, and Africa) and four functions (Economics, International Cooperation, International Law, and Consulates). The International Cooperation Bureau focuses on providing economic and technological assistance for developing countries, while the Intelligence and Analysis Service collects and analyzes information about foreign countries.

Gaimushō has two advisory committees, the Foreign Service Personnel Committee and the International Exchange Committee, both consisting of outside members from industry, academe, and NGOs (non-governmental organizations). These committees advise the foreign minister on key matters in their jurisdictions. The Foreign Service Personnel Committee submits a report every year on how to enhance *Gaimushō's* performance. Its suggestions include increasing the staff size, reinforcing early- and mid-career training, and improving the work–life balance of employees. The International Exchange Committee focuses on broad issues related to foreign relations, such as promoting cultural exchanges, expanding consulate service, protecting Japanese citizens, and cultivating connections with Japanese descendants overseas.

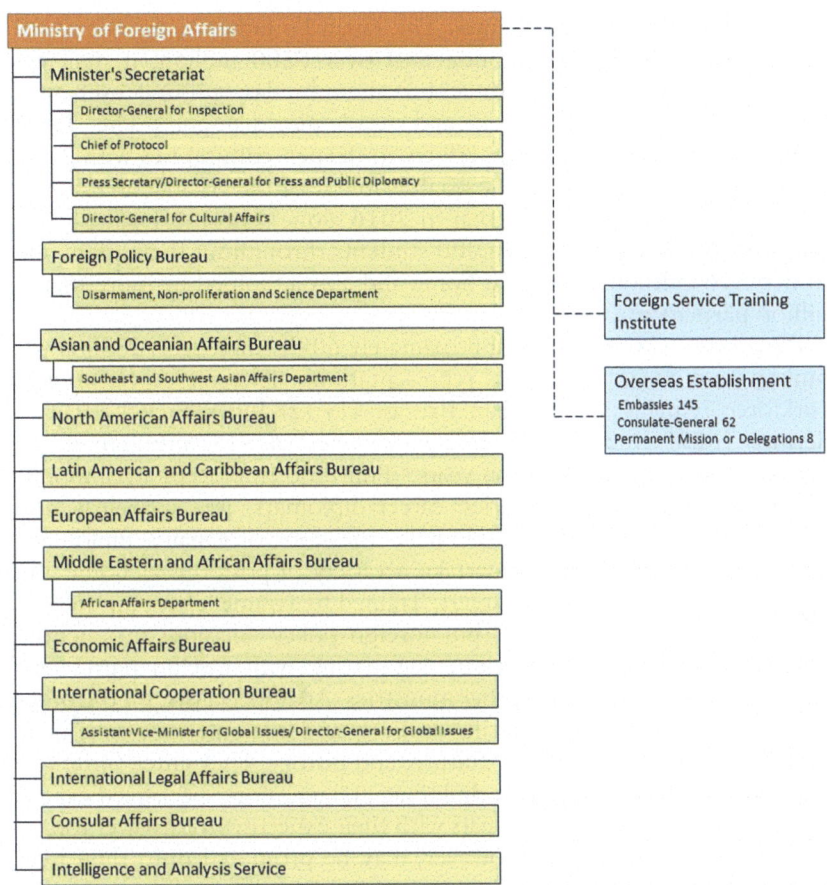

Fig. 6.1 Organization of Japan's Ministry of Foreign Affairs (*Gaimushō*) (Source: Website of the Ministry of Foreign Affairs of Japan: https://www.mofa.go.jp/about/hq/org.html)

Gaimushō administers two independent government agencies that support its missions: the Japan International Cooperation Agency (JICA) and the Japan Foundation. The JICA, staffed with approximately 2000 full-time employees, coordinates ODA with the International Cooperation Bureau. Its operations vary from providing financial assistance to dispatching emergency relief, sending technical personnel and equipment to support local Japanese companies. The Japan Foundation serves cultural diplomacy. With an annual budget of over $200 million, it manages numerous programs under three broad umbrellas: cultural exchange, Japanese language education, and academic dialogue. The Japan Foundation is recently making efforts to deepen cultural ties with Asian countries, as exemplified in the establishment of the Asia Center, a new educational exchange agency that in 2016 alone sent 364 Japanese language instructors to teach 130,000 students throughout the region, and funded 516 cultural projects at home and abroad joined by more than 1 million participants.[4]

Personnel. *Gaimushō* has approximately 6000 employees, 2550 at the ministry and 3450 at overseas representations. The size of *Gaimushō's* workforce remains smaller than that of US (28,995), French (9113), German (8292), and British foreign services (6491), although it has increased slowly in the past ten years.[5] Full-time employees at *Gaimushō* are divided into three categories: career diplomats, area specialists, and administrative staff. Career diplomats, the core of Japan's diplomatic corps, are generalists who undertake a variety of positions at home and abroad in the course of their careers. Trained to assume leadership roles in the ministry, career diplomats put foreign policy decisions into action, managing policy implementation, negotiating with foreign representatives, and coordinating with other ministries. Area specialists, on the other hand, are specialists in a specific country and region, possessing deep understanding of its language, culture, and history. They enter *Gaimushō* on a separate track from career diplomats, taking more specialized examinations, and assist career diplomats with their expertise in narrower topics. Competent area specialists, however, may be promoted onto the career track, and an increasing number of area specialists now assume leadership positions at the ranks of ambassador and bureau director. Administrative staff support the day-to-day operations at *Gaimushō* by managing administrative and technical tasks under career diplomats and area specialists.[6] In addition to full-time employees, Japanese representations overseas regularly hire part-time employees, including specialized researchers with two-year appointments who study political, economic, and cultural trends in a specific country or region. Although their expertise is essential for overseas representations, these part-time employees face severe working conditions, including low salaries and insufficient resources.

Gender Balance

Gender imbalance is one of the challenges facing *Gaimushō*'s staffing. While Japanese women outnumber men in international organizations, including the United Nations, only 20–30 percent of *Gaimushō* employees (1400–1600) are women, a figure higher than other ministries in Japan yet lower than most other countries covered in this study.[7] Gender imbalance is particularly staggering among higher-ranking officials at *Gaimushō*. All ten bureau directors are male, and only four out of 42 division directors are women.[8] Among more than 200 ambassadors, consuls, and permanent representatives, only fourteen are women. There are only seven female ambassadors, all serving in countries of little strategic importance for Japan, such as Bolivia, Ireland, Estonia, Hungary, Macedonia, Latvia, and Malawi.[9] Gender balance at *Gaimushō*, however, is improving. Following the political slogan to promote the status of women, epitomized by Prime Minister Abe Shinzō's "womenomics," *Gaimushō* has been hiring more women in the past ten years, including career diplomats. Unlike other ministries, *Gaimushō* maintains the ratio of female new hires at 30 percent. Although the *Gaimushō* leadership remains dominated by men, more women, including those who have taken maternity leave, are advancing to higher positions, setting precedents for new generations of female career diplomats.[10]

Culture

Gaimushō is part of Japan's revered bureaucracy located in Kasumigaseki, Tokyo, and elitism has long characterized the culture of Kasumigaseki—particularly so for *Gaimushō*, on par with the Ministry of Finance. As the only ministry specializing in foreign policy, *Gaimushō*, for example, used to administer special recruitment examinations separate from the one for all other ministries, a tradition that ended only in 2001. Public criticism on *Gaimushō* reached its height in the wake of an embezzlement scandal in 2001, when a high-ranking *Gaimushō* official used secret funds aimed at receiving foreign dignitaries for personal purposes, precipitating dismissal of the vice minister, as well as the ambassadors to the United States and the United Kingdom. *Gaimushō* has become more transparent and flexible since, allowing employees to communicate and cooperate not only across different bureaus within the ministry, but also with international divisions of other ministries to expedite the execution of diplomatic initiatives. One aspect of the old *Gaimushō* culture that continues to afflict its staffers is an inadequate work–life balance. The small size of Japan's diplomatic corps forces career diplomats to work overtime almost every day, leaving little time to take care of young children and ageing parents. Although *Gaimushō* has policies for paid holidays, telework, and parental leave, career diplomats can rarely use them due to the grueling workload.[11]

Recruitment and Selection

Each year, *Gaimushō* recruits 20–30 career diplomats, about 50 area specialists, and 50–60 administrative staff. Historically, male graduates from the University of Tokyo, particularly with an undergraduate degree in law, dominated the career diplomat corps, followed by graduates from other prestigious universities, including Kyōto University, Waseda University, and Keiō University. The profile of new hires, however, has diversified in recent years. Among 119 career diplomats hired between 2010 and 2014, 32 were women, 15 had graduate degrees, and 6 possessed degrees in sciences, while 65 had undergraduate law degrees.[12]

Gaimushō's recruitment process for career diplomats has three steps: career events, public service examinations, and interviews. *Gaimushō* occasionally organizes career events at the ministry, as well as at the University of Tokyo, Kyoto University, and other major universities, including recruitment seminars, panel discussions, and group discussions, all aimed at providing information about *Gaimushō* for future applicants and establishing connections with young talents. *Gaimushō* also offers summer internships every year. Sixty to seventy student interns work at different bureaus for one or two months between June and August, tasked with various low-risk assignments. The summer internships, though separate from recruitment, offer opportunities for *Gaimushō* to find potential candidates for employment.

The first step for recruitment into *Gaimushō* is the public service examinations held between April and June each year. These examinations, administered by the National Personnel Authority, are required for all ministries and agencies in *Kasumigaseki*. Applicants with (expected) undergraduate or graduate degrees who aspire to become a career bureaucrat take two sets of examinations. The first examinations consist of two groups of multiple-choice questions. The first group (2/15 of the total score) tests applicants' reading comprehension, quantitative reasoning, and basic knowledge in sciences, humanities, and contemporary issues. The second group (3/15) tests applicants' expertise in the subject of specialty, which they can choose from eight (graduate applicants) or ten fields (undergraduate applicants). *Gaimushō* mostly recruits from applicants who select public administration, politics and international relations, law, economics, or human sciences as the subject of specialty, although it also hires a few who major in natural sciences and agriculture. In 2017, one in two graduate applicants and one in seven undergraduate applicants passed the minimum score in the first multiple-choice examinations and moved on to the second examinations.

The second examinations are divided into three sections. The first section (5/15) includes two or three written questions on applicants' subjects of specialty. An applicant who specializes in politics and international relations, for example, can choose three questions from among political science, public administration, the Constitution, international relations, international law, and public policy. The second section (2/15) is a policy debate for graduate applicants and a policy essay for undergraduate applicants. In both formats, applicants read provided materials and present their views on an open-ended question. The policy essay question in 2014, for example, was "What roles do taxes play in balancing social benefits and burdens?" The third section (3/15) is a personality test—an interview with a National Personnel Authority official, who asks questions based on the applicant's academic record, extracurricular activities, or volunteer experiences. Finally, applicants with superior scores in standardized English tests, such as the Test of English as Foreign Language (TOEFL) and the International English Language Testing Service (IELTS)—usually a requirement for study abroad in the United States and Great Britain—can earn a few extra points.[13] The National Personnel Authority is responsible for grading these examinations, but independent committees of professors and practitioners oversee the multiple choice and written examinations in each specialized subject.

Only top-notch applicants can survive these rigorous examinations. In 2017, 624 among 2470 graduate applicants and 1254 among 18,121 undergraduate applicants—about one-fourth of them female—passed these examinations. The National Personnel Authority allots different numbers of successful applicants for each subject of specialty, and politics and international relations, along with law, tend to be the most competitive subjects. In 2017, only 56 among 995 test-takers in politics and international relations and 504 among 8576 in law passed the examinations. To succeed in these examinations, most applicants take classes in private schools with special know-how. Successful applicants, therefore, come from diverse academic backgrounds, with 82 universities having more than ten students passing the examinations in 2017. Students from prestigious universities, however, dominate the school ranking. In 2017, students from the University of Tokyo (372), Kyoto University (182), and Waseda University (123) became the most successful.[14] Applicants who passed the public service examinations can now apply for specific ministries and agencies.

The second stage for *Gaimushō's* recruitment is a series of interviews conducted at the ministry building in July. A successful applicant needs to visit *Gaimushō* four times in two weeks, having approximately five interviews with foreign service officers and human resource representatives each time. Interviewers ask questions based on the information sheet filled out by applicants, which lists their academic background, extracurricular activities, internships, language skills, and study abroad experience. Through this laborious process, *Gaimushō* selects 20–30 new hires from the pool of approximately 300 applicants, a competition rate much higher than most other ministries and agencies.

Gaimushō uses no standardized formula for selection in this stage. *Gaimushō* places much emphasis on soft skills, such as logical reasoning, flexible thinking, and effective communication, instead of hard skills like language ability and area specialists. *Gaimushō*, in other words, values applicants with personality and organizational fit to specific bureaus and divisions in the ministry, while shunning those more suitable to become scholars or critics.[15] *Gaimushō* does not require any foreign experience. Although many recruits have study abroad experience in English-speaking countries, *Gaimushō* occasionally hires applicants who have never been abroad. *Gaimushō* does require a high level of English proficiency, however, encouraging applicants to submit TOEFL and IELTS scores. *Gaimushō* does recruit a few master's degree holders. However, it continues to hire far more younger applicants with a bachelor's degree, signaling its preference for generalists over specialists. By design, *Gaimushō* hires few PhD holders as only applicants under the age of thirty can take the public service examinations.

Gaimushō has little difficulty retaining its top talent. Only a couple of career diplomats in a given year's cohort decide to leave. Few quit because of ideological differences with the ministry, and most do so due to unsatisfactory working conditions. The basic salaries of career diplomats stay lower than comparable positions in industry, and their social welfare package remains far from comprehensive. Contrary to the popular image of *Kasumigaseki* bureaucrats as the symbol of elitism, career diplomats at *Gaimushō* are inundated by logistical tasks that administrative staff should be responsible for, such as copying, making room reservations, and scheduling taxi rides. Worse, career diplomats no longer enjoy automatic promotion to the rank of a director at an overseas mission, a custom that discouraged many of them from quitting in the past. It is, therefore, no surprise that some career diplomats decide to take a more stimulating, lucrative job in industry before getting too old to do so. Most of them, however, not only decide to stay, but also remain highly motivated because they are proud of their service to Japanese diplomacy.[16]

Professional Development and Training

Gaimushō provides two years of initial training at the ministry for incoming diplomats. Entering *Gaimushō* in April, they spend the first month at the Foreign Service Training Institute located outside Tokyo, receiving basic training in administrative duties and foreign languages. Each year, approximately ten new hires specialize in English, five in French, and two or three in German, Spanish, Russian, Chinese, and Arabic, while only one studies Korean every few years. New hires are assigned to separate bureaus in May, where they spend the next two years. While learning the basic operations at their bureaus, young career diplomats continue language training twice a week, totaling three hours. At the beginning of the third year, they gather again at the Foreign Service Training Institute, spending two months in intensive training in foreign languages and overseas assignments, such as foreign aid management, before departing for two or three years of study abroad at universities and language institutes in their designated countries. In the United States, for instance, Japanese diplomats are usually trained at Harvard, Columbia, Tufts, Princeton, Georgetown, or other universities with prestigious programs in international affairs. Most career diplomats trained in English earn a master's degree in the United States or Great Britain, while those specializing in difficult languages such as Chinese, Russian, and Arabic often do not as they need to spend more time at a language institute. After completing their studies, career diplomats start working at overseas missions. They are assigned to new positions every two or three years thereafter, oscillating between the ministry in Tokyo and Japanese representations overseas.

The two rounds of intensive training for career diplomats in the month of their arrival at *Gaimushō* and the two months before their departure for study abroad nurture special bonds among young Japanese diplomats. Throughout both training periods, they live together at the Foreign Service Training Institute, an environment isolated from the daily duties at the ministry and suitable for developing special friendships—as well as rivalries—with their colleagues. These special ties among the same-year cohorts play important roles in the years to come. Japanese diplomats, for instance, communicate frequently with their same-year colleagues in different bureaus, a practice that ensures cross-departmental communication and assists policy implementation.[17]

After finishing their study abroad programs, career diplomats have few mid-career training opportunities. Except for language-related coursework, such as interpreter training and intensive English for specialists in other languages, *Gaimushō's* culture—one that emphasizes professional development through work—discourages mid-career diplomats above their late twenties from participating in training opportunities inside and outside *Gaimushō*. This preference for on-the-job training may derive from the old examinations administered by *Gaimushō* alone. Before 2001, numerous university students who passed the old examinations joined *Gaimushō* without completing a bachelor's degree. These old-generation officials tend to place more emphasis on practical skills acquired through work than intellectual training outside the ministry. Mid-career diplomats do have opportunities to participate in short-term professional development programs or become a research fellow for several months at universities and think-tanks overseas. Current Vice Minister Akiba Takeo, for example, studied the impact of Weapons of Mass Destruction (WMD) proliferation and East Asian security as a research fellow at Harvard University in 2008. These opportunities, however, are limited to a select group of career diplomats—usually at the rank of assistant to bureau and division directors or above—and they often find it impossible to take time off from work, even for a few weeks.[18] Mid-career training at *Gaimushō*, therefore, remains exceptional.

Critics have pointed out the inadequacy of professional development for Japanese diplomats. According to the 2017 report prepared by the Foreign Service Personnel Committee, *Gaimushō* spends only $440,000 in training its employees, a stark contrast to $11.4 million spent by the US Department of State. Even the Ministry of Foreign Affairs of South Korea, with less than half of *Gaimushō's* workforce, spends $2.7 million. The report alleges that the Foreign Service Training Institute lacks sufficient training facilities, including a reliable Wi-Fi network, making it difficult for young Japanese diplomats to use basic e-learning tools.[19] Moreover, career diplomats receive inadequate support while studying abroad. For example, they pay for textbooks and private tutors out of pocket, a condition that sometimes discourages them from investing in their language learning.[20]

The 2018 government budget plan for *Gaimushō* recognized the "life-and-death importance" of bolstering Japan's diplomatic corps. In addition to expanding the workforce by adding 90 full-time employees in the ministry and hiring more part-time staffers at overseas representations, the budget plan called for reform in training programs, both in language and in other skills. On language skills, it suggested more comprehensive English training for all career diplomats—regardless of their assigned language of expertise—and improved training in other languages of growing importance, including Chinese and Russian. Outside language skills, *Gaimushō* plans to bolster the training scheme for new hires by expanding the list of required readings and assignments, and doubling the time allotted for teaching international law, diplomatic history, and relations with neighboring countries. The budget plan also recommended expanded training of mid-career diplomats at Harvard University and the Royal Institute of International Affairs. Recognizing the importance of international law in numerous diplomatic issues in Asia, including the Senkaku/Diaoyu Island dispute, *Gaimushō* encourages mid-career diplomats to participate in English-language training programs in international law, including at the Hague Academy of International Law, the Geneva International Law Seminar, and the Rhodes Academy of Oceans Law and Policy.[21] Whether *Gaimushō* can create a new culture that allows mid-career diplomats to participate in these programs remains unclear.

LEADERSHIP

Like other foreign service bureaucracies covered in this study, *Gaimushō* has a clear hierarchy. An elite career diplomat becomes an assistant to a division director in his/her 30s, a division director in his/her 40s, a bureau director, a deputy vice minister, and, if successful, a vice minister in his/her 50s, while serving as ambassadors to major countries. In most cases, a vice minister becomes an ambassador to the United States after his/her tenure, an indication of the utmost importance *Gaimushō* attaches to the position. After reaching the end of their careers at *Gaimushō*, career diplomats assume leadership positions outside the ministry, including government agencies affiliated with the ministry, such as the Japan International Cooperation Agency (JICA) and the Japan Foundation, and international organizations such as the United Nations, the International Court of Justice, and the International Tribunal for the Law of the Sea. Most of them, however, become an administrator, advisor, or trustee in industry, academe, and NGOs.

Career diplomats win promotion based on seniority and merit. They assume higher positions without promotion examinations or certifications, although peer and supervisor evaluations are reflected in their annual assessments. *Gaimushō* previously promised career diplomats seniority-based promotion to bureau directors and ambassadors, a condition resented by non-career area specialists. *Gaimushō*, however, strives to make the promotion process more competitive, filling an increasing number of leadership positions with competent area specialists, who now occupy approximately 20 percent of ambassador positions. *Gaimushō* also tries to appoint more ambassadors from outside the ministry. Executives from banks, companies, universities, and other ministries now comprise an additional 20 percent of all ambassador posts.

Only career diplomats can assume an ambassador position in a country of strategic importance for Japan. This cautious approach derives not only from custom, but also as a reaction to the case of Niwa Uichirō, a former ambassador to China (2010–2012). A former CEO of the Itochu trading company, Niwa had extensive experience dealing with Chinese businesspeople before becoming ambassador. The Democratic Party of Japan (DPJ), which overtook the Liberal Democratic Party (LDP) as the leading party in Japan in 2009, handpicked Niwa to reduce elite *Gaimushō* bureaucrats' dominance of foreign policy. For *Gaimushō*, however, Niwa was a disaster. He was unprepared to handle a crisis over the Senkaku/Diaoyu Islands which arose during his tenure. Oblivious of the delicacies of international law and diplomatic negotiation, Niwa made careless remarks contradicting the official stance of the Japanese government, going so far as to admit the existence of a territorial dispute in the region.[22] Since this fiasco, no one outside *Gaimushō* has been appointed to an important position which may require an urgent national security response.

There are successful cases of outsider appointments, of course. The most salient example is Kitaoka Shin'ich, a former history professor at the University of Tokyo who became an ambassador to the United Nations (2004–2006) and now serves as the head of the JICA (2015–present). Besides Kitaoka, two journalists—Takashima Hatsuhisa of Japan Broadcasting Corporation and Taniguchi Tomohiko of Nikkei Business Publication, Inc.—served as a press secretary (2002–2005) and a vice press secretary (2005–2008), respectively. Although less conspicuous than these figures, executives of major Japanese trading corporations with ties to developing countries in the Middle East and Africa also have served as ambassadors to these countries.

Despite the efforts to diversify the Japanese diplomatic corps, the *Gaimushō* leadership remains dominated by those with similar backgrounds. The Faculty of Law at the University of Tokyo, in particular, continues to form a predominant group. Among the ten most recent vice ministers in the past 20 years, six are graduates from the University of Tokyo, and four from the Faculty of Law. Most leaders in *Gaimushō* come from the American school or British school, receiving training in the United States or Great Britain. In a cohort of new hires, approximately ten specialize in English as their main foreign language and study abroad in US or British universities. Only a handful of them, however, can stay in embassies and consulates in these countries after the study abroad periods, a reality that often fuels rivalry among them.[23] After studying abroad, most successful career diplomats invariably assume positions at the North American Bureau, the Asian and Oceanian Affairs Bureau, the International Legal Affairs Bureau, or the Foreign Policy Bureau before becoming a vice minister or ambassador to a major country. As a result, top officials in *Gaimushō* tend to have experience in diplomatic negotiations with the United States and Asian neighbors, along with knowledge about international law and national security. These characteristics nurture a future *Gaimushō* leadership that reproduces and reinforces Japan's basic national strategy to maintain the strong US–Japanese alliance as a backbone for dealing with regional and global issues.

Although *Gaimushō* never considers pedigree in recruitment and promotion—at least openly—some career diplomats come from prominent families. For example, Fujisaki Ichirō, a former ambassador to the United States (2008–2012), was a great-great-grandson of Itō Hirobumi, the first prime minister of Japan. His father Fujisaki Masato was also a diplomat and a former ambassador to the Netherlands (1968–1972). Saiki Akitaka, a former vice minister (2013–2016), was a son of Saiki Senkurō, a former ambassador to Argentina. Although the cases of Fujisaki and Saiki are uncommon, Japanese career diplomats, like diplomats of other countries, tend to come from the wealthiest, most educated families in the country.

Although the foreign minister had the legal right to appoint leadership positions in *Gaimushō*, the vice minister and other high-ranking officials in the ministry used to possess substantial autonomy in personnel decisions. More recently, however, the cabinet has gained growing influence on leadership appointments at *Gaimushō* and other ministries. Established by Prime Minister Abe in 2014, the Cabinet Bureau of Personnel Affairs now has the authority to appoint positions in each ministry above the rank of deputy vice minister, enabling the cabinet to promote bureaucrats loyal to it. Under this system, few career bureaucrats in *Kasumigaseki* would risk their promotion by criticizing or objecting to the cabinet's decisions. The *Gaimushō* leadership in the future, therefore, will probably reflect the preference of political leaders, especially the prime minister, more strongly than before.

Role in Foreign Policymaking

Gaimushō, as an administrative institution, assists the political leadership in foreign policy decision-making and implementation. In recent years, Prime Minister Abe (2012–present) has bolstered the leadership of his cabinet in Japanese foreign policy. Abe, for instance, makes much more frequent visits to foreign countries than his predecessors, traveling abroad almost 60 times between 2012 and 2017.[24] He often tours developing countries in Asia, promising economic and military assistance, as part of efforts to curtail the expansion of Chinese influence. Abe also tried to cultivate a close personal relationship with Trump, despite his demands on correcting the trade imbalance.

To strengthen the cabinet's leadership in national security decision-making, Abe established the National Security Council (NSC) in 2013, led by the prime minister and staffed with high-ranking officials from *Gaimushō* and the Ministry of Defense. The prototype of the NSC dates back to the Defense Council, established in 1956 and renamed the Security Council in 1986, which provided a cabinet forum to discuss national defense. As national security challenges facing Japan globalized and diversified in the post-Cold War era, the first Abe cabinet (2006–2007) tried to transform the Security Council into the NSC with authority over a wider range of issues. This plan never came to fruition, however, due to Abe's resignation following the LDP's loss in the 2007 parliamentary election. After the 2013 hostage crisis in Amenas, Algeria, where lack of coordination between ministries prevented Tokyo from formulating an effective response, the second Abe cabinet finally launched the NSC and centralized national security decision-making in the cabinet. In 2013 the NSC published a national security strategy outlining Japan's strategic goals and means to attain them.[25] Staffed with only about 60 bureaucrats from various ministries, the NSC remains in an embryonic phase, with little influence on Japanese foreign policy compared to its US counterpart.

Despite the leading role of the cabinet, influential diplomats in *Gaimushō* have played essential roles in shaping Japanese foreign policy throughout the postwar era. For example, Ushiba Nobuhiko, a former vice minister (1967–1970) and ambassador to the United States (1970–1973), assisted the cabinets of Prime Minister Satō Eisaku (1964–1972) and Tanaka Kakuei (1972–1974) in negotiations with the United States for the reversion of Okinawa and restriction of Japan's textile exports. Hashimoto Hiroshi, a former China division chief (1968–1973), persuaded Tanaka to accept the "one China" principle—a principle that Taiwan is part of the People's Republic of China—to normalize relations with Beijing in 1972, when *Gaimushō* opposed severing diplomatic ties with Taipei. More recently, *Gaimushō*, under the leadership of chief negotiator Tsuruoka Kōji, achieved the signing of the Trans-Pacific Partnership Agreement in 2016. After the Trump administration withdrew from the agreement, *Gaimushō* is now leading international negotiations with the other signatory nations to make the agreement come into effect.

Gaimushō maintains cooperation with other ministries to implement various policy initiatives. Following the Infrastructure Systems Export Strategy first formulated in 2013, the Economic Affairs Bureau, along with specialists in infrastructure projects stationed at Japanese missions overseas, coordinates infrastructure projects in foreign countries with the Ministry of Economy, Trade, and Industry, along with other ministries. Japan, for example, reached an agreement with India in 2015 to build a high-speed Shinkansen railroad between Ahmadabad and Mumbai, in which the Japanese government provides low-interest loans and technical training. *Gaimushō* also plays an important role in promoting Cool Japan—a unique aspect of Japan's national strategy since 2010, aimed at enhancing its soft power by promoting cultural products overseas. It has established taskforces in embassies and consulates in nine countries to sell Cool Japan contents, although their effectiveness remains unclear.

Gaimushō has a complex relationship with the Ministry of Defense. With rivalry dating back to the prewar competition with the army, *Gaimushō's* insecurity was exacerbated in 2007, when the Defense Agency was promoted to the Ministry of Defense, assuming larger roles in Japan's national security, including sharing military intelligence with the United States. *Gaimushō*, however, seems to have secured influence on the Japanese NSC, as seen in the appointment of Yachi Shōtarō, a former vice minister, as the first national security advisor to the prime minister (2014–present), heading the National Security Secretariat located in the cabinet. *Gaimushō*, of course, recognizes the importance of coordination with the Ministry of Defense. The Ministry of Defense, for instance, dispatches military attachés to approximately 40 embassies overseas, where they collect national security information and cultivate ties with local military officials.

Although the *Gaimushō* bureaucracy has provided stability and continuity in Japanese foreign policy in the postwar era, politics in Japan sometimes compromises its ability to implement foreign policy. In 2002, for instance, Foreign Minister Tanaka Makiko attacked *Gaimushō* officials allegedly associated with Suzuki Muneo, Tanaka's rival and a strong supporter of partnership with Russia. To assuage the hostility between the foreign minister and *Gaimushō*, Prime Minister Koizumi Jun'ichirō fired Tanaka, and Nogami Yoshiji, a vice minister affiliated with Suzuki, resigned. When the DPJ became the ruling party, Prime Minister Hatoyama Yukio promised to remove the US bases in Futemma, Okinawa out of the prefecture, instead of relocating them to a nearby location of Henoko as previously agreed—an unrealistic commitment that perplexed and angered Japanese diplomats. With the Cabinet Bureau of Personnel Affairs capable of selecting vice ministers and other leading officials in the ministry, changes in the political leadership—a frequent phenomenon in Japan before Abe's tenure—may cause a leadership shuffle at *Gaimushō* in the future, precipitating confusion and inconsistency in implementation of Japanese foreign policy.

Gaimushō uses social media tools, such as Facebook, Twitter, and YouTube, for public diplomacy. *Gaimushō* offices and overseas representations maintain approximately 200 Facebook accounts, featuring Japanese foreign policy, cultural exchanges, and local Japan-related events. The Public Diplomacy Strategy Division, the Internet Public Relations Division, and the Cultural Affairs and Overseas Public Relations Division, for instance, have special pages for cultural diplomacy, entitled "Tohoku

Experience: 40th Year of ASEAN Japan Friendship and Cooperation," "Japan Culture Spotlight," and "International Manga [comic book] Award." *Gaimushō* also manages 42 Twitter accounts. The Internet Public Relations Division's "*Gaimushō yawaraka* [soft] tweet" has the largest number of followers (330,000) and tweets about a wide range of issues entertaining for Japanese youth. *Gaimushō* has 25 YouTube channels. Its official channel features the foreign minister's activities, while the Public Diplomacy Strategy Division's channel focuses on Japanese tradition and culture, including ninja and cosplay.[26]

PREPARATIONS FOR THE FUTURE

The Diplomatic Bluebook, an annual assessment of Japanese foreign policy published by *Gaimushō*, argues that national security conditions for Japan are "increasingly severe" due to Chinese and North Korean threats, while diplomatic problems facing Japan are diversifying and globalizing.[27] *Gaimushō* is trying to reform its diplomatic corps to meet these challenges in the future. It needs to address three issues in particular: budget, staffing, and diversity.

First, *Gaimushō* is under-funded. Its original budget has not increased in the past 15 years, with the budget of $6.9 billion (735.8 billion Japanese yen) in 2003 declining to $6.3 billion (696.7 billion Japanese yen) in 2018, although the actual spending increased from $7.4 billion (788.2 billion Japanese yen) to $7.7 billion (852.1 billion Japanese yen) in the same period.[28] Economic stagnation in Japan has curtailed the growth of *Gaimushō's* budget, but the government program reviews conducted during the three years of the DPJ rule (2009–2012), which terminated such *Gaimushō* programs as public relations activities related to ODA, also account for the tight fiscal situation in the ministry. The budgetary restrictions—something out of *Gaimushō's* control—preclude the ministry from taking initiatives to strengthen its workforce, including increasing opportunities for mid-career training as advocated in the Foreign Service Personnel Committee's report.

Second, *Gaimushō* is under-staffed. Its diplomatic corps (5982) remains much smaller than foreign services of major European countries, such as France (9113), Germany (8292), and Great Britain (6491). The inadequate staff size forces career diplomats to overwork, sacrificing their work-life balance, and preventing the ministry from dealing effectively with emerging challenges facing Japan.[29] *Gaimushō* is trying to rectify this situation by recruiting more employees and allotting more human resources to bureaus and divisions of national security importance. It is, for example, planning to divide the Northeast Asia Division in the Asian and Oceanian Affairs Bureau, now staffed with only 25 members, into two divisions with more staff, each responsible for North and South Korea. The growth of the *Gaimushō* workforce, however, remains at a slow pace due partly to the budgetary restrictions.[30]

In the meantime, *Gaimushō* should improve the working conditions in the ministry. It should stop overworking career diplomats with meager tasks like copying and data input, invest in office technology to make the overall flow of operations more efficient and paperless, and make welfare systems more accessible for career diplomats. Due to lack of progress in these areas, *Gaimushō*, in the words of one career diplomat, has now ceased to be a place where most talented Japanese youth hope to work. If the current practice persists, *Gaimushō* may encounter increasing difficulty recruiting young talent in the future.[31]

Third, *Gaimushō* needs to diversify its diplomatic corps, especially at the leadership level. Western orientation has been *Gaimushō's* intellectual tradition since the Meiji era, and the American-schooled will continue to occupy leadership positions in the ministry, considering the crucial importance of the US–Japanese alliance for Japan's national security. Other groups in *Gaimushō*, particularly those specializing in languages of neighboring states, should also take charge of more important positions, including the vice minister, a position traditionally dominated by the American and French schools. Top talents from the China and Russia schools become ambassadors to China and Russia, but only a few of them assume positions at the ministry higher than bureau directors. Few members of the Korea school become an ambassador to Korea, with a recent exception of Mutō Masayoshi (2010–2012), one of the unprecedented ambassador appointments made during the DPJ rule. Of course, the United States continues to be Japan's most important ally, and English remains the most crucial language for Japanese diplomats. Yet, *Gaimushō* needs a more diverse diplomatic corps to deal with new global and regional challenges.

Acknowledgment *The author wishes to thank the diplomats and scholars consulted in researching and writing this chapter, who have chosen to remain anonymous.*

Notes

1. Tobe Ryōichi, *Gaimushō kakushin-ha—sekai chitsujo no gen'ei* [Gaimushō Reformists: Illusions of the World Order] (Tokyo: *Chūō shinsho*, 2010).
2. The proportion of Japanese military spending in GNP declined from 2.78 percent in 1952 to 1.2 percent in 1961 to less than one percent after 1967. Prime Minister Miki Takeo set an official limit for military expenditures at one percent of GNP in 1976. Although Prime Minister Nakasone Yasuhiro abolished this limit in 1986, Japanese has maintained the one-percent rule until today.
3. Ministry of Foreign Affairs of Japan, "Government Budget Plan of 2018," December 2017. http://www.mofa.go.jp/mofaj/files/000320640.pdf.
4. The Japan Foundation 2016/2017, September 2017. http://www.jpf.go.jp/j/about/result/ar/2016/pdf/dl/ar2016.pdf.
5. These figures are cited in Foreign Service Personnel Committee, "Suggestions for Strengthening the System for Implementation of Diplomacy on Both Quality and Quantitative Aspects, Including Overseas Allowances," September 2017, http://www.mofa.go.jp/mofaj/files/000302344.pdf. This chapter relies on official statistics for staff size and budget, which are not always comparable.
6. Because of their central role in *Gaimushō*, this chapter focuses on the selection, training, and promotion of career diplomats, instead of area specialists and administrative staff.
7. Forty-two percent of staff working at the ministry in Tokyo are women, but this figure includes a large number of administrative staff and temporary workers. The proportion of female employees at overseas representations is significantly lower.
8. "List of Senior Officials," Ministry of Foreign Affairs of Japan, December 28, 2018, https://www.mofa.go.jp/about/hq/list2.html. Accessed January 4, 2019.
9. "Directors of Japanese Overseas Missions," Ministry of Foreign Affairs of Japan. https://www.mofa.go.jp/about/hq/list.html. Accessed June 1, 2018.
10. Interview with Japanese career diplomat on May 27, 2018.
11. Interview with Japanese career diplomat on May 27, 2018.
12. Recruitment Pamphlet, Ministry of Foreign Affairs of Japan. http://www.mofa.go.jp/mofaj/files/000099832.pdf. Accessed March 27, 2019.
13. The National Personnel Authority administers another round of public service examinations between September and November for graduate students who passed the bar examination and undergraduate students with

expertise outside the areas outlined here. *Gaimushō* restricts undergraduate applicants in the fall round to those enrolled in universities overseas. The structure of these examinations remains similar to the spring examinations, but they put more emphasis on the ability to design and propose policies.

14. National Public Service Examinations Recruitment NAVI, the National Personnel Authority https://www.jinji.go.jp/saiyo/saiyo.html#main_and_important_bg. Accessed March 27, 2019.
15. Interview with Japanese career diplomat on May 27, 2018.
16. Interviews with Japanese career diplomats on May 27 and May 31, 2018.
17. Interviews with Japanese career diplomats on May 27 and May 31, 2018.
18. Interviews with Japanese career diplomats on May 27 and May 31, 2018.
19. Foreign Service Personnel Committee, "Suggestions."
20. Interview with Japanese career diplomat on May 31, 2018.
21. Ministry of Foreign Affairs of Japan, "Government Budget Plan of 2018."
22. In 2012, Niwa expressed opposition against Tokyo Governor Ishihara Shintarō's plan to purchase the Senkaku/Diaoyu Islands. Ishihara, along with other government officials, censured Niwa as his remarks contradicted Japan's official stance that there is no territorial dispute on these islands. Mure Dickie, "Tokyo warned over plans to buy islands," *Financial Times*, June 6, 2012.
23. Interview with Japanese career diplomat on May 31, 2018.
24. "List of the Prime Minister's Foreign Visits," Ministry of Foreign Affairs of Japan, June 14, 2018, https://www.mofa.go.jp/mofaj/kaidan/page24_000037.html. Accessed March 27, 2019.
25. Government of Japan, "National Security Strategy," December 17, 2013, https://www.cas.go.jp/jp/siryou/131217anzenhoshou/nss-e.pdf. Accessed March 27, 2019.
26. Social Media List (Ministry of Foreign Affairs, Embassies & Consulates), Ministry of Foreign Affairs of Japan, July 17, 2018, https://www.mofa.go.jp/about/list_en.html. Accessed March 27, 2019.
27. Ministry of Foreign Affairs of Japan, "Diplomatic Blue Book 2017," 2–9, http://www.mofa.go.jp/mofaj/gaiko/bluebook/2017/html/index.html. Accessed March 27, 2019.
28. Ministry of Foreign Affairs of Japan, "Government Budget Plan of 2018."
29. Foreign Service Personnel Committee, "Suggestions."
30. This chapter relies on official statistics for staff size and budget, which are not always comparable.
31. Interview with Japanese career diplomat on May 31, 2018.

REFERENCES

Dickie, M. 2012, June 6. Tokyo Warned Over Plans to Buy Islands. *Financial Times*. https://www.ft.com/content/af98fc54-aef7-11e1-a4e0-00144feabdc0. Accessed January 4, 2019.

Diplomatic Blue Book 2017, 2–9. 2017. Ministry of Foreign Affairs of Japan. http://www.mofa.go.jp/mofaj/gaiko/bluebook/2017/html/index.html. Accessed March 27, 2019.

Directors of Japanese Overseas Missions. 2018. Ministry of Foreign Affairs of Japan. http://www.mofa.go.jp/mofaj/annai/zaigai/meibo/index.html. Accessed March 29, 2019.

Government Budget Plan of 2018. 2017, December. Ministry of Foreign Affairs of Japan. http://www.mofa.go.jp/mofaj/files/000320640.pdf. Accessed March 27, 2019.

Japan Foundation 2016/2017. 2017, September. http://www.jpf.go.jp/j/about/result/ar/2016/pdf/dl/ar2016.pdf. Accessed March 27, 2019.

List of Senior Officials. 2018 June 11. Ministry of Foreign Affairs of Japan. https://www.mofa.go.jp/about/hq/list2.html. Accessed January 4, 2019.

National Public Service Examinations Recruitment NAVI. 2019. The National Personnel Authority. https://www.jinji.go.jp/saiyo/saiyo.html. Accessed March 27, 2019.

National Security Strategy. 2013, December 17. Government of Japan. https://www.cas.go.jp/jp/siryou/131217anzenhoshou/nss-e.pdf. Accessed January 4, 2019.

Organization Chart. 2017. Ministry of Foreign Affairs of Japan. https://www.mofa.go.jp/about/hq/org.html. Accessed January 3, 2019.

Prime Minister's Foreign Visits. 2018. Ministry of Foreign Affairs of Japan. https://www.mofa.go.jp/mofaj/kaidan/page24_000037.html. Accessed March 27, 2019.

Representing Japan. n.d. Recruitment Pamphlet, Ministry of Foreign Affairs of Japan. http://www.mofa.go.jp/mofaj/files/000099832.pdf.

Ryōichi, T. 2010. *Gaimushō kakushin-ha—sekai chitsujo no gen'ei* (*Gaimushō Reformers: Illusions of World Order*). Tokyo: *Chūō shinsho*.

Social Media List—Ministry of Foreign Affairs, Embassies & Consulates. 2018. Ministry of Foreign Affairs of Japan. https://www.mofa.go.jp/about/list_en.html. Accessed January 4, 2019.

Suggestions for Strengthening the System for Implementation of Diplomacy on Both Quality and Quantitative Aspects, Including Overseas Allowances. 2017. Foreign Service Personnel Committee. http://www.mofa.go.jp/mofaj/files/000302344.pdf. Accessed March 27, 2019.

CHAPTER 7

Russia

Jessica Terry, Zachary Reeves, and Jeremi Suri

EXECUTIVE SUMMARY

The Russian Ministry of Foreign Affairs has a very hierarchical and centralized structure. The bureaucratic culture shows continuity across periods—Tsarist, Soviet, and post-Soviet. This culture is evident in the modern structure and priorities of the ministry. Russian diplomats have minimal personal autonomy, and they are expected to follow specific and detailed orders from their superiors. While minor diplomatic issues in countries with low geopolitical relevance may be handled internally, any significant diplomatic action is likely to be personally delegated by Vladimir Putin. Some legacies from the Soviet era remain especially pronounced. In particular, the senior ministry leadership consists of officials who were raised and trained under the Soviet tradition. Diplomats still follow a highly professionalized and rigorous course of diplomatic training, although the communist component of the Soviet era is no longer

---

J. Terry • Z. Reeves
2018 Master of Arts Degrees, Global Policy Studies and Russian, East European, and Eurasian Studies, The University of Texas at Austin,
Austin, TX, USA

J. Suri (✉)
Lyndon B. Johnson School of Public Affairs, The University of Texas at Austin,
Austin, TX, USA
e-mail: suri@austin.utexas.edu

© The Author(s) 2020
R. Hutchings, J. Suri (eds.), *Modern Diplomacy in Practice*,
https://doi.org/10.1007/978-3-030-26933-3_7

present. The majority of recruits to the foreign service come from the Moscow State University of International Relations, which is operated by the Ministry of Foreign Affairs.

The Russian Foreign Service maintains an international reputation for professional excellence. Russian diplomats are known for their profound linguistic and cultural knowledge of assigned regions. Diplomats generally focus on one region of the world, moving from post to post while slowly rising through the ranks. Additionally, with changes in communications technologies, the Russian Foreign Service has increasingly utilized social media for purposes of public diplomacy. While the ministry is still a prestigious and valued institution in Russia, it has faced challenges in recent years which have lowered its attraction for the best potential recruits. Some causes for this reduced prestige are external factors outside the control of the government, such as the relative ease of travel outside the country today as compared with during the Soviet era. Others are internal: many students in the pool of prospective employees have cited a perceived lack of professional freedom with the ministry. As fewer of the traditionally trained Soviet era diplomats remain, the ministry will face the challenge of integrating the younger post-Soviet generation into the fabric of Russian diplomacy.

History and Culture

Russia's earliest diplomatic history begins in the ninth century, when Russian principalities sought better connections with the Byzantine Empire.[1] In the early years, Moscow inherited a political and institutional culture from the Byzantium that is, in some ways, still present today.[2] Russians borrowed the concept of "symphony"—that is, the unification of the state and the church—from the Byzantine model of diplomacy and statecraft. This resulted in a missionary concept for the early Ministry of Foreign Affairs. During the period preceding Peter the Great, the ministry focused on religion (Russian Orthodoxy), and in later eras, ideological dogmas (Marxism/Leninism and Soviet ideology) served as substitutes for religion.

The inherited Byzantine model differentiated Russian diplomacy from Asian and Western models in another important way. Recurring insecurity and weakness in Russian diplomacy derived from the Russian system of principalities, together with the ways in which Byzantine influences encouraged Orthodox administrative structures. Russian leaders reacted by emphasizing diplomatic centralization, which can still be seen in the structure of the modern Russian ministry. While little of the formal Tsarist structure exists in today's system, there are still lines of continuity that can be seen in Russian goals and objectives, especially regarding security on the Eastern border and expansion in the South.³

In the nineteenth century, two important and opposing ideological camps emerged within Russia—Slavophiles, who looked East, and the *Zapadniki*, who looked West.⁴ As Russia began to develop and expand its influence, these two philosophical camps sought to answer the important question: which path of development should Russia choose, and what would be Russia's place in the world? Those in the Slavophile camp asserted that Russia should resist Western influence and values because they would undermine what they viewed as the unique cultural heritage of Russia. The *Zapadniki* advocated for greater involvement and acceptance of the West, hoping to rectify Russia's "backwardness" in comparison to Western industrialized nations. This debate has continued since the nineteenth century and is present today in Russia's contemporary political environment and decisions regarding Russian foreign policy. Russian diplomacy has a love–hate relationship with advanced industrial countries in the West—the regime seeks to emulate many Western economic and technological developments, as it also fears the accompanying challenges to Russian political and social traditions.

Under Tsars Peter and Catherine, the diplomatic services experienced major restructuring and improvement. Both leaders looked to expand their influence outward, as Russia's unique geopolitical position—surrounded by many threatening adversaries—made foreign policy essential for survival. As Russia's involvement in foreign affairs grew, so did the strengthening of the foreign unit. Additionally, both Peter and Catherine believed in a *Zapadnik* view of progress, and both tried increasingly to westernize the foreign service and strengthen Russia's connections with the West.

The Bolshevik Revolution in 1917 essentially reset Russian/Soviet foreign relations and the development of the Ministry of Foreign Affairs. The old Tsarist system was almost entirely liquidated (including personnel during the Stalinist purges), but authoritarian practices have continued. There is still a clear, hierarchical, top-down bureaucratic structure, such that decisions can be given quickly from the top and executed by the lower levels. Additionally, normative aspects of the Soviet legacy and the Soviet approach to foreign affairs are still alive in the modern ministry, where a particular mix of Russian nationalism and anti-Westernism remains strong. The ideological component of recruitment into the government apparatus—the importance of loyalty to the state and hostility to foreign competitors—is still ever-present (although, perhaps, less intense than in the Soviet era). Conformity and the collective are valued above individual initiative. This is no surprise, considering that many leading Russian officials were products of the Soviet era—especially President Vladimir Putin and Foreign Minister Sergei Lavrov.

With the collapse of the Soviet Union, the ministry once again experienced an intense but fleeting shift to the West. Russia sought integration into the Euro-Atlantic political economic community, while maintaining a distinct set of Eurasian security and cultural obsessions.[5] When the Westernizing political urges of the early post-Cold War era conflicted with deeper security and cultural traditions, pro-Western sentiments proved short-lived. The historic battle between westernizers and Slavophiles repeated itself, and yet again, the latter grew in influence within the Russian Foreign Ministry.

The ministry underwent a complicated and painful internal transformation in the 1990s to address the political and security needs of the new international environment. Although the twenty-first century ministry is structurally different from both its Tsarist and Soviet predecessors, it has returned to many Soviet tendencies, especially regarding centralized decision-making and anti-Western hostility. As recent Foreign Minister Sergei Ivanov wrote, "Russian society looks to its own history to provide the vital reference points it needs to fill the political and psychological vacuum left by the fall of the old system."[6]

According to the ministry's own brief overview of diplomatic history, the assumption guiding today's service is the subordination of the diplomatic service to the state, and the need to aggressively defend Russian national interests in a hostile world.[7] One other important factor in evaluating today's foreign service in Russia is leadership style. Comparatively speaking, the state was more flexible and transparent under Boris Yeltsin than under Vladimir Putin. Since the early years of the post-Soviet era, the political system has moved further toward centralization and authoritarianism. Such centralization is also reflected in the bureaucracy, where Putin has appointed and promoted figures who share his aggressive and frequently anti-Western ideas, rather than a more professional approach to diplomacy. The Russian Foreign Ministry is highly politicized, as it has always been.

Profile

According to the Lowy Institute's Global Diplomacy Index,[8] Russia's diplomacy network is ranked fourth in the world in terms of extent and reach. As of 2018, the Russian diplomatic service boasts 243 total posts—142 embassies/high commissions, 89 consulates/consulates-general, 11 permanent missions, and 1 other representation. In 2015, the Russian Federation proposed a planned budget for the Ministry of Foreign Affairs for the 2016 fiscal year of 92–98 billion rubles.[9] Assuming that the budget is somewhere in the middle of these two numbers, this translates to roughly 1.5 billion US dollars. These numbers should be considered in light of the ruble's significant devaluation on the international market since 2014. In 2016, Russia's defense spending amounted to more than 4% of the country's GDP[10]; in contrast, spending on the Ministry of Foreign Affairs was 1/32nd of that number. The Russian Ministry of Foreign Affairs is composed of 10,000 employees, which includes those working in regional and functional divisions, those working as representatives and in consulate offices abroad, employees in international organizations, and those in "subordinate enterprises." Of these, 2500 are Russian diplomats posted abroad.[11]

The Russian diplomatic service does not have cones or specific career tracks; rather, there is a regional focus and a clear, hierarchical ladder for advancement in ranking.[12] The structure includes 17 regional bureaus as well as 22 functional departments (we have included the Department of International Organizations in the functional department category). The Russian Ministry of Foreign Affairs' organizational structure is currently arranged so that lower employees and departments can quickly take and execute orders from the president and the executive office. Ideas flow from the top down; there is little space for local innovation, or even experimentation.

Although we were not able to find reliable information regarding gender representation and demographic makeup of the ministry, we were able to estimate what the gender ratio might look like. A number of published articles refer to the difficulties for women to become ambassadors or enter the diplomatic service at all. An article published by the *Krasnoyarsk* branch of the ministry states: "after the 1917 transformation of the Ministry into the People's Commissariat for Foreign Affairs, the situation has not changed: the possibility of becoming ambassador was still inaccessible for the weaker sex."[13] The same article goes on to state that in today's

Russian Foreign Ministry "without a doubt, the work of a diplomat is heavy—and for women in particular it is necessary to work two to three times longer and harder to prove that, by right, you occupy a key position." In an article for *Kommersant*, a male Russian diplomat states: "the diplomatic profession involves a high degree of mobility and long trips abroad, which is in conflict with the natural destiny of a woman as mother and her family situation."[14] One mid-level female diplomat privately described the Russian Foreign Service as still shaped by a "patriarchal, militarized tradition." She claimed that there were few female diplomats, and especially few women in the highest level positions. She also pointed out that most women who were in the ministry did not have children of their own.

One source stated that a unique characteristic of the Russian Foreign Ministry is its respect for institutional memory and experience.[15] Ambassadors and diplomats for key organizations (such as the Russian ambassador to the United States) often stay in these positions much longer than in other services. With continuity in its staffing of high-level positions, the Russian Foreign Ministry has a deep institutional memory and working knowledge of certain countries and organizations. It is better prepared than most of its counterparts to nurture long-term working diplomatic relationships.

Recruitment and Selection

The vast majority of Russian diplomats come directly as graduates from the Moscow State Institute of International Relations (MGIMO).[16] MGIMO is run by the Russian Ministry of Foreign Affairs and has long played a role in preparing new bureaucrats for careers in the Ministry of Foreign Affairs. In the Soviet era, the Russian diplomatic service consisted almost exclusively of graduates from MGIMO; today, there are alternative ways to pursue a career in the Ministry of Foreign Affairs. While most career bureaucrats come from this academic institution, there are some recruits who come from other major state institutions as well.

In its recruiting, the ministry values consistent professionalism, strong analytical capabilities, evident interpersonal talents, deep writing skills, and a broad knowledge of foreign languages. Diplomatic recruits are expected to enter the ministry with mastery of at least two foreign languages.[17] Above all, the ministry emphasizes a sense of responsibility to the state, faith in the country, and defense of all points of national interest.[18] Thus, the typical Russian recruit for the diplomatic service needs to have a fierce loyalty to his/her country.

MGIMO handles the training of new recruits. In the Soviet era, training focused on ideology, so that diplomats could represent and promote the communist party in foreign countries. Now, training focuses more on classical diplomacy. Recruits undergo intensive study of foreign languages and deep training in the customs, traditions, and political history of foreign countries. To enter the MGIMO Department of International Relations, students must pass exams on history, a foreign language, and the Russian language. Students in this department also participate in intensive training which includes role-playing and situational workshops related to diplomacy and crisis management.[19] In an interview with *Russia Today* (*RT*),[20] many Russian diplomats mentioned that they had the impression that their language and theoretical training was more intensely focused than that of other nations' diplomatic services.

Despite the evident pride of current Russian diplomats in their service, the Russian Foreign Ministry has had difficulties retaining talented recruits since the end of the Soviet era.[21] The ministry is less desirable in the eyes of potential MGIMO recruits, who receive more lucrative professional offers from non-state organizations, especially private businesses. In a survey published in 2011, many MGIMO students voiced interest in pursuing alternative careers, especially in business. When asked specific questions about why they were not interested in careers within the ministry, students expressed concerns about low salaries, nepotism, cronyism, and gender discrimination. A large percentage of those surveyed stated that they were driven to pursue alternate careers by their interest to "make a difference in society" or to have greater freedom in their work. In recent years, the ministry has tried to make salaries more competitive, but the ministry has not addressed the issue of professional freedom. Often just the opposite, as Russian diplomacy has become more centralized and hierarchical.

Additionally, the decline in the foreign ministry's prestige might be due to the greater access to international travel opportunities in Russia today. In the Soviet era, employment in the ministry was one of the few avenues for foreign travel, and it brought assumptions of privilege and glamor. That is no longer the case. If anything, private travel now holds more allure for many Russian citizens.

One source stated that he believes the foreign service's prestige has rebounded since 2005. The ministry doubled salaries for diplomats after that year, and diplomats are now viewed as figures of high importance in

Russian society. Additionally, this source expressed his belief that, perhaps since there are now more lucrative alternatives to working as a bureaucrat, this has reduced pressures to keep outsiders out, thus making recruitment less about family line, status, and "eliteness" than it had been in the Soviet era.[22] Today's recruits appear motivated to join the foreign service out of patriotism and due to the relatively high level of job security in working for the government.

Professional Development and Training

The Ministry of Foreign Affairs runs its own university, the Diplomatic Academy, where mid-career level training occurs.[23] In addition to providing continued professional development for ministry officials, students unaffiliated with the ministry can also pursue advanced degrees at the Diplomatic Academy. (It is currently unclear how entry for those outside the ministry is arranged, or how rare it is for those outside the ministry to attend.) In addition to advanced degrees, the Diplomatic Academy offers training seminars for returning professionals. These seminars are two- to four-week courses on a wide range of thematic issues—Russia's foreign policy, diplomatic and consular service, international law, peacekeeping, and work with the Russian and foreign media.

In a personal interview, a source familiar with the Soviet system of training describes the training as very traditional—MGIMO provided typical classroom instruction on the history of Europe and the world, and training was strict and clinical.[24] The source also described the Russian system as emphasizing on-the-job training with diplomats expected to learn from mentors and from daily experience. There is strong continuity in substance and style from Soviet to post-Soviet training of this kind.

Between assignments at institutions abroad, diplomatic personnel are expected to spend no less than one year on assignment within one of the subdivisions of the central apparatus of the Ministry of Foreign Affairs.[25] Our information suggests that those looking to further their diplomatic career have a very clear hierarchy to climb—recruits start directly from MGIMO and then rise through secretarial ranks (third secretary, second secretary, first secretary, etc.) MGIMO's best student recruits begin as attachés; the majority of recruits start as assistants (a position which does not rank). Each promotion typically takes about three years. The Russian system is quite rigid and hierarchical.[26]

Political appointees do exist in the Russian Foreign Service. For example, Valentina Matvienko served as Soviet/Russian ambassador to the Republic of Malta and Greece. Political appointments occur most frequently during turning points in Russian history, such as after the collapse of the Soviet Union, with the logic that skilled political appointees would be better able to explain the changes within their own country and the international consequences of such changes.[27]

Leadership

The Russian Ministry of Foreign Affairs has a top-down management style with a clear hierarchical structure. Except for political appointees, Russian diplomats holding senior positions (ambassadors, generals and deputy generals, the foreign minister, etc.) have steadily climbed the hierarchical ladder over time, with some starting at the lowest level. Although a PhD is not required to enter the ministry, many of Russia's ambassadors and senior-level diplomats hold advanced academic degrees and have a long list of professional affiliations. As was the case in the Soviet era, an advanced degree carries important prestige.

Senior-level leaders in the ministry follow similar rotation patterns through parallel positions, and they often become ambassadors in their region of deepest experience. Most senior leaders have held high-level positions in some sort of functional department (for instance, Ambassador Churkin was Director of the Information Department; Ambassador Kislyak was Director of the Department of Security Affairs and Disarmament; and Ambassador Yakovenko was Director of the Department of Security Affairs and Disarmament). Almost all of the figures we examined served time in mid- to-high-level positions at the central office in Moscow. More generally, those who reached senior positions in the Russian Ministry of Foreign Affairs built a career which has demonstrated a high level of professionalism, specialized knowledge, and versatility both in Moscow and abroad. Those at high-level posts have usually remained in those positions even during shifts in leadership. The exceptions have been the moments of major institutional change, especially during the Gorbachev years.

The Russian Ministry of Foreign Affairs faces a unique problem moving forward. Most senior-level diplomats and those in senior positions in the central office of the Ministry are Soviet-trained. Like Putin and many in the state leadership, they are the legacy of the Soviet era, and their way of thinking has been shaped by the Soviet experience. In recent years, some of those in the older generation have passed away. In the coming years, the ministry will have to deal with the challenge of integrating the younger post-Soviet generation into the fabric of the leadership and its institutional culture. Generational change is happening fast in the ministry, and it is likely to be disruptive.

Role in Foreign Policymaking

Those who rise to high-ranking positions in the ministry are able to influence policy within strict limits. The strategic decisions, however, are made at the level of minister and deputy minister; even those at the level of ambassador have limited authority without prior consultation with superiors. As one official revealed in an interview with *Kommersant*, "ordinary employees simply follow instructions."[28] Current research suggests that Russian diplomats have little leeway in bilateral and multilateral negotiations. They are required to follow their given negotiation charges strictly.

Despite the perceived lack of room to maneuver in negotiations, high-level diplomats understand the official positions of the executive office to the extent that "leeway" could be viewed as unnecessary. Because of this, senior Russian diplomats conducting bilateral and multilateral negotiations go into discussions knowing exactly how much flexibility they have on each issue. This appears to be true across different missions of the ministry, with the one exception being embassies located in small countries with low geopolitical importance to Russia. Russian diplomats in those countries have suggested that their missions receive less direct supervision from Moscow, but that can change quickly in moments of crisis.

While lower level diplomats might not have much influence on foreign policy decisions, those in ministerial posts usually do. For instance, Sergei Lavrov, the current foreign minister (as of 2019), has a strong relationship with the president, a wealth of knowledge and experience, and is a strong figure in Russian foreign policy. Like many of his high-level administrative counterparts, Lavrov is the product of the Soviet era, and has shown a clarity of vision in international affairs that is remarkable. Lavrov is a fixture on the international stage (he is often involved in Russia's dealings with the UN and formerly served as the UN Permanent Representative), and while the president is firmly in control of Russian foreign policy, he is clearly influential. It is worth noting that Lavrov is now the longest-serving foreign minister in post-Cold War Russia.

Andrei Gromyko, infamously known abroad as "Mr. Nyet," served as a major Soviet example of the minister as a policy influencer for numerous general secretaries. His nickname came from frustrated Western policy-makers and was a reference to his frequent use of the veto at the UN Security Council. Gromyko served as foreign minister from 1957 to 1988—almost three decades of work at the head of the ministry. Whether or not he served as the core architect of the policies he expounded remains a mystery, but he was considered indispensable in his position as foreign minister across *four* successive leaders—Stalin, Malenkov, Khrushchev, and Brezhnev. Gromyko was the first professional diplomat to join the Communist Party's ruling Politburo, and he was the voice and the face of post-WWII Soviet diplomacy. Gromyko's acceptance into the central decision-making group proves that his value went far beyond simply his loyalty. The current Russian Foreign Ministry is acutely conscious of this history, and seeks to build on the legacy of policy influence and loyalty for its leading figures.

In recent years, the ministry has also increasingly come under the influence of the Russian Orthodox Church. In 2007, Russia passed a law aimed at uniting the interests of the Church and the Ministry of Foreign Affairs. Russian Foreign Minister Lavrov has stated that it is the ministry's intent to protect the interests of the Russian (Orthodox) diaspora abroad and facilitate their spiritual needs.[29] In recent years, the Orthodox Church has amassed considerable power among the Russian political elite, including Putin himself; the increasing influence of the Church in the work of the Ministry of Foreign Affairs can be seen as an extension of this. In 2014, Vladimir Putin stated that it was the responsibility of the Russian Federation to protect Russians abroad.[30] In a similar vein, the Russian Orthodox Church has a responsibility to Orthodox Christians throughout the world. There is a clear goal overlap here, making the Russian Ministry of Foreign Affairs and the Russian Orthodox Church ideal partners in advocating for the interests of ethnic Russians throughout the world. Observers should expect this institutional partnership to deepen in coming years.

PREPARATIONS FOR THE FUTURE

The Russian Ministry of Foreign Affairs now actively reaches out to Orthodox Christians abroad, broadening its appeal to believers in foreign countries.[31] The Russian Orthodox Church, which has periodically worked closely with the state, has its own office focused on foreign policy, the

Department of External Church Relations (DECR). Many of DECR's foreign policy objectives align with Russia's foreign policy priorities.

According to Russia's National Security Concept from the year 2000, Russia was faced with the domestic threat of "the depreciation of spiritual values," as well as the external threat of the imposition of contrary cultural and religious values in Russia by other states. Vladimir Putin, too, warns of this perceived threat. Thus, Russian foreign policy has increasingly become involved in the protection of the traditional Russian religious identity as well as the promotion of Russian Orthodoxy abroad. The Russian leadership has also endorsed Russian Orthodoxy in order to mobilize Russian nationalism both at home and abroad, especially in contested regions like the Caucasus, Ukraine, and the Baltics. The promotion of Russian Orthodox identity is a form of aggressive outreach to irredentist communities in countries of interest to Moscow.

The Russian Ministry has also made concerted efforts to improve its public diplomacy efforts in post-Soviet states.[32] As a legacy of past institutions and practices, many post-Soviet states were highly interdependent economically, and there remains a large body of Russians abroad in states no longer legally under the Russian umbrella. Russian diplomats use the term "near abroad" to assert a special relationship of influence in post-Soviet states; public diplomacy in these areas is often referred to as humanitarian cooperation. Efforts in post-Soviet states seem to be primarily driven by material and security interests, rather than being purely issues of image and reputation.

Russia has pursued a different public diplomacy strategy in the West. Many Russian public diplomacy efforts for Western audiences have centered on the practice of cultural diplomacy and focused on international media. Most recently, these efforts have included covert activities through social media, including interference in elections. Russia has also significantly updated international broadcasting and news services, cultural outreach, and support for pro-Russian think tanks abroad.[33] While the Russian goal in post-Soviet states has been to maintain interdependence and close connections, for Western audiences Moscow's aim involves bolstering the image of Russia and its friends while weakening perceived adversaries.

The Russian Foreign Ministry has energetically embraced the role of technology in aiding public diplomacy. It runs its own active and sophisticated YouTube, Twitter, and Facebook pages. In 2015, the Foreign Ministry appointed Maria Zakharova as the official spokesperson. Zakharova is ubiquitous on social media and answers questions directly from other users under the guise of what she refers to as "expert opinion," rather than "official statements." This enables Zakharova to appear as a more impartial commenter while still subtly advancing the ministry's agenda.[34]

Zakharova's approach to public diplomacy, both within Russia and beyond, coincides with the effort to rebrand and redirect the Russian Foreign Ministry. In 2013, speaking to a crowd on Diplomatic Worker's Day, Putin called for a change in the style of Russian diplomacy, urging more use of soft power to combat potential information threats. Putin focused on the use of soft power mechanisms such as promoting Russian language study abroad, promoting a positive image of Russia abroad, and integrating the Russian perspective into global information flows. Zakharova has been a bold and vocal face of this "new" Russian Foreign Ministry.

The ministry also maintains an active Twitter account, in conjunction with *RT*, to legitimize and disseminate its message to a global audience. By retweeting *RT* rather than simply putting out a message on its own, the ministry draws in international readers who may be unaware of *RT*'s direct connection to the Kremlin.[35] In general, the Russian Ministry has shown itself to be adept at utilizing new technology to reach diverse global netizens directly. We should expect more creative and covert Russian diplomatic efforts through social media in coming years. This is a priority and perceived strength within the ministry, and among its political overseers.

Acknowledgment *The authors wish to thank the following diplomats and scholars who were consulted in researching and writing this chapter:* Vladislav Zubok, Michael Kimmage, and Irvin Studin.

Notes

1. "The 210th Anniversary of the Russian Foreign Office," *Ministry of Foreign Affairs of the Russian Federation*, September 7, 2012. http://www.mid.ru/en/about/social_organizations. Accessed March 29, 2019.
2. T. V. Zonova, "Diplomatic Cultures: Comparing Russia and the West in Terms of a 'Modern Model of Diplomacy,'" *The Hague Journal of Diplomacy* 2 no. 1 (2007): 1–23.
3. Igor S. Ivanov, *The New Russian Diplomacy* (Washington: Brookings Institution, 2004).
4. "Of Russian Origin: Slavophiles and Zapadniki," *Russiapedia*, 2016. http://russiapedia.rt.com/of-russian-origin/slavophiles-and-zapadniki/. Accessed March 26, 2019.

5. Ivanov, *The New Russian Diplomacy*.
6. Ibid.
7. "Concept of the Foreign Policy of the Russian Federation," *Ministry of Foreign Affairs of the Russian Federation*, February 18, 2019. http://www.mid.ru/en/foreign_policy/official_documents/-/asset_publisher/CptICkB6BZ29/content/id/122186. Accessed March 26, 2019.
8. "Global Diplomacy Index," Lowy Institute. http://www.lowyinstitute.org/global-diplomacy-index/. Accessed March 26, 2019.
9. "2016 Spending Budget on the Foreign Ministry Could Reach Almost 98 Billion Rubles," *Russia Today*, July 10, 2015. https://ria.ru/economy/20151007/1298250077.html. Accessed March 26, 2019.
10. "The Draft Budget: Defense Spending in Russia in 2016 Will Amount to 4% of GDP," *Russia Today*, October 24, 2015. https://ria.ru/economy/20151024/1307503105.html. Accessed March 26, 2019.
11. Kseniya Gulia. "Peers of the Ministry of Foreign Affairs," *Kommersant*, February 9, 2009. http://kommersant.ru/doc/1108422. Accessed March 26, 2019.
12. "Structural Diagram of the Ministry of Foreign Affairs of Russia," *Ministry of Foreign Affairs of the Russian Federation*," October 8, 2014. http://www.mid.ru/diverse/-/asset_publisher/8bWtTfQKqtaS/content/id/679878. Accessed March 26, 2019.
13. "The Female Face of Russian Diplomacy," Representation of the Ministry of Foreign Affairs of Russia in Krasnoyarsk. http://krsk.mid.ru/zensiny-v-diplomatii. Accessed March 26, 2019.
14. Gulia, "Peers of the Ministry of Foreign Affairs."
15. International Panel on Diplomacy. Austin, January 14, 2016.
16. Yelena Biberman, "The Politics of Diplomatic Service Reform in Post-Soviet Russia," *Political Science Quarterly* 126, no. 4 (Winter 2011–2012): 669–680.
17. Gulia, "Peers of the Ministry of Foreign Affairs."
18. "Diplomatic Academy of Russian Foreign Ministry." http://www.dipacademy.ru/en/. Accessed March 26, 2019.
19. Ibid.
20. Ibid.
21. Biberman, "The Politics of Diplomatic Service Reform."
22. Authors' interview, Austin, November 13, 2016.
23. "Programmes." *Diplomatic Academy of Russian Foreign Ministry*. http://www.dipacademy.ru/programmes/. Accessed March 26, 2019.
24. Authors' interview, Austin, November 13, 2016.
25. "Model Law on Diplomatic Service (Adopted in Saint Petersburg 13 June 2000)," Levonevsky Valery Stanislavovich, 2007. http://pravo.levonevsky.org/bazazru/texts17/txt17318.htm. Accessed March 19, 2019.

26. Gulia, "Peers of the Ministry of Foreign Affairs."
27. Ibid.
28. Gulia, "Peers of the Ministry of Foreign Affairs."
29. Daniel Payne, "Spiritual Security, the Russian Orthodox Church, and the Russian Foreign Ministry: Collaboration or Cooptation?" *Journal of Church and State* 52, no. 4 (2010): 716.
30. Vladimir Putin, "Transcript: Putin says Russia will protect the rights of Russians abroad." *Washington Post*, March 18, 2014. https://www.washingtonpost.com/world/transcript-putin-says-russia-will-protect-the-rights-of-russians-abroad/2014/03/18/432a1e60-ae99-11e3-a49e-76adc9210f19_story.html?utm_term=.8dff07815a3d. Accessed March 26, 2019.
31. Robert C. Blitt, "Russia's "Orthodox" Foreign Policy: The Growing Influence of the Russian Orthodox Church in Shaping Russia's Policies Abroad," *Penn Law*, November 28, 2011. https://www.law.upenn.edu/live/files/142-blittboyd33upajintll3632011pdf. Accessed March 26, 2019.
32. Sinikukka Saari, "Russia's Post-Orange Revolution Strategies to Increase its Influence in Former Soviet Republics: Public Diplomacy 'po russkii,'" *Europe-Asia Studies* 66, no. 1 (January 2014): 54.
33. Ibid.
34. Nikolay Surkov, "Russia's Foreign Ministry's New Press Head is a Breath of Fresh Air," *Russia Beyond*, August 28, 2015. https://www.rbth.com/politics/2015/08/28/russias_foreign_ministrys_new_press_head_is_a_breath_of_fresh_air_48819.html. Accessed March 26, 2019.
35. Ilan Manor, "Is Russia Ruining Digital Diplomacy for the Rest of Us?" *USC Center on Public Diplomacy*, February 17, 2015. http://uscpublicdiplomacy.org/blog/russia-ruining-digital-diplomacy-rest-us. Accessed March 26, 2019.

REFERENCES

2016 Spending Budget on the Foreign Ministry Could Reach Almost 98 Billion Rubles. 2015, July 10. *Russia Today*. https://ria.ru/economy/20151007/1298250077.html. Accessed March 26, 2019.

Biberman, Y. 2011. The Politics of Diplomatic Service Reform in Post-Soviet Russia. *Political Science Quarterly* 126 (4): 669–680.

Blitt, R.C. 2011, November 28. Russia's "Orthodox" Foreign Policy: The Growing Influence of the Russian Orthodox Church in Shaping Russia's Policies Abroad. *Penn Law*. https://www.law.upenn.edu/live/files/142-blittboyd33upajintll3632011pdf. Accessed March 26, 2019.

Concept of the Foreign Policy of the Russian Federation. 2019. Ministry of Foreign Affairs of the Russian Federation. http://www.mid.ru/en/foreign_policy/official_documents/-/asset_publisher/CptICkB6BZ29/content/id/122186. Accessed March 26, 2019.

Diplomatic Academy of Russian Foreign Ministry. 2019. Diplomatic Academy of (the) Russian Foreign Ministry. http://www.dipacademy.ru/en/. Accessed March 26, 2019.

Global Diplomacy Index. 2017. Lowry Institute. http://www.lowyinstitute.org/global-diplomacy-index/. Accessed March 26, 2019.

Gulia, K. 2009, February 9. Peers of the Ministry of Foreign Affairs. *Kommersant*. http://kommersant.ru/doc/1108422. Accessed March 26, 2019.

Ivanov, I.S. 2004. *The New Russian Diplomacy*. Washington: Brookings Institution.

Manor, I. 2015, February 17. Is Russia Ruining Digital Diplomacy for the Rest of Us? *USC Center on Public Diplomacy*. http://uscpublicdiplomacy.org/blog/russia-ruining-digital-diplomacy-rest-us. Accessed March 26, 2019.

Model Law on Diplomatic Service. 2007. Levonevsky Valery Stanislavovich. http://pravo.levonevsky.org/bazazru/texts17/txt17318.htm. Accessed March 19, 2019.

Of Russian Origin: Slavophiles and Zapadniki. 2016. *Russiapedia*. http://russiapedia.rt.com/of-russian-origin/slavophiles-and-zapadniki/. Accessed March 26, 2019.

Payne, D. 2010. Spiritual Security, the Russian Orthodox Church, and the Russian Foreign Ministry: Collaboration or Cooptation? *Journal of Church and State* 52 (4): 712–727.

Programmes. n.d. Diplomatic Academy of (the) Russian Foreign Ministry. http://www.dipacademy.ru/programmes/. Accessed March 26, 2019.

Putin, V. 2014, March 18. Transcript: Putin Says Russia Will Protect the Rights of Russians Abroad. *Washington Post*. https://www.washingtonpost.com/world/transcript-putin-says-russia-will-protect-the-rights-of-russians-abroad/2014/03/18/432a1e60-ae99-11e3-a49e-76adc9210f19_story.html?utm_term=.8dff07815a3d. Accessed March 26, 2019.

Saari, S. 2014. Russia's Post-Orange Revolution Strategies to Increase Its Influence in Former Soviet Republics: Public Diplomacy "po russkii". *Europe-Asia Studies* 66 (1): 50–66.

Structural Diagram of the Ministry of Foreign Affairs of Russia. 2014. Ministry of Foreign Affairs of the Russian Federation. http://www.mid.ru/diverse/-/asset_publisher/8bWtTfQKqtaS/content/id/679878. Accessed March 26, 2019.

Surkov, N. 2015, August 28. Russia's Foreign Ministry's New Press Head Is a Breath of Fresh Air. *Russia Beyond*. https://www.rbth.com/politics/2015/08/28/russias_foreign_ministrys_new_press_head_is_a_breath_of_fresh_air_48819.html. Accessed March 26, 2019.

The 210th Anniversary of the Russian Foreign Office. 2012, September 7. Ministry of Foreign Affairs of the Russian Federation. http://www.mid.ru/en/about/social_organizations. Accessed March 29, 2019.

The Draft Budget: Defense Spending in Russia in 2016 Will Amount to 4% of GDP. 2015, October 24. *Russia Today*. https://ria.ru/economy/20151024/1307503105.html. Accessed March 26, 2019.

The Female Face of Russian Diplomacy. n.d. Representation of the Ministry of Foreign Affairs of Russia in Krasnoyarsk. http://krsk.mid.ru/zensiny-v-diplomatii. Accessed March 26, 2019.

Zonova, T.V. 2007. Diplomatic Cultures: Comparing Russia and the West in Terms of a "Modern Model of Diplomacy". *The Hague Journal of Diplomacy* 2 (1): 1–23.

CHAPTER 8

Turkey

Zuli Nigeeryasin, Evan W. Burt, and Jeremi Suri

EXECUTIVE SUMMARY

The Turkish Ministry of Foreign Affairs (MFA) is characterized by a strong decision-making apparatus in Ankara, with prime ministerial and presidential involvement in decisions that affect the core national security interests of the country. The individual autonomy of officers in the MFA therefore varies according to the issue, with latitude frequently granted for input on lower priority concerns. Historically, entrance to the MFA was informally restricted to a privileged coastal elite channeled through an educational pipeline centered on Ankara University. The MFA's membership has, however, diversified considerably in recent years. Turkish diplomats are lauded for their firm negotiation skills and deep preparation—qualities that are emphasized in their initial training. Language instruction and requirements

---

Z. Nigeeryasin
2018 Master of Arts Degrees, Global Policy Studies and Asian Studies,
The University of Texas at Austin, Austin, TX, USA

E. W. Burt
2018 Master of Arts Degrees, Global Policy Studies and Middle Eastern Studies,
The University of Texas at Austin, Austin, TX, USA

J. Suri (✉)
Lyndon B. Johnson School of Public Affairs, The University of Texas at Austin, Austin, TX, USA
e-mail: suri@austin.utexas.edu

for new officers reflect the services' Kemalist roots and Western orientation, with French, German, and English emphasized. Promotion is regulated through a meritocratic examination process as well as the development of professional networks, but promotion is generally linear, at fixed time intervals for a successful candidate. As the service and its mission grow, Turkey faces a challenge to supplement its traditionally generalist service with linguistic and regional expertise in countries and regions where the republic has not historically had strong ties. Under the leadership of Ahmet Davutoğlu, the MFA's role in foreign policy making increased and Turkey accrued considerable soft power. As events continue to unfold in anticipation of major governmental reforms (especially in the aftermath of an attempted coup), it is likely that further changes in the MFA's capabilities and role are in store.

History and Culture

The MFA has its roots in the *Reis ul-Kuttab* (Chief of the Scribes) of the Ottoman Empire. Foreign Ministry literature describes the MFA as having four generations of diplomats. The first, ushered during the Ottoman *Tanzimat* period, brought about the beginnings of formal diplomacy; the second, with the founding of the Turkish Republic, had to achieve recognition and manage relations in the context of the early wars faced by the Turkish state. Throughout the Cold War, the third generation of Turkish diplomats served as balancers in the context of bipolar superpower politics. The fourth and latest generation of Turkish diplomats must now contend with issues raised by Turkey's emergence as a true regional power.[1]

The secular nationalist philosophy of Turkey's founder, Mustafa Kemal Ataturk, undergirds the modern Turkish State. "Peace at Home, Peace in the World" continues to inform the culture of the MFA, which frames the legacy of Ataturk as a firm commitment to rationalism, respect for sovereignty, and peaceful negotiation.[2] Ataturk's vision of the Turkish Republic also centered on the modernization and westernization of Turkey without losing its core Eastern values. This modernization was only made possible by establishing very close linkages with the West, and the foreign policy apparatus of the emerging Kemalist state was tightly crafted and proscribed around securing ties with Western Europe and America. The other plank of a Kemalist foreign policy, respect for sovereignty and a commitment to peace, was secured through treaty obligations reflected in the Balkan *Entente* and the Saadabad Pact. These agreements secured peaceful relationships in Turkey's two major neighboring regions and prevented Turkish entry into World War II. Turkey's armed forces have frequently intervened directly in Turkey's democratic politics to ensure the continuity of secular policy and political control, as in the coups of 1960, 1971, 1980. Military influence in Turkey's politics and foreign policy declined sharply following the election of the Justice and Development Party (AKP) in 2002.

In recent history, the MFA has prioritized securing trade and security ties with the West, but the post-2000s government of the AKP party under Recep Tayyip Erdoğan has dramatically expanded the country's ties to its eastern neighbors. This pivot has been accompanied by a new foreign policy, dubbed "Neo-Ottomanism" by some, which seeks to reassert the Turkish State's leading role in Middle Eastern politics. Sakarya University scholars Murat Yeşiltaş and Ali Balcı term this new foreign policy "vision-oriented" because it attempts to anticipate crises and create innovative policy positions in regions where Turkey has not encountered problems or traditionally had much involvement.[3]

"Neo-Ottomanism" has roots in the liberal economic reforms of the 1980s, and the corresponding social transformation of the country from a secular and fundamentally western-oriented political base to a more religious and middle class composition. Though its historical western orientation is still reflected in language requirements for Foreign Service Officers (FSOs) and the incorporation of Ataturk's biography and ideas in the MFA's public materials, Turkey's rapidly expanding non-Western economic and political ties and the restoration of full civilian control of its foreign policy have driven a fundamental re-envisioning of Ankara's diplomatic strategy. Turkey's foreign policy goals have evolved from seeking Western recognition and support to projecting soft power and attempting to influence neighbors more directly, although former Foreign Minister Ahmet Davutoğlu has rejected the hegemonic implications of the term "Neo-Ottomanism."[4]

Turkey's expanded global reach has been fueled by continual economic expansion and a period of relative peace in the country's longstanding internal conflict with Kurdish militant groups, such as the Kurdistan Worker's Party (PKK). With Turkey's currency dropping sharply against the dollar, decreasing economic growth and renewed unrest in the southeast, future expansion of influence is an open question. Opinion polling in Turkey's near abroad shows the flip-side of deeper involvement in regional affairs, as public perception of Turkey's friendliness has fallen sharply in the Middle East in recent years, particularly in countries which have had a contentious relationship with Turkey, such as Syria and Egypt.[5] Though Turkish soft power may be at an inflection point, Turkey remains a more influential presence abroad than before. That is unlikely to change any time soon.

Profile

The Republic of Turkey had a total of 39 diplomatic and consular missions abroad in 1924.

The number of missions increased to 234 missions by 2016. These missions include 135 Embassies, 13 Permanent Representations to international organizations, 84 Consulate Generals, 1 Consular Agency, and 1 Trade Office.[6]

Much of this expansion is recent. In 2002, the Turkish Foreign Service consisted of 163 representations, 12 of which were in Africa.[7] In 2018, Foreign Ministry Spokesman Hami Aksoy announced Turkey had built the fifth largest diplomatic network in the world, with 239 foreign missions.[8] In particular, Turkey added 29 new representations in Africa between 2002 and 2014. President Erdoğan further announced in September 2018 that Turkey had increased the number of its embassies in Africa from 12 in 2002 to 41, with plans to open 13 more across the "important" continent.[9] This growth has both provided Turkey with new opportunities and posed the MFA with a corresponding new set of challenges, as we will discuss further.

The Turkish Foreign Service consists of 1202 Foreign Service Officers,[10] 948 Consular, Linguistic and Cultural Officers, 14 Foreign Policy Experts (FPEs), and 4330 other personnel.[11] The total number of employees is 6583 as of 2015; 2217 are career diplomats. This represents a slight increase in the number of career diplomats compared to a 2013 report of the MFA, which listed 1199 Foreign Service Officers, 884 Consular, Linguistic and Cultural Officers, and 21 Foreign Policy Experts.[12] The average age of the career diplomats is under 40; the ministry encourages people to apply to the MFA at a young age, after graduating from college. Approximately 25% of MFA employees are women and 37 of them are ambassadors[13]—a large increase from just over 20 in 2013.[14] A number of highly respected recent Turkish ambassadors have been women.[15]

The rapid increase in women's representation among diplomats in the Turkish MFA shows a serious effort toward achieving gender diversity.

Still far from achieving an equitable balance of 50% woman ambassadors, Turkey's current 16% representation is significant progress. We have been unable to find data on the ethnic makeup of the Turkish MFA. The MFA budget increased from barely 2 million Turkish lira in 2015 to nearly 2.7 million Turkish lira (approximately 900 million US dollars) in 2016. Compared to the budget of the Ministry of National Defense (22 billion lira) or even the Ministry of Religious Affairs (5 billion lira), the budget of the MFA is small; less than 1% of government expenditures are devoted to the MFA Budget.

Recruitment and Selection

The MFA recruits by career track, with four broad "cones" available to aspiring candidates sorted through three exam processes. These are the Foreign Policy Expert (FPE), Foreign Service Officer (FSO), Consular Officer (CO), and Cultural and Linguistic Specialist (CLS) tracks. Foreign Policy Experts research regions, countries, and thematic issues and work in Ankara formulating the strategic foreign policy approaches to be executed abroad by Foreign Service Officers, who constitute the regular diplomatic track of the MFA. Cultural and Linguistic Specialists aid FSOs in their work by providing translation and expert subject knowledge, while Consular Officers serve Turkish nationals abroad. The ministry's hiring practices clearly favor candidates with a good education and deep linguistic skills.

Turkey recruits by examination. The CLS and CO tracks are recruited through the same examination, while there are separate examinations for FSOs and FPEs. FSO candidates are tested on their broad foreign policy knowledge, as well as their knowledge of three major foreign languages: French, English, and German. Advanced knowledge is required of English, or of the other two languages plus a minimum of English, but fluency beyond these levels helps to advance a candidacy.[16] Foreign Policy Expert candidates must pass three sequential tests: the standard Civil Servant Selection Examination (KPSS), which tests for math, geography, history, and knowledge of Turkish national institutions, language, and literature; a Supplementary Language Examination; and then finally a Foreign Ministry Adequacy Exam, which is both written and oral and covers law, economics, international relations, and political science. Candidates who pass the written test are ranked by testing scores, and the oral examination then selects assistant FPEs from this pool.[17] Four times as many candidates pass the written examination as there are available positions.

Most candidates who enter the service have degrees in international relations, law, economics, or public administration.[18] Historically, Ankara University was a major educational pipeline for entrance to the Ministry of Foreign Affairs[19] It is now common for officers to have different educational backgrounds.[20] Similarly, it was historically unexceptional for MFA officers to never have been east of Ankara, though this is no longer the case.[21]

There is a maximum age of entry established for these cones, which is 31 for the Foreign Service Officer, Consular Officer, and Cultural and Linguist Specialist tracks, and 35 for Foreign Policy Experts possessing the equivalent of a master's degree or 37 for FPEs possessing PhDs. Also notable is that all men entering the Ministry of Foreign Affairs must have served the full term of their mandatory military conscription service in order to be considered for selection. Between 1998 and 2006, nearly 42% of MFA employees had a family background in public service, with 7% having a family background in the MFA itself.[22]

Foreign Policy Experts constitute an in-house academic team of chief policy strategists who research and coordinate policy from Ankara. This feature is somewhat distinct from other services, which we have surveyed, and reflects the centralization and cohesion of foreign policy decision-making in the MFA. Assistant FPEs are promoted to the elite pool of Foreign Policy Experts through a thesis writing and defense process which typically takes two years to complete.[23]

Professional Development and Training

Most professional development is centralized in the Diplomacy Academy of Turkey. The most important responsibility of the Diplomacy Academy is training new diplomats. Recruited employees from the FSO, CLS, and CO tracks go through Basic Training as well as Preparatory Training, each of which lasts between two weeks and three months. Both courses are completed by examination.[24]

Basic Training covers administrative procedures as well as an orientation to the mission of the Ministry of Foreign Affairs.[25] Preparatory Training includes theoretical and practical coursework covering international relations, economics, history, law, and public administration Additional professional topics include internal organization, diplomatic protocol, negotiation techniques, information technology, consular issues, and advanced foreign language training. Attention is also paid to personal development in literature, arts, cinema, and public speaking.[26] Additionally, the remainder of a year-long candidacy period for these officers includes an internship requirement where new employees work at government agencies in capacities related to their fields of specialization.[27] Through this combination of rigorous training and early learning experiences, new Turkish diplomats are well prepared when they take on their early assignments.

Meritocratic examinations are used for promotion as well as selection. Career diplomats (excluding FPEs) must pass the Progress and Consular Adequacy Exam, which determines eligibility for higher promotion, six to nine years (six for FSO, nine for CLS and CO) into their service. Failure to pass results in retention of rank, but an inability to progress further ahead in the hierarchy.[28] Preexisting academic achievement is used to regulate advancement through the ranks. For instance, to advance from the position of third secretary normally requires three years of service, but requires only two years with a master's degree and one year with a doctorate.[29] Additional considerations for promotion within the Turkish MFA include a demonstrable mastery of policy issues, oral presentation, negotiation skills, and solid internal relationships within the MFA.[30]

Assignment order is tightly regulated. FSOs must spend at least two years and may spend no more than five years abroad in any given country, as well as spending two years at the MFA in Ankara.[31] Candidates express their preferences by rank ordering ten postings, but assignment is based on the Ministry's needs and individual skills of FSOs.[32] There is no "hardship pay" for difficult or dangerous postings, although there has been a limited implementation of a year's reduction in promotion time for assignments considered more difficult for aspiring officers.[33] FPEs may not be posted abroad unless appointed for a special mission; they typically spend the majority of their careers in Ankara. FSOs, on the other hand, are encouraged to work outside of the MFA in international organizations for as many as six years (previously, nine years were permitted). They retain insurance and financial assistance and are promoted on regular schedule while working outside the MFA. Currently, it is estimated that 10% of FSOs pursue this option.[34] The position of FSO remains highly prestigious in Turkish society, ameliorating the impact on morale of the rigid assignment system. Although external analysis would suggest that the absence of hardship pay and rigidity in assignment allocation instigates morale problems, the position of FSO is still a highly prestigious one in Turkish society.

There is little mid-career training for the typical Turkish diplomat. Sources at the Turkish Embassy cited the tough near abroad of Turkey as a natural incentive for quickly acquiring a depth of historical, cultural, and policy knowledge in the place of a mid-career training program.[35] Additionally, the meritocratic examination process which determines advancement incentivizes continuous academic study. Nonetheless, as Turkey expands its reach globally, greater regional and linguistic specialization beyond the horizons of the Turkish near abroad is becoming more desirable.[36] The current Turkish diplomatic service is considered to be more generalist in its orientation, but the MFA is actively developing its specialist capacities. Between 2013 and 2014, the ministry sent 40 diplomats to complete master's level coursework in regional studies, and the ministry estimated that it annually sends 30 new diplomats to complete coursework in linguistic and regional studies, following its current distributional needs.[37]

The Turkish MFA uses its Diplomacy Academy to offer training to foreign diplomats, especially those from countries where Turkey hopes to increase its influence. The Academy teaches these foreign diplomats subjects such as economics, international politics, political science, history, art, and literature with a special focus on the Turkish authors. The Academy also provides courses on specific international issues, with special attention paid to Turkey's policy positions. In the last decade, the Diplomacy Academy has trained around 800 foreign diplomats from Africa, Southeast Asia, Latin America, the Balkans, the Caucasus, the Middle East, and Eastern Europe.

Leadership

The Turkish Ministry of Foreign Affairs has not historically hosted many political appointees, although a law allowing political appointments across government was adopted as early as 1965.[38] A 2002 survey found nine Ambassadors had been appointed from outside the MFA, out of a total of 135 embassies,[39] and the total number of political appointees has never exceeded ten.[40] Political appointments are discouraged within the MFA due to the small size of most Turkish embassies and the Turkish Foreign Service in general.[41] A highly controversial reform passed in 2010 that allows these political appointees to the MFA to secure high-level internal positions at the MFA after serving their initial terms.[42] Ambassadors are given a two-week training program at the Diplomacy Academy that aims at preparing them for their new leadership and management responsibilities.[43] Leadership roles assigned in the MFA include positions roughly equivalent to Ambassador, Deputy Chief of Mission, Deputy Chief of Advisors, Consul-General, First Deputy Chief, Deputy Chief, First Secretary, Second Secretary, and Third Secretary (Attaché). An additional senior position, the Constant Representative, serves as the highest Turkish official representative to international organizations. CLS track diplomats are capable of achieving Consul-General rank, but no further. FSOs may be promoted to Ambassadorial rank.[44]

The Turkish MFA divides its career diplomats into six ranks, with the sixth and lowest rank made up of entry-level FSOs through Third Secretaries. There is a minimum length of service at positions within each rank in order to advance to higher ranks. Sixth to Fifth ranks require three years of service; Fifth to Fourth ranks require three years of service; Fourth to Third require two years of service; Third to Second require four years of service; and rising from the Second rank to the First requires six years of service. Promotion to the highest First rank positions requires recommendation by the MFA commission and the approval of the Foreign Minister. In addition to the minimum amount of time the Fifth- and Sixth-rank FSOs need to spend in their rank, they are also required to take a midcareer adequacy exam to advance to higher ranks. Fifth-rank Consular Officers and Cultural and Linguistic Specialists who are successful in the adequacy exam are given a title with the recommendation of the MFA commission, and the approval of the Foreign Minister.

Track changes are possible through an adequacy exam. Officers from one track may switch to another if they succeed at that track's adequacy exam. For those who pass the adequacy exam, the MFA commission recommends a title according to the years in service in the MFA. The appropriate titles are given with the approval of the Foreign Minister.

The average age of Turkish ambassadors sampled in our research is 56, with the youngest born in 1968 and the oldest born in 1954. Most of them graduated from Ankara University at some point in their education, reflecting the university's role as a pipeline to the MFA. Two ambassadors were educated abroad, both in France. All hold bachelor's degrees in political science, economics, or international relations. Three hold master's degrees, and two have doctorates. Most began their service in the MFA in the 1980s, although Ambassador Çavuşoğlu began his appointment as Foreign Minister by merit of his political career.

All of the sampled diplomats speak some combination of English, French, and German. The only official among them who speaks additional languages that we know of is Ambassador Çavuşoğlu, who speaks Japanese in addition to English and German. Most are lifelong diplomats, although Ambassador Kiliç began his service in the Ministry of Tourism and Ambassador Musa has career linkages with Turkish intelligence services. It seems a common practice to serve in the ministry itself on a specific policy area before being promoted to ambassador. Nearly half of the sampled Turkish ambassadors served in NATO (North Atlantic Treaty Organization) or the United Nations in some capacity, and the Foreign Minister served in the Parliamentary Assembly of Council of Europe, reflecting the value the Turkish MFA places on multilateral work for its leaders. The broad trajectory of their careers does not seem to have been affected by changes in political leadership in Turkey. Experienced ambassadors have served under many different administrations with no noticeable reduction or change in their ranks. This remains true for the most recent years of political turmoil in Turkey.

Role in Foreign Policy

Historically, the Turkish military has had a strong influence in foreign policy decision-making. Previous military leaders viewed themselves as guardians of the Turkish Republic's secularism, and prior to the twenty-first century, the Turkish military staged three coups against civilian governments, although power was ultimately restored to civilian hands in each instance. These circumstances began to change with President Turgut Özal's liberalization project in the 1980s, but the pace of civilian dominance accelerated rapidly under the AKP government of the 2000s.

In 2010, the Turkish government opened a major criminal investigation against senior military officials. Under this investigation, 365 suspects including journalists, military figures, and civilian leaders were arrested and put on trial for charges of conspiracy.[45] An attempted coup in the summer of 2016 prompted a further curtailment of military influence in Turkey and jeopardized the military's enduring prestige. Purges resulting from this attempted coup have affected various levels of government, and, as of this writing in 2019, the long-term effects for this event on the MFA cannot be determined. It would appear that the Turkish military has become a much less significant player in foreign policy decision-making. Always a powerful influence on Turkish foreign policy, the Turkish president has in recent years become the dominant force in the nation's decision-making.

The Turkish Foreign Ministry has been very influential in forming Turkey's modern foreign policy, especially under former Foreign Minister Ahmet Davutoğlu. As in many parliamentary systems, the Foreign Minister serves by appointment of the Prime Minister, and all top-level ministerial positions in the MFA require approval of the Foreign Minister. The influence that individual posts have in the foreign policy-making process and the method by which reports and policy proposals are filtered through the ranks of the MFA has much to do with whether the posting or policy issue is of critical importance to the current Turkish administration. Issues of great importance—such as the unfolding crisis in Syria, the Cyprus conflict, and Iraqi policy—are tightly controlled by the president.[46] Other MFA postings appear to have broader latitude to participate in the policy-making process with Ankara.[47]

Recent constitutional reforms in Turkey have changed a great many things about the Turkish political system, some of which have bearing on the MFA's future role in foreign-policy decision-making. Previously, the Turkish Grand National Assembly (GNA) had power to supervise and issue orders to the Council of Ministers regarding specific policy matters.[48] By way of example, during the Second Iraq War, the legislature severely curtailed US authorization to base forces in Turkey and prohibited Turkish troop participation in the conflict. After the recent constitutional changes, the GNA no longer has this power. The executive branch's supervisory power over the MFA has, consequently, greatly expanded. During the Prime Ministry of Ahmet Mesut Yılmaz (Motherland Party), the Minister of Foreign Affairs İsmail Cem (Democratic Left Party) was from a different political party and answerable to different constituents than the Prime Minister. Coalition politics in Turkey produced the opportunity for a more independent Foreign Ministry. Since then, Turkey has moved from a model where the MFA was accountable to the executive first and the legislature second, to a model where the MFA is accountable to the executive alone. Whether this enhances or curtails the independence of the MFA will be determined by the relationship of the Turkish President with the Turkish Foreign Minister.

Preparations for the Future

The AKP Party of Turkey has put forth a new vision, which has guided Turkey's foreign policy development since the early 2000s. Murat Yeşiltaşve and Ali Balcı explain that this new vision emphasizes a radical redefinition of Turkey's traditional self-conception as a mixed Eastern-Western Power.[49] This redefinition highlights soft power, public diplomacy, international institution building, and proactive diplomatic maneuvering to achieve Turkish core interests. Crucial to this redefinition of Turkish foreign policy is the concept of "Center State," which breaks with the traditional view of Turkey as a bridge between the West and the East, representing the best values of the former, and minimizing the static and presumed negative identity of the latter.[50] Turkey's ability to maneuver on a cross-cultural level is now promoted as a springboard from which to build new multilateral institutions and accrue greater influence in existing international organizations.[51]

In a moment dominated by transnational issues such as migration, climate change, and terrorism, Turkey intends to use its position as "Center State" to lead a regional order which draws on cultural and historical ties. This "Neo-Ottomanist" multilateral stance is reflected in increasing participation in organizations such as the Organization of Islamic Cooperation, the Economic Cooperation Organization, the African Union (as a Member Observer), the European Council, the Organization for Security and Cooperation in Europe, the United Nations Security Council, and the G20.

Turkey has taken advantage of the new multilateral and institution-focused posture of the MFA to establish strong bilateral economic relationships with other countries through its membership in international institutions. Turkish accession to Member Observer status within the African Union has enabled it to access African Development Bank funds for its companies working on the continent—Turkish–Kenyan trade, in particular—and has burnished Turkey's image as a player in African development alongside the United States and China.[52]

Turkey's public diplomacy has been guided by a hyperconscious internal evaluation of Turkey's public image and its many international detractors.[53] Turkey's Foreign Minister and the MFA maintain active Twitter accounts, and they tweet frequently in both Turkish and English. As Turkey strives for a more prominent role in global politics, the MFA's activities in public diplomacy will likely grow. This will be both a challenge and an opportunity for a well-educated, but not always well-prepared, service.

Acknowledgment *The authors wish to thank Ebru Aydoğan, David Judson, and Tugay Tunçer for assistance in researching and writing this chapter.*

Notes

1. "Brief History of the Ministry of Foreign Affairs of the Republic of Turkey." *Republic of Turkey Ministry of Foreign Affairs*. 2011. http://www.mfa.gov.tr/turkiye-cumhuriyeti-disisleri-bakanligi-tarihcesi.en.mfa. Accessed March 27, 2019.
2. "Turkish Foreign Policy During Ataturk's Era." *Republic of Turkey Ministry of Foreign Affairs*. 2011. http://www.mfa.gov.tr/turkish-foreign-policy-during-ataturks-era.en.mfa. Accessed March 27, 2019.
3. Murat Yeşiltaş and Ali Balcı. "A Dictionary of Turkish Foreign Policy in the AK Party Era: A Conceptual Map." *Center for Strategic Research*. May 2013, 10. http://sam.gov.tr/wp-content/uploads/2013/05/SAM_Papers7.pdf. Accessed March 27, 2019.
4. Richard Falk, "Turkey's New Multilateralism: A Positive Diplomacy for the Twenty-First Century." *Global Governance* 19, no. 3 (2013), 365.
5. Umut Uras, "Turkey's Popularity Dives in MENA Region Poll." *Al-Jazeera*, December 4, 2013. http://www.aljazeera.com/news/middleeast/2013/12/turkey-popularity-dives-mena-region-poll-201312471328507508.html. Accessed March 27, 2019.
6. Figures listed for 2016. "Brief History of the Ministry of Foreign Affairs of the Republic of Turkey." *Republic of Turkey Ministry of Foreign Affairs*. 2011. http://www.mfa.gov.tr/turkiye-cumhuriyeti-disisleri-bakanligi-tarihcesi.en.mfa. Accessed March 27, 2019.
7. Yuksel Serdar Oguz, "Turkey Boasts No. 5 Diplomatic Network in the World," *Anadolu*, September 2, 2018. https://www.aa.com.tr/en/infographics/turkey-boasts-no-5-diplomatic-network-in-the-world/1058710. Accessed March 27, 2019.
8. Ibid.
9. "Turkey Aims to Open More Embassies in Africa, Says Erdoğan," *Hurriyet*, September 7, 2018. http://www.hurriyetdailynews.com/turkey-aims-to-open-more-embassies-in-africa-says-erdogan-136561. Accessed March 27, 2019.
10. The term Foreign Service Officer is used because the role of this track is broadly analogous with the work of American FSOs. The more direct translation of the Turkish career title is Career Civil Servant.
11. This includes 2858 contract personnel, 961 domestic civil servants, 17 advisors, 13 economic advisors, 9 legal advisors, 454 security personnel, 4 press and communication advisor, 14 administrative auditor and other staff

members responsible for different tasks. "2015 Annual Report by Turkish Foreign Ministry." *Republic of Turkey Ministry of Foreign Affairs*, June 27, 2016, 7. http://www.mfa.gov.tr/data/BAKANLIK/2015-faaliyet-raporu_.pdf. Accessed March 27, 2019.
12. "2013 Annual Report by Turkish Foreign Ministry." *Republic of Turkey Ministry of Foreign Affairs*, 2014, http://www.mfa.gov.tr/site_media/html/2014_mali_rapor.pdf. Accessed March 27, 2019.
13. Nazlı Yüzbaşıoğlu, "Turkey's New Africa Strategy and Women's Progress," *Anadolu*, March 7, 2016. http://aa.com.tr/tr/turkiye/turkiyenin-afrika-aciliminda-kadin-atilimi/532810.
14. "The Turkish MFA is 93 Years Old..." *Republic of Turkey Ministry of Foreign Affairs*, 2011. http://www.mfa.gov.tr/disisleri-bakanligi-93-yasinda.tr.mfa. Accessed March 27, 2019.
15. Interview with a former American Ambassador to Turkey, 12/16/2016.
16. "Turkish Constitutional Law No. 657." *Republic of Turkey Ministry of Foreign Affairs*. 2011. http://www.mfa.gov.tr/bakanliktaki-temel-memuriyet-kategorileri.tr.mfa. Articles 48, 59 and 60. Accessed March 27, 2019.
17. "Dışişleri Uzmanliği Yönetmeliği (Rules for Foreign Specialization)," *Republic of Turkey Ministry of Foreign Affairs*. (n.d.), http://www.mfa.gov.tr/data/BAKANLIK/Mevzuat/15-uzman.pdf. Accessed March 27, 2019.
18. Interviews with diplomats assigned to the Turkish Embassy in Washington, DC. December 15, 2016.
19. Ibid.
20. Ibid.
21. Interviews with diplomats assigned to the Turkish Embassy in Washington, DC. December 15, 2016.
22. "Meslek Memurluğu (Occupations)." *Republic of Turkey Ministry of Foreign Affairs*. (n.d.), http://www.mfa.gov.tr/meslek-memurlari.tr.mfa. Accessed March 27, 2019.
23. "Dışişleri Uzmanliği Yönetmeliği (Rules for Foreign Specialization)."
24. "Career Diplomat Promotion Act." *Republic of Turkey Ministry of Foreign Affairs* (n.d.), http://www.mfa.gov.tr/diplomatik-kariyer-memurlari-gorevde-yukselme-yonetmeligi.tr.mfa. Accessed March 29, 2019.
25. "Basic Training Program." http://diab.mfa.gov.tr/en/education-programs-2/diplomatic-studies-program/basic-training-program/. Accessed October 25, 2016.
26. "Preparatory Training Program." *Republic of Turkey Ministry of Foreign Affairs* (n.d.), http://diab.mfa.gov.tr/en/education-programs-2/diplomatic-studies-program/preparatory-training-program/. Accessed October 25, 2016.

27. "Career Diplomat Promotion Act."
28. "Turkish Constitutional Law No. 6004." *Grand National Assembly of Turkey.* https://www.tbmm.gov.tr/kanunlar/k6004.html. Articles 10 and 11. Accessed March 27, 2019.
29. "Career Diplomat Promotion Act."
30. Interviews with diplomats assigned to the Turkish Embassy in Washington, DC. December 15, 2016.
31. "Meslek Memurluğu (Occupations)."
32. Interviews with diplomats assigned to the Turkish Embassy in Washington, DC. December 15, 2016.
33. Ibid.
34. Ibid.
35. Ibid.
36. Ibid.
37. "65 New Representations in 13 Years." *Turkish Prime Ministry Office of Public Diplomacy,* http://kdk.gov.tr/sayilarla/13-yilda-65-yeni-temsilcilik-turkiyenin-yurtdisindaki-temsilcilik-sayisi-228e-cikti/41. Accessed February 20, 2017.
38. "Turkish Constitutional Law No. 657."
39. Zeynep Gürcanlı, "Dışişleri'nde yeni dönem" *Hurriyet,* August 3, 2013, http://www.hurriyet.com.tr/disislerinde-yeni-donem-24450429. Accessed March 27, 2019.
40. Interviews with diplomats assigned to the Turkish Embassy in Washington, DC. December 15, 2016.
41. Ibid.
42. "Turkish Constitutional Law No. 6004."
43. "Training Program for The Officials Appointed As Ambassador for The First Time," *Diplomacy Academy.* (n.d.). http://diab.mfa.gov.tr/ambassador.en.mfa. Accessed March 27, 2019.
44. "Career Diplomat Promotion Act."
45. Emre Peker. "Hundreds Convicted in Turkish Coup Trial." *Wall Street Journal,* September 21, 2012. https://www.wsj.com/articles/SB10000872396390444032404578010383839076610#articleTabs%3Darticle. Accessed March 27, 2019.
46. Interviews with diplomats assigned to the Turkish Embassy in Washington, DC. December 15, 2016.
47. Ibid.
48. Amendment to Article 87. Metin Feyzioğlu, "Turkish Constitutional Changes." *Turkish Bar Association.* http://anayasadegisikligi.barobirlik.org.tr/Anayasa_Degisikligi.aspx. Accessed March 27, 2019.
49. Yeşiltaş and Balcı. "A Dictionary of Turkish Foreign Policy in the AK Party Era."

50. Ibid., 9.
51. Ibrahim Kalın, "Türk Dış Politikası Ve Kamu Diplomasisi (Turkish Foreign Policy and Public Diplomacy)," *Republic of Turkey Prime Ministry Office of Public Diplomacy*, 2010. http://www.kamudiplomasisi.org/makaleler/makaleler/94-tuerk-di-poltkasi-ve-kamu-dplomass. Accessed March 27, 2019.
52. J. Cannon Brendon "Turkey in Kenya and Kenya in Turkey: Alternatives to the East/West Paradigm in Diplomacy, Trade and Security." *African Journal of Political Science and International Relations* 10, no. 5 (2016): 57.
53. Ibrahim, "Türk Dış Politikası Ve Kamu Diplomasisi."

References

Annual Report by Turkish Foreign Ministry. 2014. Republic of Turkey Ministry of Foreign Affairs. http://www.mfa.gov.tr/site_media/html/2014_mali_rapor.pdf. Accessed March 27, 2019.
———. 2015. Republic of Turkey Ministry of Foreign Affairs. http://www.mfa.gov.tr/data/BAKANLIK/2015-faaliyet-raporu_.pdf. Accessed March 27, 2019.
Brendon, J.C. 2016. Turkey in Kenya and Kenya in Turkey: Alternatives to the East/West Paradigm in Diplomacy, Trade and Security. *African Journal of Political Science and International Relations* 10 (5): 56–65.
Brief History of the Ministry of Foreign Affairs of the Republic of Turkey. 2011. Republic of Turkey Ministry of Foreign Affairs. http://www.mfa.gov.tr/turkiye-cumhuriyeti-disisleri-bakanligi-tarihcesi.en.mfa. Accessed March 27, 2019.
Dışişleri uzmanliği yönetmeliği (Rules for Foreign Specialization). n.d. Republic of Turkey Ministry of Foreign Affairs. http://www.mfa.gov.tr/data/BAKANLIK/Mevzuat/15-uzman.pdf. Accessed March 27, 2019.
Falk, R. 2013. Turkey's New Multilateralism: A Positive Diplomacy for the Twenty-First Century. *Global Governance* 19 (3): 353–376.
Feyzioğlu, M. n.d. *Turkish Constitutional Changes*. Turkish Bar Association. http://anayasadegisikligi.barobirlik.org.tr/Anayasa_Degisikligi.aspx. Accessed March 27, 2019.
Gürcanlı, Z. 2013, August 3. Dışişleri'nde yeni dönem. *Hurriyet*. http://www.hurriyet.com.tr/disislerinde-yeni-donem-24450429. Accessed March 27, 2019.
Kalın, I. 2010. *Türk dış politikası ve kamu diplomasisi* (Turkish Foreign Policy and Public Diplomacy). Republic of Turkey Prime Ministry Office of Public Diplomacy. http://www.kamudiplomasisi.org/makaleler/makaleler/94-tuerk-di-poltkasi-ve-kamu-dplomass. Accessed March 27, 2019.
Meslek memurluğu (Occupations). n.d. Republic of Turkey Ministry of Foreign Affairs. http://www.mfa.gov.tr/meslek-memurlari.tr.mfa. Accessed March 27, 2019.

Oguz, Y.S. 2018, September 2. Turkey Boasts No. 5 Diplomatic Network in the World. *Anadolu.* https://www.aa.com.tr/en/infographics/turkey-boasts-no-5-diplomatic-network-in-the-world/1058710. Accessed March 27, 2019.

Peker, E. 2012, September 21. Hundreds Convicted in Turkish Coup Trial. *Wall Street Journal.* https://www.wsj.com/articles/SB10000872396390444032404578010383839076610#articleTabs%3Darticle. Accessed March 27, 2019.

The Turkish MFA Is 93 Years Old… 2011. Republic of Turkey Ministry of Foreign Affairs. http://www.mfa.gov.tr/disisleri-bakanligi-93-yasinda.tr.mfa. Accessed March 27, 2019.

Training Program for the Officials Appointed as Ambassador for the First Time. n.d. Diplomacy Academy. http://diab.mfa.gov.tr/ambassador.en.mfa. Accessed March 27, 2019.

Turkey Aims to Open More Embassies in Africa, Says Erdoğan. 2018, September 7. *Hurriyet.* http://www.hurriyetdailynews.com/turkey-aims-to-open-more-embassies-in-africa-says-erdogan-136561. Accessed March 27, 2019.

Turkish Constitutional Law No. 6004. n.d. Grand National Assembly of Turkey. https://www.tbmm.gov.tr/kanunlar/k6004.html. Accessed March 27, 2019.

Turkish Constitutional Law No. 657. 2011. Republic of Turkey Ministry of Foreign Affairs. http://www.mfa.gov.tr/bakanliktaki-temel-memuriyet-kategorileri.tr.mfa. Accessed March 27, 2019.

Turkish Foreign Policy During Ataturk's Era. 2011. Republic of Turkey Ministry of Foreign Affairs. http://www.mfa.gov.tr/turkish-foreign-policy-during-ataturks-era.en.mfa. Accessed March 27, 2019.

Uras, U. 2013, December 4. Turkey's Popularity Dives in MENA Region Poll. *Al-Jazeera.* http://www.aljazeera.com/news/middleeast/2013/12/turkey-popularity-dives-mena-region-poll-201312471328507508.html. Accessed March 27, 2019.

Yeşiltaş, M., and A. Balcı. 2013. *A Dictionary of Turkish Foreign Policy in the AK Party Era: A Conceptual Map.* Center for Strategic Research, May 2013, p. 10. http://sam.gov.tr/wp-content/uploads/2013/05/SAM_Papers7.pdf. Accessed March 27, 2019.

Yüzbaşıoğlu, N. 2016, March 7. Turkey's New Africa Strategy and Women's Progress. *Anadolu.* http://aa.com.tr/tr/turkiye/turkiyenin-afrika-aciliminda-kadin-atilimi/532810.

CHAPTER 9

United Kingdom

Adam Crawford, Annika Rettstadt,
and Robert Hutchings

EXECUTIVE SUMMARY

As a former imperial power, the British Government has retained a strong global perspective in its diplomatic relations worldwide. The Foreign and Commonwealth Office (FCO) is an elite, highly regarded, diplomatic service with rigorous standards for recruitment, training, and employee conduct both at home and abroad. It has a distinctive diplomatic culture—of pragmatism, realism, and commitment to a rules-based international order—that continues to bear the imprint of what was once called "the Foreign Office mind."

An organization led primarily by career civil servants, the FCO and its organizational culture are viewed internally as honest, meritocratic, and open to creative thinking. The FCO has also emphasized empowering lower level staff to engage in more significant policy work at earlier stages of their

---

A. Crawford • A. Rettstadt
2018 Master of Arts Degrees, Global Policy Studies and Middle Eastern Studies, The University of Texas at Austin, Austin, TX, USA

R. Hutchings (✉)
Lyndon B. Johnson School of Public Affairs, The University of Texas at Austin, Austin, TX, USA
e-mail: rhutchings@austin.utexas.edu

© The Author(s) 2020
R. Hutchings, J. Suri (eds.), *Modern Diplomacy in Practice*,
https://doi.org/10.1007/978-3-030-26933-3_9

careers, such as drafting policy memoranda, and exercising greater autonomy while in post abroad, particularly in social media communications.

Over the last several decades, the FCO's initial training program had focused on developing strong managerial skillsets in an effort to produce agile policy generalists. Recent training reforms aim to strengthen the FCO's regional and linguistic expertise, such as the opening of the Diplomatic Academy in 2015. The FCO promotes staff through a somewhat *laissez-faire* bidding process whereby FCO employees bid for jobs, and if selected, submit to a rigorous review process that includes interview panels, role-playing, and a mix of written and interactive exercises that focus on core competencies such as judgment, communication, and influence.

The FCO is working to embrace "digital diplomacy" by expanding its technological capabilities and empowering its staff to operate in a networked global environment. The FCO has granted significant autonomy to its diplomats abroad to utilize social media in creative ways with little oversight from London. Additionally, in response to a department-wide review in 2015, the FCO has made a significant investment in a technology overhaul program that seeks to update embassy communications technology as well as personal mobile technology that can deliver real-time information and communications to FCO's diplomats around the globe.

The FCO faces significant challenges, including a sharply reduced budget, the transfer of key functions such as foreign assistance and trade to other ministries, and the growing centralization of policy making in the office of the prime minister. "Brexit"—the decision to exit the European Union—has created additional problems as the Foreign Office is obliged to reorient its global vision after nearly half a century of merging much of its foreign policy to a common EU foreign policy. Voices within the FCO and outside express deep concern about Britain's ability to adapt to this new environment as "an island apart," to borrow the title of a recent article in the British press, yet the UK faces this future with a skilled and resilient diplomatic corps. Unwelcome though it is to almost everyone in the FCO, Brexit may wind up giving the Foreign Office a new lease on life as it is obliged to manage Britain's global interests in this new era.

History and Culture

As an island nation with a vast empire for much of its modern history, the UK depended on conciliatory and agile diplomacy to maintain a European balance of power and maritime supremacy. The UK continues to aspire to major roles in former imperial areas, such as the Middle East, South Asia, and East Africa. In this way, the UK still perceives itself as a world power, which may affect the FCO's internal culture and how they practice diplomacy with foreign communities and governments. Traditionally, British diplomats are known for their professionalism and objectivity, but also for caution and extreme pragmatism.

The story of modern British diplomacy traces its roots back to the eighteenth century and the appointment of the first Secretary of State for Foreign Affairs, Charles James Fox, just one year prior to the signing of the Treaty of Paris that brought the American Revolutionary War to its conclusion. Foreign Secretary Fox would be the only British Foreign Secretary to preside over a diminution of the British Empire until the turn of the twentieth century. The Foreign Office of the nineteenth century oversaw what historians have called Britain's "imperial century." Britain's imperial project placed enormous strain on the ministries of state, particularly the Foreign Office, precipitating a sizable increase in the number of Foreign Office personnel and leading eventually to the commissioning of new office space to the south of 10 Downing Street. The Foreign Office, along with the India Office, opened the doors to their new building in 1868, a building that subsequently housed both the Colonial and Home offices. That opulent and grandiose building that represented the nerve center of the British Empire continues to serve as the base of operations for the modern Foreign and Commonwealth Office (FCO). It should, therefore, come as no surprise that Britain's imperial legacy permeates the culture of the modern FCO; indeed, the "Commonwealth" component of the FCO's name is itself a reference to the UK's imperial past.

The current iteration of the FCO has existed in a similar form since the Crowe Reforms of 1906 that molded the Foreign Office into a modern vehicle for the exercise of diplomacy.[1] Later reforms in the 1920s combined the Foreign Office and the Diplomatic Service, excluding the Consular Service that remained independent. The UK also established the Commercial Diplomatic Service under the Department of Overseas Trade that fell under the purview of the Foreign Office. In the early 1940s, the Foreign Office underwent an additional internal reform process that consolidated the Diplomatic, Consular, and Commercial Diplomatic Services, creating the present-day Foreign and Commonwealth Office.[2]

Contemporary British diplomatic culture springs from the earlier imperial period of British history and from what once was called the "Foreign Office mind." The term reflected certain specific characteristics of British diplomats of that era: education at one of the nine elite "public schools," graduation from Oxford or Cambridge, verbal virtuosity, independent wealth that required no salary, and a strong sense of British exceptionalism and personal duty. It "reflected the social, political and intellectual concerns of Britain's foreign policy elite" and the "emphasis which senior diplomats placed on applying conventional norms of decency and gentlemanly conduct to international relations."[3] The words may sound quaint, but the diplomatic style will be recognizable to diplomats dealing with their British counterparts today.

The "Foreign Office mind" also connoted a shared worldview. As an island nation on the exposed flank of Europe but with a vast empire stretching around the globe, Britain developed a foreign policy based on certain enduring principles, including maritime supremacy, free trade, balance of power politics, and a rules-based international order.[4] These principles produced a diplomatic style that favored pragmatism over grand strategic design, giving British diplomacy what Sir Harold Nicolson called a "peculiar quality of empiricism" that focused on the practicalities of managing an empire.[5] It also focused on maintaining equilibrium among the major powers, as expressed in Lord Palmerston's famous dictum that Britain had neither permanent allies nor permanent enemies but rather permanent interests[6] and in Sir Eyre Crowe's classic balance of power argument in "Memorandum on the Present State of British Relations with France and Germany" of January 1907.

In the aftermath of World War II, with British power in decline and the empire in retreat, Winston Churchill sought to update this worldview by envisioning Britain at the center of "three circles" of interest: the Atlantic circle (anchored by the US–British "special relationship" and later North Atlantic Treaty Organization [NATO]), the European circle (later the European Union), and the Commonwealth circle (encompassing what was once the British Empire).[7] Although more rallying cry than sober analysis, the "three circles" concept shaped British thinking for more than half a century—and indeed has echoes in the UK's National Security Strategy documents of 2010 and 2015, notwithstanding the constriction of all three circles at the time those documents were produced.[8]

Clearly a great deal has changed since Palmerston's or even Churchill's time: The Foreign Office, while still elite, has become more open and meritocratic, as have Oxford and Cambridge themselves. Britain's place in the global system likewise has changed dramatically with the loss of empire, the erosion of maritime supremacy, and relative economic decline, among many other things. The "Foreign Office mind" seems to belong to another era altogether.

But what of the underlying worldview? This has proved more durable. British diplomacy is still guided by certain core principles: a belief that Britain should be a major player on the world stage, and a commitment to free trade, to the importance of the armed forces as ultimate guarantor of British security, and to international order.[9] In a speech on May 29, 2018, Tom Tugendhat, Chair of the Foreign Affairs Committee of the House of Commons, made a ringing call for active British diplomacy in support of a "rules-based international order" and a foreign policy that is "an expression of our national identity projected into the world."[10] These are words that could have as easily been spoken two centuries ago. At the same time, critics complain that commitment to a "big" foreign policy, driven by "memories of past grandeur, facilitated by a too slowly reduced military establishment" have "played a detrimental part in delaying Britain's adjustment to its true place in the world."[11] The current debate over the meaning of the current rallying cry of "Global Britain" reflects this strategic uncertainty and confusion.

British diplomats, still regarded as among the best in the world, possess some distinctive attributes. British diplomats still favor practical solutions over grand strategic statements and continue to exhibit powerful drafting and speaking skills. They are known for being conscientious, intelligent, loyal, attentive to detail, and "guided by interests rather than sentiments." As legatees of "the Foreign Office mind," however, they are also criticized for being prone to "inside the box" thinking and to being reactive and defensive rather than proactive.[12] The American political scientist Kenneth Waltz once characterized the Foreign Office style in terms that may sound demeaning but actually capture the essence of the art of diplomacy:

> [T]o proceed by a sidling movement rather than move directly toward an object, to underplay one's hand, to dampen conflicts and depreciate dangers, to balance parties off against each other, to compromise rather than fight, to postpone decisions, to obscure issues rather than confront them, to move as it were by elision from one position in policy to another.[13]

Profile

Mission

The FCO aims to promote the UK's national security and economic interests, and provide support to British citizens and businesses abroad.[14] According to the FCO's "Priority Outcomes," the main diplomatic priorities are protecting their citizens, expanding soft power, and promoting prosperity.[15] As part of an emphasis on measuring outcomes, the FCO conducts an annual internal review, which analyzes its performance with regard to its efficacy in achieving the Priority Outcomes.[16]

An internal "Future FCO" report released in 2016 argued that the diplomatic service is too hierarchical and generally deficient in linguistic and regional expertise. The report cited internal concerns over poor language skills, outdated technology, and paralyzing risk aversion. Additionally, the report claimed that some British diplomats use social media platforms, such as WhatsApp, to discuss sensitive subjects while abroad.[17] Other reports alleged that today's FCO is a timid organization partially due to a department-wide perception that failure is not an option.[18]

Conversely, sources within the FCO have described it in far more favorable terms. One source described the organizational culture as "honest, creative, and open," and as a place where diplomats are actively encouraged to express their views, even when such views are contrary to the prevailing viewpoint among the senior management. The FCO does not maintain a dissent channel similar to that of the US State Department, but British diplomats report that they feel empowered to criticize within a culture that it less prone to politicization than is the case in the US system, where politically-appointed officials abound even at senior working levels. The FCO is also characterized by a healthy delegation of authority to junior-level policy officers. It is not uncommon for junior staff at the FCO to draft policy memoranda that are seen by the senior management, and in some cases, by the Foreign Secretary.

Budget

The FCO net expenditure for FY 2016–2017 was £1.98 billion ($2.55 billion), a decrease of £51 million from 2015–2016.[19] This represents less than one-tenth of 1% of the UK's gross domestic product (GDP).[20] Comparatively, the UK allocated a little over 2% of its GDP to national security and defense spending.[21] For a historical comparison, the FCO budget for FY 2003–2004[22] was more than double the current FCO budget as a percentage of GDP.[23] The FCO has objected that the budget cuts imposed upon them have moved beyond "trimming fat," and instead have begun to threaten operational capabilities.[24] Recent parliamentary reviews also assert that the government has not funded the FCO properly, particularly in light of the growing responsibilities of the FCO post-Brexit.[25] The "Future FCO" report asserted that the UK's "global diplomatic network is the same size as France's…at 75% of their cost."

Human Resources and Diplomatic Network

For a nation with a population just under 65 million (23rd largest in the world), the size of the UK's diplomatic network is notable at the fifth largest in the world. As of 2017, the FCO employed 12,865 total staff, of which a third are posted abroad, and the remaining two-thirds are based in the UK. Budget austerity has led the FCO to rely heavily on the recruitment of foreign nationals to staff its overseas posts. Approximately two-thirds of the total FCO staff are locally engaged foreign nationals and the remaining one-third of the FCO staff are UK nationals. As of FY 2015–2016, the FCO operates in 236 postings abroad, including 149 embassies, 60 consulates, and 9 permanent missions.[26]

Unlike the US State Department, the FCO does not use a cone or track system to classify employees. The FCO maintains five employment "bands"—A, B, C, and D, and the SMS (Senior Management Structure).[27] Bands A and B are restricted to administrative and clerical staff, and bands C and D include the policy and diplomacy employees, although it is not unheard of for some B band employees to serve some policy or diplomatic functions.[28] The FCO recruits generalists or specialists based on existing organizational needs; however, as of a 2010 budgetary spending freeze, the FCO restricted recruitment to specialists only (C band or above) until 2016 when it resumed A and B band recruitment.[29] C+ band recruitment is limited to the Civil Service Fast Stream recruitment system, which requires thematic or regional expertise and a university degree (equivalent to a bachelor's degree in the United States).[30] Despite the resumption of recruitment at the A and B bands, sources at the FCO have suggested that they continue to struggle in filling some of the low level domestic positions. Relatively low starting salaries and the high cost of living in metropolitan London are the most likely culprits for the difficulty in recruitment.

The salary structure for the employment bands is as follows: A band (22–26 thousand USD/annum), B band (27–33 thousand USD/annum), C band (34–49 thousand USD/annum), and D band (52–68 thousand USD/annum).[31]

British diplomats are expected to be foreign policy generalists, but they normally acquire some degree of regional or thematic expertise through what are called "career anchors"—"areas to which officers may return multiple times over their careers."[32] The acquisition of "career anchors" is increasingly tied to promotion, according to the FCO's written submission to the House of Commons Foreign Affairs Committee.[33]

Organizational Structure

The head of the UK's diplomatic service is the Permanent Under-Secretary for Foreign Affairs. Just beneath the Permanent Under-Secretary are a number of individual directorates, including "Operations, Economic and Consular, Central Group, Political, Defense and Intelligence, Europe and Globalization, Finance, and UK Trade and Investment."[34] Each directorate includes a number of units that work on thematic, regional, or cross-cutting issue areas. The FCO is led at the ministerial level by three Ministers of State. The ministerial level includes the Secretary of State for Foreign and Commonwealth Affairs ("the Foreign Secretary"), followed by two Ministers of State (one for Europe and the Americas, and the other for the Commonwealth and the UN).

RECRUITMENT AND SELECTION

The FCO hires via two streams, the fast stream (A) and the main stream (B). The more senior stream has faster promotion and focuses on policy and high-level diplomacy. To qualify for the faster stream, applicants must have a good university degree and be seeking a career in diplomacy. Entrance testing entails two working days of individual and group exercises, interviews, and written tests, with a focus less on specific knowledge than on reasoning and problem-solving ability, resiliency, and the ability to influence others.[35] According to a report by the UK's Civil Service, the FCO seeks recruits who exhibit ten specific characteristics.[36] The Civil Service application process may also include online aptitude tests, a competency questionnaire, a personality test, and an in-person assessment and interview.[37]

As in other diplomatic services, the FCO has only belatedly focused on diversity in hiring and promotion. A report from the UK's National Audit Office stated that the FCO is not meeting its diversity goals for senior management positions in terms of gender, ethnicity, and disability.[38] Internal sources from the FCO claim that they greatly value diversity, yet its employees remain, as one FCO employee described, "too pale, male, and stale." These sources stated that concerted efforts are being made to create a more diverse workforce in order to accurately represent the UK abroad. There is a strong belief that current attempts to improve diversity will increase efficacy as well. Having been criticized for what some perceive as its elitist, narrow minded, and "Oxbridge" mentality, the FCO views increased diversity as a step to break free of those notions.

In recent years, the FCO distributed a report detailing their hiring practices and diversity among employees. In the A–D employment bands, the FCO has made considerable progress in achieving gender diversity. The gender breakdown for the A–D bands is 53% male and 47% female.[39] The report also found that the FCO continues to lag behind its diversity targets in terms of ethnicity, disability, sexual orientation, and religion.[40] Overall, employees in the A-D bands are 88% white, 12% black and other ethnic minorities, and 6% disabled. The senior management structure continues to trail in all diversity targets. The SMS is 30.1% female, 4.1% black and other ethnic minority, and 9.9% disabled.[41] One bright spot is in the Fast Stream recruitment for 2015–2016 where 42% of entrants were female and 35% of entrants were of an ethnic minority background.

Interestingly, the "Future FCO" report devoted relatively little attention to recruitment and selection, focusing more on organization, training, and culture. It did, however, urge the FCO to recruit a more diverse workforce and to pay more attention "upstream" to helping those who do enter the FCO to "thrive" as they move through their careers.[42] At FCO headquarters on King Charles Street in London, there is a prominent display of women and individuals of color currently in senior positions—presumably, to offset the overwhelmingly white male images found almost everywhere else in the building.

Professional Development and Training

Historically, the FCO has focused on elite recruitment rather than diplomatic training in developing skilled diplomats. The organization has traditionally relied on recruiting highly educated candidates from elite academic institutions, i.e. Oxford and Cambridge, providing modest entry-level training and acculturation, and subsequently leaving them to navigate the rest of their careers with relatively little formal training or direction from management.

Upon entry, all new staff are required to attend a two-week training process that helps the recruits understand their role in the FCO, the FCO's role in the UK government, and the requirements of the Civil Service Code, which "sets out the standards of [behavior] expected" of all UK civil servants "based on the core values which are set out in legislation."[43] The FCO also utilizes the initial training period to acculturate its new staff to the mission and values of the organization. Additionally, new recruits are required to undertake courses on security, conduct, information management, diversity at work, health and safety, and finance. Policy recruits have additional requirements, such as attending an international policy skills course, as well as intensive language instruction, depending on the results of the candidate's language aptitude test.[44]

Typically, new FCO recruits spend their first 12–18 months on a home tour based at one of the FCO offices in the UK before being sent on their first overseas posting. FCO staff bidding for an overseas posting must submit to an interview before a three-person panel made up of senior level staff members (at least one of which must be a woman and/or an ethnic minority). If the employee is unsuccessful in securing the post, the review panel offers feedback to the employee in order to assist them with their professional development. Overseas postings vary in their lengths depending on location (some hardship posts can be as short as six months, i.e. Afghanistan), but the majority of overseas tours last three to four years.

In 2015, the FCO established the Diplomatic Academy to address the lack of a universal and systematized training and development program.[45] The program offers three different levels of training—Foundation, Practitioner, and Expert—to assist employees in all employment bands. Much of the Academy's training program takes place on a digital platform (including a mobile app) rather than face-to-face, and the pace of training is largely self-directed.[46] Staff members seeking promotion are now required to have completed various diplomatic academy modules, mostly focused on management training, before they apply for more senior positions. The FCO's main training program, "Diplomacy 20:20," has been criticized by successive House of Commons Foreign Affairs Committee reports for excessive focus on "managerialism" at the expense of core diplomatic skills.[47] As a response to such complaints, in 2016 the Diplomatic Academy added a Trade Policy and Negotiations faculty.[48]

In addition to its internal training mechanisms, the FCO maintains a partnership with King's College in London that delivers training courses to FCO staff working on or in the South Asia region and Afghanistan.[49] The one to five day program at King's includes plenary and group discussions which address "the modern history of states in the region and their interrelations, domestic politics and culture, the role of extra-regional powers, business and economic opportunities, and key policy issues affecting the region." Similarly, the London School of Economics and Political Science (LSE) offers an "Economics for Foreign Policy Program" tailored for members of the UK Foreign Service.[50] The LSE program provides participants with "well-rounded knowledge of economic and political issues...[the] ability to converse easily using economic terminology with a high degree of accuracy and a reasonable level of sophistication." According to LSE, over 1400 FCO staff have participated in the program. Beyond its academic ties with King's College and the LSE, the FCO also conducts an annual joint diplomatic training conference with its French counterpart, the Ministry of Foreign Affairs. The aim of the conference is not only to expand the knowledge base of the participating diplomats, but also to develop "institutional and personal ties" between members of the two organizations.[51]

In 1999, the FCO established Assessment and Development Centres (ADCs) as the means of promoting staff to the Senior Management Structure. The FCO now uses the ADC mechanism for the promotion of all staff at and above the B band.[52] In order to apply for a slot in the ADC, the applicant must have served a minimum of two years in their current employment band. Applicants with a minimum of two years but less than five years' experience in their current employment band must also procure a letter of recommendation from his or her senior manager, which assesses whether the candidate possesses the required competencies to sit for the ADC. Those candidates with at least five years of experience in their current employment band do not require a letter of recommendation.

The ADC process is a mix of written and interactive exercises (including role-playing) that tests candidates' core competencies "such as problem solving and judgment, managing external relationships, and communicating and influencing."[53] The FCO has argued that the ADC's have proven quite effective in "improving the quality of leaders and managers" throughout the organization.[54] However, concerns remain over the lack of emphasis on regional and linguistic expertise in the ADC system; the worry among several observers is that the ADC mechanism is tailored to rewarding managerial skills rather than traditional diplomatic skills. If a candidate is successful in the ADC and transitions to a new role, he or she is expected to produce a personal development plan with their manager within six weeks of taking on a new role. These personal development plans detail what skills and knowledge the employee will need to cultivate to be successful in their role. The ADC examination for promotion to ambassadorial level is said to be a tough one, focusing mainly on management, human resources, resiliency, and leadership.

Leadership

In order to be considered for promotion, FCO employees must spend at least five years in their current grade and subsequently receive a letter of recommendation from their senior manager. The letter must include clear indication of the employee's potential and the strength of their established skill-set. In the promotion process, a review board consisting of five to six senior-level FCO employees assesses the candidate's performance. Throughout the assessment, the candidate completes several interactive exercises, such as interviews and role-playing, in order to determine their overall performance and eligibility for promotion. If the employee is not promoted after their initial request, they must wait a period of one to three years to further develop their skills and become better prepared for promotion.[55]

Promotion to the highest level—the Senior Management Structure, or SMS—is determined by a Board chaired by the Permanent Undersecretary and is based on performance reviews, hiring managers' recommendations, and interviews. For the most senior positions, the Foreign Secretary, and sometimes the Prime Minister, has the final say.[56] Interestingly, the "Future FCO" report, replete with recommendations on other topics, has little to say about senior level appointments aside from a vague appeal for "World Class Heads of Mission."[57]

The great majority of high-ranking diplomats have spent their entire career working for the FCO. Most entered as junior-level officers either immediately after graduation from university, or after a few years of working at a think tank or policy research organization. The majority of ambassadors have served under several administrations under different political parties. Some have also had previous outside experience working for the government in other departments or ministries, such as the Department for International Development (DFID). There is a wide variety of career paths on the way to reaching ambassadorial rank. Some have served mainly in one region; most have moved among different regions and functional specializations. Unlike the pattern in the United States, there are very few political appointees in the UK's Diplomatic Service, and those few generally have relevant experience in other government positions, such as chief of staff to the prime minister.

In October 2018, Foreign Secretary Sir Jeremy Hunt announced that in order to "broaden the pool of talent we tap into for our Ambassadors," the FCO would open up the process to external candidates, especially those with commercial background. When asked for further details by the House of Commons Foreign Affairs Committee, he said that these would not be political appointments and the announcement "does not represent a significant change in recruitment policy.[58] Given the damaging effects of the widespread use of political appointments in the US Department of State, it seems likely that the British government will resist going down the same road.

Role in Foreign Policy Making

Formally, under the "Westminster model," the Cabinet wields ultimate decision-making authority, and it is the Cabinet Office that coordinates policy among ministries and departments. The Foreign Secretary, like all cabinet ministers, must be an elected member of the House of Commons or a member of the House of Lords, but the FCO is an apolitical, professional public service, led by a Permanent Under-Secretary. The actual role of the FCO in the foreign policy decision-making process varies widely with each new government and Prime Minister. Whether or not the Foreign Secretary operates as the chief foreign policy advisor in the UK government depends a great deal on the extent to which the Prime Minister chooses to delegate foreign policy strategy and decision-making to the Foreign Secretary and the FCO.[59] That said, there has been a gradual centralization of power in the Prime Minister's office at No. 10 Downing Street, and a drift toward "presidentialism" in foreign policy making.

Under Prime Minister Tony Blair and the New Labor government of the early 2000s, the FCO saw its role in foreign policy decision-making severely sidelined. Blair continued the precedent established by some of his predecessors of working "in small ad hoc committees of his most trusted civil servants" rather than with the entire Cabinet.[60] During the

Iraq War beginning in 2003, Blair cut out a number of ministers, including Foreign Secretary Jack Straw, from his Defence and Overseas Policy Committee, as he found the committee "too unwieldy."[61] Critics called the practice "sofa government," meaning that policy was worked out informally with a small set of advisors, without structure or the participation of key ministers. In the run-up to the war, in a manner very similar to that of the Bush Administration in the United States, Blair disregarded warnings coming from the FCO and elsewhere, and exerted pressure on the Joint Intelligence Committee to exaggerate the threat.[62] In a widely resented departure from customary practice, he also extended decision-making authority to political appointees, bypassing the FCO. Such, at least, were the findings of the Chilcot Inquiry.[63]

The FCO also saw its role in foreign policy diluted with the transfer of key functions to other departments: foreign aid to the Department for International Development (DFID) in 1997, foreign trade to the Department for International Trade in 2016, and European policy to a complex web of policy actors including the Prime Minister's office, the UK Permanent Representation to the EU in Brussels, the European Secretariat in the Cabinet Office, and two separate Cabinet sub-committees.[64] To this should be added the longstanding, and far from cordial, rivalry between the FCO and the Treasury, or Exchequer.

As a response to this fragmentation of foreign policy and a reaction to "sofa government," Prime Minister David Cameron established in May 2010 a National Security Council (NSC) to oversee a more structured decision-making process. Unlike its counterpart in the United States, the UK's NSC was established through an administrative rather than a statutory act, meaning that the council derives its power solely from prime ministerial prerogative.[65] The NSC comprises the prime minister (who serves as chairperson) and a number of senior ministers from departments with national security related portfolios, including the Ministry of Defense, the Exchequer, the Department for International Development, and the Foreign and Commonwealth Office, among others. The national security secretariat, led by the Prime Minister's National Security Advisor, after consultation with the Prime Minister and other relevant departmental ministers, sets the agenda for the meetings of the NSC. According to the UK's Cabinet Office, the UK NSC acts solely as a forum for advisory activity rather than as a distinct executive body with intrinsic decision-making authority. One level down, in a rough analog to the NSC Deputies Committee in the United States, is the National Security Administrative Group.

It is probably too early to render a judgment on the NSC's effectiveness, and whether it has strengthened or weakened the FCO's role. On the one hand, it has formalized the centralization of decision-making and empowered other cabinet offices, leading Former Foreign Secretary William Hague to conclude that the NSC has, in some ways, supplanted the Foreign Secretary as "the principal adviser to the Prime Minister on foreign affairs."[66] On the other hand, the NSC has created a formal structure that guarantees the FCO, in the person of the Foreign Secretary, a seat at the high table. The FCO actually has another seat at the table, in that the position of National Security Advisor has been effectively "captured" by the FCO, which has supplied all but one of the advisors to date. Most of the briefing material for the NSC comes from the FCO, which also provides some 90% of the staff of the Joint Intelligence Committee, so the Foreign Office shapes the agenda in multiple ways. Kim Darroch, former British ambassador to the United States and a former National Security Advisor (2012–2015), argues that the NSC gives the FCO a platform to project its foreign policy priorities and creates an environment more likely to generate "cross-Whitehall support."[67] Similarly, a parliamentary review of the FCO's role in foreign policy making hailed the creation of the NSC as a means of "binding the Prime Minister to a collective decision-making forum, of which the Foreign Secretary is a principal member."[68]

The Department for International Development (DFID), the UK department responsible for the administration of foreign assistance and development funds, continues to operate independently of the FCO. The Foreign Affairs Committee review of the FCO's role suggests some difficulty among high-level ministers of "[reconciling] DFID's separate existence."[69] Some witnesses suggested that, at times, DFID has operated as an "alternative overseas representative" of the UK government, at the expense of the FCO, particularly with regard to UK foreign policy in Sub-Saharan Africa.[70] The budget disparity between the two departments has also created an imbalance; while the FCO's budget has been continually cut in recent years, DFID's budget has been shielded from cuts.[71] There appears to be a growing consensus that the organizational missions of the FCO and DFID must be more closely aligned.

Budget cuts have clearly contributed to the FCO's struggle to retain primacy within the government. In 2016, former Permanent Under-Secretary Simon Fraser testified that budget cuts have severely limited the

FCO's ability to staff its embassies with "the right people with the right training."[72] As a point of reference, the FCO's latest budget was only about twice as large as the UK's annual foreign aid to Ethiopia.[73]

Preparations for the Future

In light of all these factors—severe budget cuts, the loss of control of essential aspects of foreign policy, and the "tug-of-war with the Cabinet office"—Tom Tugendhat, Chair of the Foreign Affairs Committee of the House of Commons, stated bluntly that the FCO had "lost its way" and that its "role in directing foreign policy has been gradually hollowed out."[74] His was but one of a number of sharply critical and self-critical appraisals of the FCO's challenges.

A widely read article of October 2018 in Prospect magazine cited a number of such laments. Former Permanent Under-Secretary Peter Ricketts said the FCO has "no clout," and Ricketts' successor Simon Fraser criticized it for being "timid."[75] Brexit—the decision to leave the EU—has been profoundly unsettling and disorienting for British diplomats, for whom the EU has been at the center of British foreign policy for 45 years. "Global Britain," the Government's rallying cry for British policy in a post-EU era, has been criticized as "a slogan without any content."[76] In its reviews of 2010 and 2012, the House of Commons Public Administration Select Committee accused the UK government more broadly of having "all but lost the capacity to think strategically" and for its "inability to express coherent and relevant strategic aims,"[77] referring particularly to the 2010 Security and Defence Strategic Review.

One should not take all these lamentations at face value. For one thing, Britain has always had an admirable capacity for self-evaluation and self-criticism, in contrast to the smug complacency one often finds in other capitals. In a way, much of the criticism has less to do with the FCO or the British government as a whole than with the difficult strategic environment in which Great Britain now finds itself. As noted earlier, each of Churchill's "three circles"—Commonwealth, Europe, and the "special relationship" with the United States—are constricting. It is hardly surprising that the FCO has been unable to articulate a compelling vision for "Global Britain," since no one else has been able to do so, either. With Britain looking more like "an island apart" (to borrow the title of the October 2018 Prospect magazine article cited above) and with the erosion of power that Britain has experienced, it is hard to see the country as the "bridge," "pivot," or "hub" at the center of a networked world, as Churchill once envisioned,[78] no matter how clever the strategic design.

It is nonetheless true that the FCO faces significant challenges, starting with the budget. The FCO has the lowest median pay of any government department for middle managers and ranked 48th out of 48 in the annual Government "staff survey" of how staff felt about pay.[79] Its "Future FCO" report of 2016, prepared by British diplomat Tom Fletcher, made a ringing appeal to "unchain the FCO" by raising pay, improving language and geographic competency, increasing tour lengths to deepen expertise, replacing "managerialism" with a new focus on strategic thinking, accelerating the use of social media, and modernizing its technology for the digital age.[80] Similarly, the November 2018 "Delivering Global Britain" report of the House of Commons Foreign Affairs Committee urged the FCO to prioritize strategic thinking and core diplomatic skills, and to embrace "digital diplomacy" by encouraging diplomats to show initiative and empowering them to take risks.

In recent years, the FCO began using various social media platforms to establish a new form of public outreach, but their success thus far is unclear.[81] A number of FCO diplomats have noted the importance of using social media and new technologies to create a better public understanding of FCO's mission.[82] FCO's leadership actively encourages employees to use social media freely. Domestically, they ask officers to use specific hash-tags that support British campaigns. With regard to foreign postings, there is not a clear process or set of guidelines for officers, and the FCO, like other diplomatic services, struggles to transform the hierarchical, top-down organizational structure of the past into one that is decentralized and networked.[83]

Administratively, FCO has also taken steps to eliminate administrative duties for junior-level officers, ultimately allowing them to advance and acquire relevant expertise earlier in their careers. For example, all visa work abroad is exported to local support staff, giving junior foreign officers an opportunity to work elsewhere in the embassies. This recent change not only removes an aspect of "busy work" from younger diplomats, but also offers them a chance to make more substantive contributions to UK foreign policy while working in their initial posting abroad.

As concerns public diplomacy, Hugo Swire, a former FCO Minister of State, claimed that a poll from "YouGov" affirmed the UK's strong reputation abroad, and emphasized the importance in maintaining a positive image abroad.[84] One FCO report on public diplomacy included research that explained how the international community perceives the UK's diplomatic service. According to the 2010 Anholt Nation Brand Index, the FCO is viewed as "fair, innovative, diverse, confident, and stylish," but also "arrogant, stuffy, old-fashioned and cold."[85] A separate report from the FCO encouraged active engagement with local communities abroad as a way to counter those negative perceptions.[86] To promote public engagement and an "outward facing" mentality among diplomats despite the security risks they face in many posts, the FCO provides risk management training to prepare for posting abroad.[87]

The greatest immediate challenge facing the FCO is, of course, preparing for Brexit. The newly created Department for Exiting the European Union focuses on the many organizational and procedural changes associated with detaching British diplomacy from that of the European Union. Difficult as it was for British diplomacy to integrate itself into the EU, reverse engineering the process is likely to prove even more difficult—not only for Britain but also for the EU, whose foreign and security policy benefited so greatly from British diplomatic skill. The "E-3" of France, Germany, and Britain will continue providing a platform for joint action on the part of Europe's most significant powers, but day-to-day foreign policy making will be challenging for both the EU and for the UK.

Clearly, it will take some time for Great Britain to "find its way." Much depends on how the exit from the European Union plays out, whether NATO remains a viable and vibrant alliance, and whether the United States returns to a more active and responsible global role after the destabilizing policies of the Trump Administration. With its European and North American allies seemingly unwilling to offer much help, the UK may be left to its own devices in a way not seen for generations. In this challenging new environment, it is even possible that "Brexit," perversely, might give the FCO and its skilled, resilient diplomatic corps a new lease on life in managing Britain's global interests.

Acknowledgment *The authors wish to thank the following diplomats and scholars who were consulted in researching and writing this chapter:* Gill Bennett, John Bew, Keith Hamilton, Matthew Harries, Stephen Hickey, Matthew Moody, Pauline Neville-Jones, Patrick Salmon, and Liane Saunders.

Notes

1. For brief discussion, see Edward T. Corp, "Sir Eyre Crowe and the Administration of the Foreign Office, 1906–1914," *The Historical Journal* 22, no. 2 (June 1979): 443–454.
2. Frank Ashton-Gwatki. "Foreign Service Reorganization in the United Kingdom." *International Affairs* (Royal Institute of International Affairs 1944–) 22, no. 1 (1946): 57–74.
3. T.G. Otte, *The Foreign Office Mind: The Making of British Foreign Policy, 1865–1914* (Cambridge: Cambridge University Press, 2011), 6 and 12.
4. Sir Harold Nicolson, *Diplomacy* (Oxford: Oxford University Press, 1963), 132–135.
5. Ibid., 132. See also Sir Ernest Satow, *A Guide to Diplomatic Practice* (Cambridge: Cambridge University Press, 2011; first published in 1917). 183–184; and Prime Minister William Gladstone's letter to Queen Victoria, April 17, 1869, as cited in Nicolson, 137.
6. The precise quote from his March 1, 1848 remarks in the House of Commons is, "We have no eternal allies, and we have no perpetual enemies. Our interests are eternal and perpetual, and those interests it is our duty to follow." Quoted in William Safire, "Friends More than Interests," February 7, 1991. *New York Times*.
7. "Conservative Mass Meeting: a speech at Llandudno, 9 October 1948," in *Europe Unite: Speeches, 1947 & 1948* (London: Cassell, 1950), 416–418.
8. David Sanders and David Patrick Houghton, *Losing an Empire, Finding a Role: British Foreign Policy Since 1945* (London: Palgrave Macmillan, 2nd edition, 2017), 1–11, esp. 1–3.
9. Laurence Martin and John Garnett, *British Foreign Policy: Challenges and Choices for the Twenty-First Century* (London: Royal Institute of International Affairs, 1997), 83–85.
10. Tom Tugendhat, "Address to the Royal United Services Institute, May 29, 2018." https://rusi.org/event/tom-tugendhat-defending-rules. Accessed November 28, 2018.
11. Martin and Garnett, *British Foreign Policy*, 6–7.
12. Otte, *The Foreign Office Mind*, 394–395. See also the critiques discussed at the end of this chapter, many of them coming from the FCO itself.
13. Kenneth Waltz, *Foreign Policy and Domestic Politics* (Boston: Little, Brown & Co., 1967), 7–8.
14. "About Us." *Foreign and Commonwealth Office*. Accessed October 11, 2016. https://www.gov.uk/government/organisations/foreign-commonwealth-office/about.

15. "FCO Public Diplomacy: The Olympic and Paralympic Games 2012." House of Commons Foreign Affairs Committee. January 26, 2011. Accessed October 24, 2016. http://www.publications.parliament.uk/pa/cm201011/cmselect/cmfaff/581/58102.htm. According to a report released by the FCO, soft power is used to "describe governments' ability 'to get what (they) want through attraction rather than coercion or payments.' Soft power 'arises from the attractiveness of a country's culture, political ideals, and policies. When (its) policies are seen as legitimate in the eyes of others, (its) soft power is enhanced."
16. "Foreign and Commonwealth Office Annual Report and Accounts 2015–2016." Foreign and Commonwealth Office. July 20, 2016. Accessed October 24, 2016. https://www.gov.uk/government/uploads/system/uploads/attachment_data/file/539413/FCO_Annual_Report_2016_ONLINE.pdf.
17. Patrick Wintour. "Internal report slams culture in UK Foreign Office." *The Guardian*. May 9, 2016. Accessed October 11, 2016. https://www.theguardian.com/politics/2016/may/09/internal-report-slams-culture-in-uk-foreignoffice. See also "Future FCO" (London: Foreign and Commonwealth Office, 2016). Accessed January 26, 2019. https://www.gov.uk/government/publications/future-fco-report.
18. Brian Brady. "Foreign Office is beset by culture of timidity, say staff." *Independent*. March 21, 2009. Accessed October 11, 2016. http://www.independent.co.uk/news/uk/politics/foreign-office-is-beset-by-culture-of-timidity-saystaff-1651331.html.
19. "A Short Guide to the Foreign and Commonwealth Office" (London: National Audit Office, October 2017), 4. https://www.nao.org.uk/report/a-short-guide-to-the-foreign-and-commonwealth-office/. Accessed January 26, 2019.
20. Includes staff costs and expenditures on programs and consular services.
21. Ibid.
22. For the FCO budget during FY 2003/2004, we used currency rates reported from 2003.
23. "Chapter 3: Comparative Data." Italian Ministry of Foreign Affairs. 2003. Accessed October 24, 2016. http://www.esteri.it/MAE/doc/chapter3.pdf.
24. Philip Hammond, "Government Response to the House of Commons Foreign Affairs Committee Report HC 605 of Session 2014–15." Foreign and Commonwealth Office. June 2015. Accessed November 15, 2016. https://www.gov.uk/government/uploads/system/uploads/attachment_data/file/435544/50038_Cm_9058_Gov_to_HC_Accessible_v0.2.pdf.
25. Ibid.

26. "Annual Report and Accounts."
27. "FCO Staff and Salary Data." Foreign and Commonwealth Office. July 21, 2016. Accessed September 17, 2016. https://www.gov.uk/government/publications/foreign-office-staff-and-salary-data.
28. "Further written evidence from the Foreign and Commonwealth Office." UK Parliament. November 25, 2010. Accessed October 10, 2016. http://www.publications.parliament.uk/pa/cm201012/cmselect/cmfaff/665/665we03.htm.
29. The FCO defines generalists as "staff who rotate through a variety of roles" vs. specialists who "take up a specific role requiring specialist skills, i.e. research analyst or lawyer." Due to the 2010 spending freeze, recruitment had been limited to specialist recruitment only through the Civil Service Fast Stream, however, recently the FCO has begun recruiting generalists at the A and B bands, in part due to criticisms that the Fast Stream system was too elitist. "Working for FCO." Foreign and Commonwealth Office. Accessed September 17, 2016. https://www.gov.uk/government/organisations/foreign-commonwealth-office/about/recruitment.
30. Ibid.
31. "FCO Staff and Salary Data."
32. "Delivering Global Britain: FCO Skills," HC 1254, Foreign Affairs Committee, House of Commons, 28 November 2018, 10.
33. Ibid.
34. "Annual Report and Accounts."
35. Interviews at the FCO and with former senior British diplomats, London, October 29 and 30, 2018.
36. "Civil Service Competency Framework: 2012–2017." Civil Service Human Resources. Accessed October 11, 2016. https://assets.publishing.service.gov.uk/government/uploads/system/uploads/attachment_data/file/436073/cscf_fulla4potrait_2013-2017_v2d.pdf; The "Competency Framework" provides ten key characteristics of a successful Civil Service employee: seeing the big picture, making effective decisions, changing and improving, leading and communicating, building capability for all, collaborating and partnering, achieving commercial outcomes, delivering value for money, managing a quality service, and delivering at pace. According to the report, this framework is used for recruitment and promotion considerations.
37. "Prepare for Civil Service Online Test." Job Test Prep. Accessed October 24, 2016. https://www.jobtestprep.co.uk/civil-service-online-test#e-tray-exercise; The Civil Service's online testing consists of numerical and verbal reasoning, an abstract reasoning test, a situational judgment test (which tests the applicant's potential responses to certain work scenarios), a personality exam, a Watson Glaser test (a multi-faceted exam that tests

the applicant's critical thinking skills), and an in-person assessment and interview at the Civil Service Assessment Centre. At the Centre, applicants spend a day completing a number of exercises, including a writing exam, further aptitude tests, presentations, role-playing work scenarios, and team building activities. Applicants may be asked to participate in several interviews, which include questions regarding their applications, qualifications, and the Civil Service Competency Framework.
38. "A Short Guide." See also Natalie Gil, "The Foreign Office Has Traditionally Been a Place for Eccentric Males." *The Guardian*, 2014, accessed October 11, 2016, https://www.theguardian.com/public-leaders-network/2014/jun/18/foreign-officeeccentric-males-women-pay-gap.
39. "Annual Report and Accounts."
40. Foreign and Commonwealth Office (FCO) Diversity and Equality Report 2014–15. Foreign and Commonwealth Office. 2015. Accessed September 17, 2016. https://www.gov.uk/government/uploads/system/uploads/attachment_data/file/450587/FFFCO827_Equality_Report_2015_v5.pdf.
41. "Annual Report and Accounts."
42. "Future FCO," 28.
43. FCO, "Further written evidence."
44. Ibid.
45. "Opening of New Diplomatic Academy." Gov.uk. Accessed October 11, 2016. https://www.gov.uk/government/publications/opening-of-new-diplomatic-academy.
46. "Diplomatic Academy," Foreign and Commonwealth Office, 2015. https://assets.publishing.service.gov.uk/government/uploads/system/uploads/attachment_data/file/402469/Diplomatic_Academy_launch_brochure_Jan_2015_FINAL.pdf, accessed January 21, 2019.
47. "Delivering Global Britain: FCO Skills." (Written Evidence from the Foreign and Commonwealth Office)," Global Britain: FCO Skills, HC 1254, Foreign Affairs Committee, House of Commons, 28 November 2018. Accessed January 26, 2019. https://publications.parliament.uk/pa/cm201719/cmselect/cmfaff/1254/125404.htm. 4–6.
48. "Delivering Global Britain," 4.
49. "Foreign and Commonwealth Office Training." King's College London. 2019. Accessed January 26, 2019. https://www.kcl.ac.uk/sspp/departments/kii/executiveeducation/fco-training.aspx.
50. "Economics for Foreign Policy: Customized Courses for the FCO." London School of Economics and Political Science. 2019. Accessed January 25, 2019. https://www.slideshare.net/lseenterprise/economics-for-foreign-policy-customised-courses-for-the-fco.

51. "Joint training for French and British Diplomats." Gov.uk. June 19, 2014. Accessed November 16, 2016. https://www.gov.uk/government/world-location-news/joint-training-for-french-and-british-diplomats.
52. "Role of the FCO in UK Government." UK Parliament. Accessed January 26, 2019. https://www.parliament.uk/business/committees/committees-a-z/commons-select/foreign-affairs-committee/inquiries1/the-role-of-the-fco-in-uk-government/.
53. Ibid.
54. Ibid.
55. "Further Written Evidence from the Foreign and Commonwealth Office." UK Parliament. November 25, 2010. Accessed October 10, 2016. http://www.publications.parliament.uk/pa/cm201012/cmselect/cmfaff/665/665we03.htm.
56. "Delivering Global Britain": Written evidence from the Foreign and Commonwealth Office (SK10004), 6; Andrew Levi, "British Foreign Office Personnel Rules: Introduction" http://unpan1.un.org/intradoc/groups/public/documents/NISPAcee/UNPAN007287.pdf. Accessed February 2, 2019.
57. "Future FCO," 8–9.
58. "Delivering Global Britain," 13–14.
59. Ibid.
60. Paul Williams, "Who's Making UK Foreign Policy?" International Affairs (Royal Institute of International Affairs 1944–) 80, no. 5 (2004): 911–929. http://www.jstor.org/stable/3569478.
61. Ibid.
62. Interviews with senior FCO officials, past and present, London, October 29 and 30, 2018. For discussion, see Jamie Gaskarth, *British Foreign Policy* (Cambridge, UK: Cambridge University Press, 2014), 12–19. For analysis of similar distortions in the US decision to go to war, see Robert Hutchings, "America at War, 2003–5," chapter 5 in *Truth to Power: A History of the U.S. National Intelligence Council*, ed. Robert Hutchings and Gregory Treverton (Oxford University Press, 2019).
63. Commissioned by Prime Minister Gordon Brown in 2009 under the chairmanship of Sir John Chilcot, The Iraq Inquiry, as it was also known, was issued in 2016: https://webarchive.nationalarchives.gov.uk/20171123123237/http://www.iraqinquiry.org.uk/.
64. Williams, "Who's Making UK Foreign Policy?"
65. Jon Lunn, Louisa Brooke-Holland, and Claire Mills. "The UK National Security Council." United Kingdom House of Commons Library 7456. January 11, 2016.
66. Ibid.

67. Joe Devanny and Josh Harris, "The National Security Council: National Security at the Centre of Government." 2014. Accessed November 16, 2016. http://www.instituteforgovernment.org.uk/sites/default/files/publications/NSC%20final%202.pdf.
68. "Role of the FCO."
69. Ibid.
70. Williams, "Who's Making UK Foreign Policy?"
71. Ibid.
72. "Equipping the Government for Brexit." House of Commons Foreign Affairs Committee. July 19, 2016. Accessed November 15, 2016. http://www.publications.parliament.uk/pa/cm201617/cmselect/cmfaff/431/431.pdf.
73. Ibid.
74. Tugendhat, "Address to the Royal United Services Institute."
75. Steve Bloomfield, "An island apart: the inside story of how the Foreign Office is failing to prepare for Brexit," *Prospect*, October 15, 2018.
76. Ibid.
77. Cited in Timothy Edmunds, "Complexity, Strategy and the National Interest," in Timothy Edmunds, Jamie Gaskarth, and Robin Porter, eds. *British Foreign Policy and the National Interest* (New York: Palgrave Macmillan, 2014), 171.
78. Sanders and Houghton, *Losing an Empire*, 1–2 and 286–287.
79. "Delivering Global Great Britain."
80. "Future FCO."
81. "Foreign Office@foreignoffice." Foreign and Commonwealth Office Twitter Page (n.d.). Accessed October 6, 2016. https://twitter.com/foreignoffice; "Foreign Office@foreignoffice," Foreign and Commonwealth Office Facebook Page (n.d.). Accessed October 6, 2016. https://www.facebook.com/foreignoffice/.
82. Greg Quinn, "British Diplomacy in the Information Age." Foreign and Commonwealth Office. 2014. Accessed September 19, 2016. https://www.gov.uk/government/speeches/british-diplomacy-in-the-information-age; William Hague, "The best diplomatic service in the world: strengthening the Foreign and Commonwealth Office as an institution." Foreign and Commonwealth Office. September 8, 2011. Accessed October 11, 2016. https://www.gov.uk/government/speeches/the-bestdiplomatic-service-in-the-world-strengthening-the-foreign-and-commonwealth-office-as-an-institution; Joe Devanny, "Austerity, Reform and Leadership: The View from the Foreign Office." July 16, 2015. Institute for Government. Accessed October 12, 2016. http://www.instituteforgovernment.org.uk/blog/12151/austerity-reform-and-leadership-the-view-from-the-foreignoffice/.

83. Interview with FCO employee.
84. Hugo Swire, "Foreign Office Minister speaks about Britain's reputation in the world." Foreign and Commonwealth Office. September 18, 2012. Accessed October 11, 2016. https://www.gov.uk/government/news/foreign-office-ministerspeaks-about-britain-s-reputation-in-the-world.
85. "FCO Public Diplomacy."
86. Jolyon Welsh and David Fearn, D "Engagement: Public Diplomacy in a Globalised World." Foreign and Commonwealth Office. 2008. Accessed October 31, 2016. https://www.uscpublicdiplomacy.org/sites/uscpublicdiplomacy.org/files/useruploads/u26739/Engagement_FCO.pdf.
87. Interview with FCO employee.

REFERENCES

A Short Guide to the Foreign and Commonwealth Office. 2017, September 29. London: National Audit Office. https://www.nao.org.uk/report/a-short-guide-to-the-foreign-and-commonwealth-office/. Accessed January 26, 2019.

About Us. 2016. Foreign and Commonwealth Office. https://www.gov.uk/government/organisations/foreign-commonwealth-office/about. Accessed October 11, 2016.

Annual Report and Accounts. 2016, March. Foreign and Commonwealth Office. https://www.gov.uk/government/uploads/system/uploads/attachment_data/file/539413/FCO_Annual_Report_2016_ONLINE.pdf. Accessed October 24, 2016.

Ashton-Gwatkin, F. 1946. Foreign Service Reorganization in the United Kingdom. *International Affairs (Royal Institute of International Affairs 1944–)* 22 (1): 57–74.

Bloomfield, S. 2018, October 15. An Island Apart: The Inside Story of How the Foreign Office Is Failing to Prepare for Brexit. *Prospect.* https://www.prospectmagazine.co.uk/magazine/foreign-office-brexit-failure-steve-bloomfield. Accessed January 26, 2019.

Brady, B. 2009, March 21. Foreign Office Is Beset by Culture of Timidity, Say Staff. *Independent.* http://www.independent.co.uk/news/uk/politics/foreign-office-is-beset-by-culture-of-timidity-saystaff-1651331.html. Accessed October 11, 2016.

Churchill, Winston. 1950. Conservative Mass Meeting: A Speech at Llandudno, 9 October 1948. In *Europe Unite: Speeches, 1947 & 1948*, ed. R.S. Churchill. London: Cassell.

Civil Service Competency Framework: 2012–2017. n.d. Civil Service Human Resources. https://assets.publishing.service.gov.uk/government/uploads/system/uploads/attachment_data/file/436073/cscf_fulla4potrait_2013-2017_v2d.pdf. Accessed October 11, 2016.

Comparative Data. 2003. Italian Ministry of Foreign Affairs. http://www.esteri.it/MAE/doc/chapter3.pdf. Accessed October 24, 2016.

Corp, E.T. 1979. Sir Eyre Crowe and the Administration of the Foreign Office, 1906–1914. *The Historical Journal* 22 (2): 443–454.

Delivering Global Great Britain: FCO Skills (Written Evidence from the Foreign and Commonwealth Office). 2018, November 28. Foreign Affairs Committee, House of Commons. https://publications.parliament.uk/pa/cm201719/cmselect/cmfaff/1254/125404.htm. Accessed January 26, 2019.

Devanny, J. 2015, July 16. Austerity, Reform and Leadership: The View from the Foreign Office. *Institute for Government*. http://www.instituteforgovernment.org.uk/blog/12151/austerity-reform-and-leadership-the-view-from-the-foreignoffice/. Accessed October 12, 2016.

Devanny, J., and J. Harris. 2014, November. The National Security Council: National Security at the Centre of Government. http://www.instituteforgovernment.org.uk/sites/default/files/publications/NSC%20final%202.pdf. Accessed November 16, 2016.

Diplomatic Academy. 2015. Foreign and Commonwealth Office. https://assets.publishing.service.gov.uk/government/uploads/system/uploads/attachment_data/file/402469/Diplomatic_Academy_launch_brochure_Jan_2015_FINAL.pdf. Accessed January 21, 2019.

Economics for Foreign Policy: Customized Courses for the FCO. 2019. London School of Economics and Political Science. https://www.slideshare.net/lseenterprise/economics-for-foreign-policy-customised-courses-for-the-fco. Accessed January 25, 2019.

Edmunds, T. 2014. Complexity, Strategy and the National Interest. In *British Foreign Policy and the National Interest*, ed. T. Edmunds, J. Gaskarth, and R. Porter, 171–187. New York: Palgrave Macmillan.

Equipping the Government for Brexit. 2016, July 19. House of Commons Foreign Affairs Committee. http://www.publications.parliament.uk/pa/cm201617/cmselect/cmfaff/431/431.pdf. Accessed November 15, 2016.

FCO Public Diplomacy: The Olympic and Paralympic Games 2012. 2011, January 26. House of Commons Foreign Affairs Committee. http://www.publications.parliament.uk/pa/cm201011/cmselect/cmfaff/581/58102.htm. Accessed October 24, 2016.

FCO Staff and Salary Data. 2016, July 21. Foreign and Commonwealth Office. https://www.gov.uk/government/publications/foreign-office-staff-and-salary-data. Accessed September 17, 2016.

Foreign and Commonwealth Office (FCO) Diversity and Equality Report 2014–15. 2015. Foreign and Commonwealth Office. https://www.gov.uk/government/uploads/system/uploads/attachment_data/file/450587/FFFCO827_Equality_Report_2015_v5.pdf. Accessed September 17, 2016.

Foreign and Commonwealth Office Annual Report and Accounts 2015–2016. 2016, July 20. Foreign and Commonwealth Office. https://www.gov.uk/government/uploads/system/uploads/attachment_data/file/539413/FCO_Annual_Report_2016_ONLINE.pdf. Accessed October 24, 2016.
Foreign and Commonwealth Office Training. 2019. King's College London. https://www.kcl.ac.uk/sspp/departments/kii/executiveeducation/fco-training.aspx. Accessed January 26, 2019.
Foreign Office@foreignoffice. n.d.-a. Commonwealth Office Facebook Page. https://www.facebook.com/foreignoffice/. Accessed October 6, 2016.
———. n.d.-b. Foreign and Commonwealth Office. Twitter Account. https://twitter.com/foreignoffice. Accessed January 26, 2019.
Further Written Evidence from the Foreign and Commonwealth Office. 2010, November 25. UK Parliament. http://www.publications.parliament.uk/pa/cm201012/cmselect/cmfaff/665/665we03.htm. Accessed October 10, 2016.
Future FCO. 2016. London: Foreign and Commonwealth Office. https://www.gov.uk/government/publications/future-fco-report. Accessed January 26, 2019.
Gaskarth, J. 2014. *British Foreign Policy*. Cambridge, UK: Cambridge University Press.
Gil, N. 2014, June 18. The Foreign Office Has Traditionally Been a Place for Eccentric Males. *The Guardian*. https://www.theguardian.com/public-leaders-network/2014/jun/18/foreign-office-eccentric-males-women-pay-gap. Accessed January 26, 2019.
Hague, W. 2011, September 8. *The Best Diplomatic Service in the World: Strengthening the Foreign and Commonwealth Office as an Institution*. Foreign and Commonwealth Office. https://www.gov.uk/government/speeches/the-bestdiplomatic-service-in-the-world-strengthening-the-foreign-and-commonwealth-office-as-an-institution. Accessed October 11, 2016.
Hammond, Philip. 2015. *Government Response to the House of Commons Foreign Affairs Committee Report HC 605 of Session 2014–15*. Foreign and Commonwealth Office. https://www.gov.uk/government/uploads/system/uploads/attachment_data/file/435544/50038_Cm_9058_Gov_to_HC_Accessible_v0.2.pdf. Accessed November 15, 2016.
Hutchings, R. 2019. America at War, 2003–5. In *Truth to Power: A History of the U.S. National Intelligence Council*, ed. R. Hutchings and G. Treverton. New York: Oxford University Press.
Joint Training for French and British Diplomats. 2014, June 9. *Gov.uk*. https://www.gov.uk/government/world-location-news/joint-training-for-french-and-british-diplomats. Accessed November 16, 2016.
Lunn, J., L. Brooke-Holland, and C. Mills. 2016, January 11. *The UK National Security Council*. United Kingdom House of Commons Library 7456.
Martin, L., and J. Garnett. 1997. *British Foreign Policy: Challenges and Choices for the Twenty-First Century*. London: Royal Institute of International Affairs.

Nicolson, H. 1963. *Diplomacy*. Oxford: Oxford University Press.
Opening of New Diplomatic Academy. 2015. *Gov.uk*. https://www.gov.uk/government/publications/opening-of-new-diplomatic-academy. Accessed October 11, 2016.
Otte, T.G. 2011. *The Foreign Office Mind: The Making of British Foreign Policy, 1865–1914*. Cambridge, UK: Cambridge University Press.
Prepare for Civil Service Online Test. n.d. *Job Test Prep*. https://www.jobtestprep.co.uk/civil-service-online-test#e-tray-exercise. Accessed October 24, 2016.
Quinn, G. 2014, September 19. *British Diplomacy in the Information Age*. Foreign and Commonwealth Office. https://www.gov.uk/government/speeches/british-diplomacy-in-the-information-age. Accessed September 19, 2016.
Role of the FCO in UK Government. 2010, May 12. *UK Parliament*. https://www.parliament.uk/business/committees/committees-a-z/commons-select/foreign-affairs-committee/inquiries1/the-role-of-the-fco-in-uk-government/. Accessed January 26, 2019.
Sanders, D., and D.P. Houghton. 2017. *Losing an Empire, Finding a Role: British Foreign Policy Since 1945*. London: Palgrave Macmillan.
Satow, E. 2011 [1917]. *A Guide to Diplomatic Practice*. Cambridge: Cambridge University Press.
Swire, H. 2012, September 18. *Foreign Office Minister Speaks About Britain's Reputation in the World*. Foreign and Commonwealth Office. https://www.gov.uk/government/news/foreign-office-minister-speaks-about-britain-s-reputation-in-the-world. Accessed January 26, 2019.
The Report of the Iraq Inquiry. 2016, July 12. *The National Archives*. https://webarchive.nationalarchives.gov.uk/20171123123237/http://www.iraqinquiry.org.uk/. Accessed January 26, 2019.
Tugendhat, T. 2018, May 29. Address to the Royal United Services Institute. https://rusi.org/event/tom-tugendhat-defending-rules. Accessed January 26, 2019.
Waltz, K. 1967. *Foreign Policy and Domestic Politics*. Boston: Little, Brown & Co.
Welsh, J., and D. Fearn. 2008. *Engagement: Public Diplomacy in a Globalised World*. Foreign and Commonwealth Office. https://www.uscpublicdiplomacy.org/sites/uscpublicdiplomacy.org/files/useruploads/u26739/Engagement_FCO.pdf. Accessed October 31, 2016.
Williams, P. 2004. Who's Making UK Foreign Policy? *International Affairs (Royal Institute of International Affairs 1944–)* 80 (5): 911–929.
Wintour, P. 2016, May 9. Internal Report Slams Culture in UK Foreign Office. *The Guardian*. https://www.theguardian.com/politics/2016/may/09/internal-report-slams-culture-in-uk-foreignoffice. Accessed October 11, 2016.
Working for FCO. 2016. Foreign and Commonwealth Office. https://www.gov.uk/government/organisations/foreign-commonwealth-office/about/recruitment. Accessed September 17, 2016.

CHAPTER 10

United States

Ronald McMullen

EXECUTIVE SUMMARY

America's diplomatic service, with nearly 7900 Foreign Service Officers (FSOs), is the largest in the world. Well-funded by global standards and operating 277 diplomatic posts abroad, the US Department of State engages in continuous diplomacy to foster America's interests and values around the world. At times, however, it struggles to adapt to changes in American political leadership, deal with the rising influence of other foreign affairs agencies, overcome bureaucratic inertia in Washington, harness technological change, and address the increased importance of non-traditional issues.

For over a century, most American diplomats were wealthy amateurs or well-connected political appointees. The merit-based Foreign Service was created in 1924 and modernized in 1980. Foreign Service Officers (FSOs) are selected though a highly competitive process that weeds out about 97% of applicants. A typical successful candidate is a 31-year-old woman with an advanced degree, strong language aptitude, and significant international experience. A US diplomat (a term used interchangeably herein with Foreign Service Officer) will spend about two-thirds of his or her career working abroad in one of five career tracks.

R. McMullen (✉)
Ambassador in Residence, University of Iowa, Iowa City, IA, USA
e-mail: rhutchings@austin.utexas.edu

Today, the US diplomatic service shares space at embassies and consulates with more than two dozen other US government agencies. These other agencies comprise 40% of the American staffing at posts worldwide. Political appointees fill about 30% of ambassadorships and most top State Department positions in Washington. Domestically, Civil Service employees now significantly outnumber their Foreign Service colleagues. Heightened foreign affairs engagement in recent decades by the military, intelligence community, and other executive branch agencies, both in Washington and overseas, has further diffused the traditionally preeminent foreign policy role of the US diplomatic service.

History and Culture

A bronze statue of an avuncular Benjamin Franklin greets new American diplomats reporting for duty at the Foreign Service Institute (FSI). His is a fitting welcome, being America's first diplomat, as Jeremi Suri notes in his introduction to this volume. For many Europeans of his day "Franklin *was* America, and the enormous respect accorded Franklin extrapolated to the American cause."[1] In a number of interesting ways, Ben Franklin still serves as a role model for American diplomats. He was a brilliant generalist with no formal training in diplomacy, was highly adept at persuasion, developed useful personal networks, and spent years overseas at some cost to his personal and family's well-being. A skilled writer, Franklin was largely self-taught, adapted quickly to changing environments, and was highly curious about the world. Are Benjamin Franklin's attributes and skills, one wonders, still relevant to American diplomacy some 250 years later?

In July 1789, George Washington signed legislation creating the Department of Foreign Affairs. The new constitution gave the president the power, in some cases shared with the Senate, to make treaties and appoint and receive American and foreign ambassadors. As the tiny federal government had only three departments that year (Foreign Affairs, later joined by War and Treasury), several domestic duties accrued to the Department of Foreign Affairs, such as overseeing the census, managing the mint, and safeguarding the Great Seal of the United States. These additional responsibilities prompted the name to be changed to the generic Department of State. "Despite surrendering most of its domestic duties in the nineteenth century, the Department found itself stuck with the name," as G.R. Berridge observes.[2]

During the country's first century, many American diplomats were self-financed dilettantes. They were outnumbered around the world by American consuls who provided services to American companies, ships, and travelers for a fee. Appointments to the separate diplomatic and consular services were secured via political connections. In 1832, Senator William Marcy of New York, defending a controversial ambassadorial appointment made by Andrew Jackson, claimed that "to the victor belong the spoils ..."[3] President Jackson honed the spoils system to a fine art.

His successors followed suit; by Abraham Lincoln's time, the patronage system had nearly gotten out of hand. When actor James Hackett from Ford's Theater camped outside Lincoln's office, hoping for a diplomatic appointment to London, the president told an aide, "Oh, I can't see him; I can't see him. I was in hopes he had gone away."[4] It got worse.

The spoils system raged unchecked—in 1881, a lawyer from Illinois named Charles Guiteau lobbied President Garfield for a diplomatic appointment to Vienna. When that post was filled, he set his sights on the Paris consulship. When he didn't get that either, he shot the president twice at point-blank range. Two years after President Garfield's assassination, Congress passed the Pendleton Civil Service Reform Act to (mostly) replace the spoils system with one based on merit rather than connections or political affiliation.

After World War I, in which more than 117,000 Americans died, Representative John Rogers of Massachusetts led the struggle to modernize and professionalize the diplomatic service. "The promise of good diplomacy is the greatest protector of peace," Rogers believed.[5] In 1924, the US Foreign Service was born when Congress passed the Rogers Act, which merged the diplomatic and consular services. Candidates entered the Foreign Service by competitive examination, promotions were based on merit, and pay and benefits were standardized. In 1925, Clifton Wharton became the first African American Foreign Service Officer to enter by competitive exam. His 40-year career included serving as ambassador to Norway.

America's global engagement during and after World War II saw the Foreign Service balloon from just 840 members in 1940 to 7710 a decade later.[6] Post-war institutions and developments such as the United Nations (UN), the Bretton Woods system, the Marshall Plan, and the Cold War kept American diplomats at the forefront of international affairs. As the globe became a geopolitical chessboard, even previously sleepy backwaters like Laos, Nicaragua, and Zaire became "strategic" and the US diplomatic presence approached universality. Today, the United States still has resident embassies in 170 of the world's 195 countries, a worldwide presence that is more a reflection of precedent and globalization than grand strategy.

Alarm bells rang in the Western world in 1949, when the Soviets exploded their first atomic bomb and China fell to Mao Zedong's forces. In January 1950, Alger Hiss, a former Soviet spy working as an attorney at the State Department, was convicted of perjury. Two weeks later, Senator Joseph McCarthy declared that he had a list of 205 Communist Party members who were "working and shaping policy" at the Department of State. McCarthy's Red Scare led to the dismissal of hundreds of State Department personnel on security grounds, including 414 suspected gay and lesbian employees deemed "susceptible to blackmail and … exposed to other pressures because of the highly unconventional character of their personal relationships."[7] It took the State Department years to recover lost trust and influence, a process some say remains incomplete.

Richard Nixon fulminated in 1972 that he aimed to "ruin the Foreign Service. I mean ruin it—the old Foreign Service—and to build a new one. I'm going to do it."[8] He resigned in disgrace before he could carry out his threat, but his frustrations were widely shared.

In the late 1970s, Representative Jim Leach of Iowa (a former FSO) and others began crafting legislation to update the country's creaky, outmoded diplomatic framework. The resulting 159-page Foreign Service Act of 1980 fashioned a modern personnel system that is the basis of today's Foreign Service. The Act's objective was "to strengthen and improve the Foreign Service of the United States." It created the Senior Foreign Service (SFS), added benefits and allowances, standardized pay scales, shored up the retirement system, institutionalized the grievance procedure, and expanded Congressional oversight.

The professionalization of the Foreign Service fostered a culture that was increasingly cosmopolitan, elite (if not elitist), upper-middle class, and quietly patriotic. It prized the ability to write policy-framing analyses (such as George F. Kennan's "Long Telegram" from Moscow), influence foreign decision makers, and win friends for America abroad. Plum overseas assignments were highly valued; many hoped hardship tours or postings to Washington would be rewarded with a desirable onward assignment. Professional advancement depended on how well one operated within the system. Loyalty was expected, and one's corridor reputation and networking skills complemented (or outweighed) formal performance evaluations.

"Pale males from Yale" is how critics often characterized the Foreign Service, dominated as it was by white men from selective universities since its founding. Until 1971, female Foreign Service Officers had to resign if they wed, and until 1972, married FSOs' evaluations included a section on the (unpaid) contributions of their wives. Minorities were also underrepresented: "in 1976, only 4 percent of Foreign Service officers were black," reflected former ambassadors Thomas Pickering and Edward Perkins.[9] The Foreign Service Act of 1980 stipulates that "the Foreign Service should be representative of the American people" and mandates "vigorous implementation of policies and procedures, including affirmative action programs," to ensure equal opportunity and equitable treatment.[10]

In 1976, FSO Alison Palmer launched a class action lawsuit alleging the Department discriminated against female diplomats in hiring, assignments, and promotions. In 1985, Walter Thomas initiated a similar complaint, citing discrimination against African American Foreign Service Officers. The plaintiffs won a series of judgments in 1989 and following years resulting in new assignments, retroactive promotions, back pay, and revised entrance exam scores for over a thousand female or African American officers and applicants. Complying with the Palmer and Thomas consent decrees remains a hallmark of personnel management within the State Department.

In 1991, Mikhail Gorbachev dissolved the Soviet Union, leading Americans to question the nature and degree of US global engagement in an uncertain new world order. Taxpayers, many argued, deserved a peace dividend, which Bill Clinton's Secretaries of State Warren Christopher and Madeleine Albright delivered. Both of them shrank and realigned the State Department from its Cold War configuration. New diplomats were hired at below the rate of attrition, despite the need to staff a score of new embassies in countries emerging from the former Soviet Union and Yugoslavia.

The US Information Agency and the Arms Control and Disarmament Agency were unhappily folded into the State Department in 1999. Staffing more embassies while reducing the overall number of employees—doing more with less—left the Department in a serious bind. "By 2001 more than seven hundred Foreign Service and six hundred civil service positions had no one in them. Training and leave were routinely curtailed," noted Harry Kopp and John Naland.[11]

Al-Qaida's attacks of September 11, 2001 and President Bush's subsequent Global War on Terrorism, thus, caught the US diplomatic service in a weakened state. Two outgrowths of 9/11 further challenged the Foreign Service: (1) a change in regulations required millions more visa applicants to be interviewed by US officials, and (2) diplomats were called to help transform and "democratize" Afghanistan and Iraq after the ouster of the Taliban and Saddam Hussein regimes. The decade of expeditionary diplomacy that followed 2001 saw diplomats kitted out in helmets and flak vests as they became engaged in what Secretary Condoleezza Rice termed transformational diplomacy.

Rice, pondering terrorists' motivations, came to see democracy and good governance as the antidote to terrorism. In a 2006 speech at Georgetown University, she said that the goal of transformational diplomacy was "to work with our many partners around the world, to build and sustain democratic, well-governed states that will respond to the needs of their people and conduct themselves responsibly in the international system."[12]

The Foreign Service Institute held workshops on the basics of transformational diplomacy, a supposedly new approach that prioritized interagency action and results over reporting and analysis. For many FSOs, especially in the management, consular, and public diplomacy cones, this represented no great change from normal operations. Political and economic officers, however, were less clear about their role in building and sustaining democratic, well-governed states amid ongoing wars.

Despite being ill-prepared and uncertain about their functions, Foreign Service personnel helped staff the super-sized embassies in Kabul and Baghdad and the dozens of Provincial Reconstruction Teams (PRTs) across war-torn Afghanistan and Iraq—all on a voluntary basis. The Department incentivized volunteers for the one-year assignments by offering generous pay, approving quick curtailments from disliked jobs, promising to link assignments to a desired next post, and raising expectations that promotion boards would favor those who had done their duty. By 2012, the year after the last PRT closed, approximately 40% of the Foreign Service had reportedly served in Afghanistan or Iraq as expeditionary diplomats.[13]

Individually, some diplomats, like their predecessors in the rural pacification program in Vietnam decades earlier, contributed to notable successes in dangerous, unfamiliar settings. FSO Michael McClellan, who served in Iraq in 2007, described a part of one day like this:

> A couple of incoming rockets hit right outside the palace, knocking a chunk out of the fountain. We dive under our desks, wait for the "all clear," and then get back to work ... Diplomacy in a war zone is not the usual Foreign

Service assignment, but such assignments are becoming increasingly common. We have a vital role to play in conflict zones and, personally, my year in Baghdad has been the most rewarding assignment of my career.[14]

Overall, however, neither the Foreign Service nor the US government as a whole demonstrated the ability to conduct nation-building efficiently in Iraq or Afghanistan. Even had the Foreign Service been fully staffed, better trained, and more closely coordinated with other US government agencies, it seems unlikely that Afghanistan and Iraq could have been quickly transformed into peaceful, prosperous democracies.

The 2016 election of Donald Trump presented the State Department with a host of new challenges, including a proposed 31% cut in the foreign affairs budget (rejected by Congress) and the devaluing of institutions, agreements, alliances, and diplomatic norms undergirding the post-war liberal international system. Secretary Rex Tillerson presided over a year-long hiring freeze, numerous senior-level vacancies, and plummeting morale. President Trump's transactional "America First" approach to diplomacy seemed to undermine long-standing American efforts to promote democracy, human rights, and the rule of law. The Trump White House frequently expressed disdain for the advice of professionals in intelligence, diplomacy, security, legal, and other fields, and the president, sometimes, announced unscripted foreign policy initiatives or taunts via Twitter. Diplomatic, in the sense of being courteous or well-mannered, is a not term often associated with President Trump's style of global engagement.

Profile

"The United States diplomatic corps needs to be in every corner, every stretch of the world, executing missions on behalf of this country," Secretary of State Mike Pompeo told assembled State Department employees in May 2018.[15] His use of the phrase "diplomatic corps" was meant to be blurrily inclusive, as the State Department crowd consisted of Civil Service employees, FSOs, Foreign Service specialists, political appointees, contractors, interns, and others. Normally, the term diplomatic corps refers to the body of foreign diplomats posted in a capital city, but it often means just the foreign ambassadors as a group, as in "the diplomatic corps was convoked by the foreign minister today." Pompeo sought to reconfirm the Department's commitment to the "universality" of America's diplomatic engagement, downplay divisions or differences among State Department employees, and reenergize the organization after the funk many employees felt following Tillerson's year as secretary.

The State Department's 7895 Foreign Service Officers are confirmed by the Senate, commissioned by the president, and sworn to support and defend the US constitution. According to the Foreign Service Act of 1980, they are to be characterized by excellence and professionalism and are "to provide the highest caliber of representation in the conduct of foreign affairs."[16] Sometimes called Foreign Service generalists, they spend about two-thirds of their careers abroad staffing 277 US embassies, consulates, and other posts. Although they are generalists, each is hired in one of five career tracks (informally called "cones")—political, economic, public diplomacy, consular, or management—in which they will serve the bulk of their assignments.

FSOs make up less than 11% of the State Department's full-time, permanent staff of 75,382.[17] State is the only cabinet-level department made up mostly of non-Americans. Globally, "locally employed staff" comprise 66% of State Department employees. Many of these foreign nationals serve as embassy clerks, translators, receptionists, or drivers; about 37,000 of the approximately 50,000 foreign national employees work as security guards at American diplomatic posts.[18] Locally employed staff, who outnumber Americans at most posts, provide continuity and unsurpassed local knowledge. Working for the US embassy brings status, good pay by local standards, and, in some cases, the opportunity to immigrate to the United States after a successful career. Such benefits are well earned in the many countries where foreign nationals serve at a great risk to themselves and their families.

The Foreign Service's 5801 specialists include doctors, diplomatic security agents, couriers, IT specialists, construction engineers, office management specialists, and others. Unlike FSOs, they do not enter primarily by competitive exam, but are hired based on qualifications and experience. Like FSOs, specialists spend about two-thirds of their careers abroad. The Bureau of Diplomatic Security has a large number of Foreign Service security specialists, about 300 of whom work abroad. Another 1200 or so are assigned domestically, in part to staff dozens of investigative field offices across the United States.[19]

More members of the Civil Service work in the State Department than do either FSOs or Foreign Service specialists. Most of the 10,191 Civil Service employees spend all their careers in Washington and can remain in the same job for decades. The only way they can be promoted is to move to a higher grade job.

Additionally, more than 100 working-level political appointees in the Department fill "special assistant" or similar positions, often given to campaign staffers.[20] The State Department offers internships to about 2000 university students each year, with half interning in Washington and half overseas. The State Department has some 3300 overseas short-term positions filled by family members of American employees at post. EFMs (for "Eligible Family Members") teach English, answer the mail, serve as community liaison officers, and carry out other support jobs at embassies and consulates.

Nobody knows exactly how many contractors work at or for the State Department, but their number is in thousands. Some are hired individually on personal services contracts. Many more are hired for projects and programs by well-connected institutional contractors.[21] For example, in 2007, the State Department's counter-narcotics program for Afghanistan and Pakistan contracted with DynCorp, a Virginia-based company, to train and support Afghan and Pakistani anti-drug forces and programs. Some 1200 DynCorp contractors or subcontractors were on the ground in Afghanistan and Pakistan. Of those, about 700 were "shooters" (i.e., armed security contractors) from the United States, Bosnia, South Africa, Nepal, and elsewhere. DynCorp operated a small fleet of helicopters and airplanes, had fortified residential compounds, and drove bulletproof SUVs around Afghanistan.[22] None of the 1200 contractors was a State Department employee, but some confusingly described themselves as working "for" or "with" the State Department.

Thus, FSOs make up a small portion of State Department employees; an FSO's co-workers might be Foreign Service specialists, locally employed staff, Civil Service employees, interns, political appointees, personal service contractors, or EFMs. A few other federal agencies also employ FSOs, such as the US Agency for International Development and the Departments of Commerce and Agriculture, but 90% of FSOs work for State. Each agency hires and promotes FSOs separately and slightly differently.

At embassies, FSOs often work in the section corresponding to their career track (political, economic, management, consular, or public diplomacy) headed by a section chief. Section chiefs report to the deputy chief of mission (DCM), who in turn is supervised by the ambassador or chief of mission. Most consulates and consulates general are located in important cities outside the capital and are "constituent posts" of an embassy. The FSO who heads a consulate general is called the principal officer or consul general (a term that can confusingly also mean the embassy's consular section chief).

In Washington, the secretary and deputy secretary supervise the half dozen or so undersecretaries, who oversee a "family" of bureaus working on similar issues. The bureau is the main work unit in the Department. Headed by an assistant secretary, bureaus typically have about 210 employees and are subdivided by office and, then, country "desk." For example, between the desk officer for Ireland and the secretary are six layers of bureaucracy: deputy office director, office director, deputy assistant secretary, principal deputy assistant secretary, assistant secretary, undersecretary, and the deputy secretary. The Department's bureaucracy is turfy, slow, and dauntingly hierarchical.

The State Department's 25 or so functional bureaus each deal with a set of related issues (e.g., the Bureau of Population, Refugees, and Migration) and are mainly staffed by Civil Service employees. In contrast, Foreign Service members form a majority in the six regional bureaus dealing with specific geographic areas.[23] FSOs who serve in Washington prefer to work in one of the regional bureaus, in part because they control most overseas assignments. Accordingly, an FSO interested in Japan might pursue a domestic assignment in the Bureau of East Asia and Pacific Affairs. If she does well in the bureau, she may have the inside track for an onward assignment to Embassy Tokyo or Consulate General Sapporo.

Recruitment and Selection

The three-stage Foreign Service Officer selection process is famously competitive; over the past decade, less than 3% of those who start the process landed jobs. About 15,000–20,000 people take the Foreign Service Officer Test (FSOT) in a normal year, although a surge of patriotism saw over 31,000 applicants in 2002. In 2017, the year of the Trump/Tillerson hiring freeze, just 9500 people took the exam.[24] The FSOT, which is free to take, tests job knowledge and English expression, and requires applicants to write a short essay and provide biographic information. In most years, about 40% of those taking the FSOT pass and move on to the second stage, the Qualifications Evaluation Panel (QEP).

The QEP, added in 2007, employs a "total-candidate" approach to winnow out those not possessing the right stuff. Candidates, after submitting six short personal narratives, are rank ordered based on education and work experience, language aptitude, and other attributes. The QEP yields a more diverse candidate pool for the Foreign Service Oral Assessment (FSOA) than did the pre-2007 practice of relying solely on the written exam. Typically, about 30% of candidates pass the QEP.

Given projected needs of the service by career track, top-ranked candidates in each cone are invited to Washington to take the FSOA. In a tense, day-long series of activities, candidates participate in small group simulations, are individually interviewed by a battery of examiners, and do a management-oriented "in-box" exercise. At the end of the grueling day, candidates are told on the spot whether or not they passed. If they fail, they are free to start over at the FSOT stage. The 40% or so who pass the FSOA are taken into another room and begin filling out the massive security clearance questionnaire.

FSOA passers, then, must receive a Top Secret security clearance, pass a suitability review, and get a medical clearance for world-wide availability. The security clearance aims to weed out actual or potential spies or terrorists, while the suitability review tries to screen out those unfit on other grounds (spouse beaters, chronic bankrupts, and the like).

To summarize, of every 100 people who take the written exam, about 40 pass and continue to the Qualifications Evaluation Panel. At the QEP stage, approximately 12 pass and are then invited to the Oral Assessment. Of the dozen who take the FSOA, maybe five pass. Of those five, perhaps one fails to get all three clearances. The four remaining candidates are placed on a waiting list called the register.

The four candidates who made it to the register are ranked by FSOT results and other factors. They join other candidates already on the register. Veterans get a bit of extra credit, as do those fluent in "critical-needs" languages like Arabic, Mandarin, or Dari. Candidates with top rankings are offered jobs as positions become available. Those who don't get off the register within 18 months are out—they can reapply by starting over at the FSOT stage. Making it onto the register but not landing a job is referred to as "dying on the vine." This might eliminate the lowest ranked of our four remaining candidates. At the end of the year-long process, out of the original 100 applicants, just three will have secured jobs as Foreign Service Officers.

How does the State Department select FSOs from among the many highly qualified candidates? While every human interaction involves some subjectivity, the Bureau of Human Resources' Board of Examiners is trained to assess candidates objectively at each stage of the process based on selection criteria called the 13 Dimensions. Candidates receive a score on each dimension, the individual dimension scores are added together, and then candidates are rank ordered by total score. Those at the top move on to the next stage of the process—a few are ultimately offered jobs. The dimensions are: composure, cultural adaptability, experience and motivation, information integration and analysis, initiative and leadership, judgment, objectivity and integrity, oral communication, planning and organizing, resourcefulness, working with others, written communication, and quantitative analysis. During the Oral Assessment, the examiners strive to maintain strict professional neutrality to avoid any unintended clues or special encouragement to candidates. Well-prepared candidates come to the FSOA primed to demonstrate and explain their personal competence in each of the 13 dimensions.

In addition to this highly competitive traditional route into the Foreign Service, about 60 new FSOs enter each year via the Pickering and Rangel fellowship programs aimed at increasing the number of minorities, women, and candidates with financial need. Successful applicants for the Pickering and Rangel fellowships receive funding for a two-year master's degree and two paid summer internships. After completing his or her master's degree, a fellow may skip the FSOT and QEP portions of the selection process and go right to the oral assessment. Those who pass the FSOA, and the vast majority do, bypass the register and go directly into the next A-100 orientation class. The Pickering and Rangel programs each offer about 30 fellowships a year, with successful candidates selected from a pool of hundreds of applicants. FSO Derek Hogan was named ambassador to Moldova by President Trump in 2018, the first Pickering fellow to make it to the ambassadorial ranks since the program's founding in 1992.

The intake of new FSOs considerably varies by year. During the "peace dividend" era of the 1990s, only about 150 new officers were hired per year, fewer than the number of FSOs who retired, died, or resigned.[25] In 2001, incoming Secretary Colin Powell, aghast at the vacancies, staffing gaps, and lack of training opportunities for FSOs, proposed a three-year hiring surge called the Diplomatic Readiness Initiative. Its objective was to "provide us with the additional personnel to fill vacancies, create a training float, provide bench strength to respond to crises and minimize staffing gaps."[26] Secretary Powell argued that the Department needed an excess of personnel over positions to enable in-service training (the "training float") while simultaneously avoiding debilitating staffing gaps. The Initiative largely succeeded in getting more FSOs on board—467 new officers were hired in 2002 alone.[27] Nonetheless, wars in Afghanistan and Iraq meant that Powell's 15% training float never materialized—most of the Initiative's substantial staffing increase was "absorbed by the demand for personnel in Afghanistan and Iraq."[28]

During the era of expeditionary diplomacy, staffing gaps and vacancies reappeared, prompting Secretary Hillary Clinton in 2009 to launch an initiative called Diplomacy 3.0, aimed at growing the Foreign Service by 25%. Clinton's plan got off to a good start, as 716 new officers were hired in 2010, perhaps the largest annual intake in modern times.[29] Due to budget restraints and sequestration, however, Diplomacy 3.0 was not sustainable; by 2013, the number of new FSOs fell to 234.

Women, a majority of US college graduates, now also make up a majority of incoming FSOs. An informal analysis of group photos of recent A-100 classes suggests that women constitute slightly more than half of new American diplomats. When considering all ranks, 41% of FSOs were women in 2018. Women are a smaller minority among Foreign Service specialists (just 29% of the total), but outnumber men among the State Department's Civil Service employees. By career track, women are relatively overrepresented in the consular and public diplomacy cones.

Minority recruitment, in contrast, has been more of a challenge for the Foreign Service. Among other efforts to increase minority recruiting, the Department assigns 16 officers to the Diplomats in Residence program to conduct outreach and recruitment on college campuses with substantial numbers of minority students. Data on incoming minority FSOs are difficult to parse out. Some insights can be gleaned from the promotion statistics broken down by race and ethnicity of 904 relatively junior officers competing in 2017 for promotion to FS-03, which typically happens after an FSO's second assignment. Of this group, 7% were African American, 7% Hispanic, and 8% Asian. The number of Asians, combined with those listed as "multi-race," was larger than the collective total of African Americans and Hispanics. All told, 78% of the group consisted of non-Hispanic white officers.[30] Based on this analysis, whites, Asians, and "multi-race" individuals make up a larger percentage of relatively junior Foreign Service Officers than they do of the general American population of 25–34-year-olds.[31]

While there is no education or work experience requirement for becoming a Foreign Service Officer, a majority of new FSOs have an advanced degree and several years of real-world experience.[32] Some have served in the military or Peace Corps, and many have taught or studied overseas.

Others have worked abroad for faith-based or non-governmental organizations. New American diplomats are well-traveled, bright, tech-savvy, and are, on average, about 31 years old.

Professional Development and Training

Enthusiastic new Foreign Service Officers report for duty at the Foreign Service Institute (FSI), a leafy campus in northern Virginia that originally housed a finishing school for young women and later served as the World War II cryptology base that cracked key Japanese codes. Some might snap a selfie with the statue of Ben Franklin before filing in to join 40–90 other new FSOs in a six-week orientation course still called A-100 (after the course's room number in another building in a previous century). Classmates become professional peers and often lifelong friends. After receiving the "bid list" of open assignments, A-100 class members indicate their relative preference for each posting. Some are eager to head off to Bamako as assistant general services officer, hoping to avoid being sent to Tijuana as vice consul. Others feel just the opposite. Assignments are announced on "Flag Day" amid excitement, joy, and sometimes dismay. (Officers are presented with the national flag for their first post, sometimes prompting a scramble to identify the nation that matches the flag.)

Entry-level officers (ELOs) undertake at least one consular tour in their first two assignments, regardless of cone. The State Department faces a global tsunami of visa applications—one consulate in southern China issued over one million visas in 2015.[33] The United States is one of the world's top destinations for immigrants and visitors, most of whom need visas. In addition, some nine million Americans live abroad and rely on embassies for a variety of citizen services. Since 9/11, increased scrutiny of visa applicants has meant more consular officers interviewing applicants. Despite the rise in the number of entry-level consular officers doing visa interviews, there are relatively few mid-level consular positions. Rather than hire large numbers of new consular cone FSOs (who would eventually face problems getting promoted into the small number of mid-level consular jobs), the Department requires all officers to do a consular tour to help with the huge workload. Recently, a program for short-term American hires called Consular Fellows was created to help alleviate staffing shortfalls in high-demand consular sections around the world.

Assigning first-tour officers to visa mills is not ideal, but it does have a couple of positive impacts: it thickens the skin and shrinks the head. Vice consuls can be subjected to lies, threats, bribes, and constant cajoling from visa applicants, everyday acquaintances, and even other embassy employees. It teaches them to be tough, principled, and polite in the face of adversity. It also is a humbling, grinding experience. Interviewing 100 Dominicans a day who want to visit their cousins in New York is not glamorous or fun. It teaches humility and perspective to inexperienced diplomats, some of whom might have harbored inflated views of their rightful place in America's foreign policy apparatus.

Before heading to their first assignment, FSOs commonly spend months in training at FSI. After A-100, entry-level officers (ELOs) can spend up to six months of language training, in addition to taking various tradecraft, area studies, and specialized classes at FSI. An ELO going to Rio de Janeiro as vice consul might get six months of Portuguese language training, take the rigorous nine-week consular tradecraft course, enroll in the basic South America area studies course on the history, culture, politics, and economics of the region, participate in the week-long Foreign Affairs Counter-Threat security course (sometimes called "flash-bang"), and take the mandatory short courses on sexual harassment prevention and safeguarding classified information.

Tradecraft courses run from the general to the specialized. For example, prior to their initial assignments, political officers take the basic three-week "Political Tradecraft" course at FSI to further develop professional skills and attitudes. Reporting and analysis, advocacy, contact building, briefing skills, and the context of global issues are stressed. Later in their careers, they take more specialized courses, such as the three-day class on "International Terrorism: Understanding the Threat and Formulating the Response" or "International Negotiation: Art and Skills." Upon his or her first assignment as an embassy's political section chief, an officer would take the week-long "Political Counselor Seminar" that focuses on more complex political and leadership skills and perspectives.

After two tours, usually both overseas, most FSOs get "tenure" and return to the Department for their third tours. Many hope one day to become an ambassador, but the nearer term career focus for most is to earn a favorable annual Employee Evaluation Report (EER), secure a good onward assignment, and get promoted to the next highest rank quickly. The Foreign Service is an "up-or-out" system in which officers must advance to the next rank within a given number of years.

Promotion numbers are limited, competitive, and granted on merit. Who gets promoted and why?

An FSO's performance is evaluated annually by his or her supervisor (the rating officer) on six "core precepts": leadership skills, managerial skills, interpersonal skills, communication and foreign language skills, intellectual skills, and substantive knowledge. Substantive knowledge, for example, includes familiarity with foreign cultures, professional expertise, institutional knowledge, and other factors. These areas are graduated by rank; entry-level officers have lower standards on each precept than do mid-level or senior officers. The reviewing officer (the rating officer's boss), then, comments on the FSO's performance and can agree or disagree with the rating officer's evaluation. The employee is permitted a final comment, after which the entire Employee Evaluation Report goes to the promotion panel for rank ordering.

FSOs compete for promotion against others at their grade for a limited number of available positions at the next highest rank. Career tracks also come into play, as there must be a rough match by cone (economic, management, consular, etc.) of those promoted to the number of available positions in their career track at the next highest rank. It is a complicated, time-consuming, and closely scrutinized process.

There is no real numerical or categorical summary of the EER; the evaluation is entirely prose. Thus, an employee whose supervisor is a talented writer has a better chance of promotion than others. Events on the ground also influence promotions; heroic leadership in the wake of a natural or man-made disaster provides richer EER fodder than does a competent performance in a sleepy backwater or quiet cubicle.

Officers cannot rest on their laurels or afford to get a bland evaluation, which could lead to being forced out for "time in class," similar to a shot-clock violation in basketball. Furthermore, every year a few low-ranked officers at each grade are "selected out" for poor performance.

Like any organization, the Foreign Service has a unique culture, quite different from that of the military or even from the State Department's Civil Service employees. The Foreign Service values improvization, intuition, and experience. Most FSOs are slightly introverted, service-oriented, and have a high need for affiliation. While the military spent most of the 25 years between the fall of Saigon and the fall of the World Trade Center planning and exercising, US diplomats were out in the field *doing* diplomacy.

Continuous diplomacy was vital during the Cold War to counter ongoing Soviet and other Communist efforts and to promote American interests and values. It continues apace in the post-Cold War era in the face of

Islamist terrorism and the increasing importance of transnational issues such as pandemics, refugee flows, the globalized economy, human trafficking, and environmental issues. US diplomats are engaged on a daily basis to build ties with their host governments, international organizations, third-country diplomats, and the general public of the host countries.

Globalization, the faster movement of people, things, and money due to advances in telecommunications and transportation, makes continuous diplomacy indispensable. For instance, sudden refugee flows from an Ebola-stricken region of Congo into South Sudan could have bilateral, regional, and global implications. American diplomats in the South Sudanese capital of Juba need to have excellent working relations with local officials, international organizations like the World Health Organization, UN peacekeepers, governors and other provincial strongmen, and opposition figures to help coordinate a response to a potential catastrophic jump of Ebola into war-torn South Sudan.

The array of bilateral and multilateral issues addressed by each embassy is large and growing. Embassies lobby their host governments for supporting votes in the United Nations and other international organizations, even when the issue is not directly relevant to the bilateral relationship. US diplomats posted in Paramaribo, for example, may seek Suriname's support in the UN General Assembly on an upcoming vote on whaling.

This decades-long experience of planning versus doing (as some diplomats oversimplified the decades after Vietnam) affected both the military and the Foreign Service. When thrust together in nation-building operations in Afghanistan and Iraq, diplomats and soldiers found pronounced differences in each other's perspectives and approaches. The 1998 article by FSO Rosemary Hansen and LTC Rick Rife called "Defense is from Mars, State is from Venus" was widely read by diplomats and military officers trying to decipher the strange customs of the other.[34]

Compared to FSOs, the State Department's Civil Service employees (many of whom dislike the term "civil servant") as a group are more diverse, more female, less well educated and paid, and have been in their current jobs much longer. The two different personnel systems have produced two different organizational cultures. At times, they complement each other. Relations between FSOs and Civil Service employees are generally constructive, although some Civil Service employees view FSOs working in Washington as transient upstarts and a few FSOs see Civil Service employees as stodgy clock punchers. The Bureau of Human Resources, usually headed by a Foreign Service Officer, is overwhelmingly staffed by Civil Service employees. The two cultures, therefore, both influence the Department's assignments, promotions, and other aspects of the institution's personnel management, but many FSOs feel the Civil Service culture is paramount in this key bureau.

Most FSOs can expect to serve for 20–30 years, steadily moving up the ranks from the entry-level grade FS-05 (similar to a lieutenant) to that of FS-01 (equivalent to a full colonel). FSOs can retire at age 50 if they have 20 years of service. As most enter at about age 30, the age "50 with 20" years mark often coincides. Officers at the FS-01 rank may "open their window" to compete for promotion into the Senior Foreign Service (SFS), which has three grades equivalent to one-, two-, and three-star generals. Those who don't make it within six years must retire.

Assignments as deputy chiefs of mission, principal officers, and ambassadors are highly prized and extremely competitive. Most are drawn from the ranks of the Senior Foreign Service. These plum jobs often go to FSOs with extensive regional experience, outstanding corridor reputations, and an influential senior proponent in the relevant regional bureau and in HR.

The 1011 SFS members were 89% white and 68% male in 2018. They are relatively well paid, with base salaries ranging from $126,148 to $189,600.[35] Starting FS-05s, in contrast, make $45,319 a year (77% of the 2016 median US household income).

"We have a retention problem," said Linda Thomas-Greenfield, a former director general of the Foreign Service, in the 2014 PBS documentary "The Foreign Service in Search of Diversity." Overall, the Foreign Service has a very high retention rate by federal government standards. Minorities and women, however, drop out more often than white males, as seen by the large percentage of white males in the Senior Foreign Service.

Why? Some clues about relative success are available in the promotion statistics of the 904 second-tour FSOs discussed above. More men than women were promoted (38% of men vs. 30% of women). The promotion rate of Hispanics was significantly below that of non-Hispanics (27% vs. 36%). By race, Asians were promoted at a higher rate (42%) than whites (35%) or African Americans (31%). Of the 316 officers promoted to FS-03 in 2017, 19 were African American.[36] Slow merit-based promotion rates can lead to discouragement, which can prompt resignations.

What accounts for these discrepancies? Institutional bias could be the answer, despite the fact that only one of the past seven directors general of the Foreign Service (the head of human resources) has been a non-Hispanic white male. Random chance could play a role. Perhaps, some officers came into the job better prepared for success in the Foreign Service than others. The overseas work environment also influences performance—minority and female officers encounter substantial discrimination in some societies, making it more difficult for them to excel at their jobs. Female FSOs in "tandem couples" also tend to become the "trailing spouses," often accepting less advantageous positions to serve together with FSO spouses at the risk of undercutting their own career growth. The Department's usual response to the ongoing retention problem is to encourage more mentoring.

"Take care of your people," said Colin Powell as he addressed State Department employees in 2003, adding, "How do you take care of them? You train them."[37] Previously, the State Department's capstone senior training experience was the prestigious Senior Seminar, which paired 15 rising State Department employees with an equal number of members of other foreign affairs agencies for an intensive, nine-month seminar on US foreign policy.

Secretary Powell scrapped the Senior Seminar (which he deemed too small) in favor of leadership and management training along each step of an FSO's career. Mid-level FSOs now take three leadership courses at FSI. Once promoted into the Senior Foreign Service, officers take another two-week leadership course, while the first deputy chief of mission assignment is preceded by a three-week long leadership seminar. Those selected for ambassador attend yet another leadership course at FSI. FSOs who become ambassadors will have taken at least six leadership courses at FSI, in addition to a dozen area studies, language, and tradecraft courses over the years.

Professional development opportunities for FSOs include year-long assignments to academic institutions where FSOs take courses and can earn a master's degree. Each year, over 100 slots are available at Princeton, the National Defense University, the Army War College, the National Intelligence University, and elsewhere. These opportunities have begun to attract serious bidders, and most are filled every year. The Department also deploys about 35 officers as faculty advisors to teach at West Point, Georgetown, George Washington, and other universities.[38]

Traditionally, FSOs have not viewed academic and faculty advisor assignments as career enhancing, although this is changing. Many Millennials view an advanced degree as imperative for a post-Foreign Service career. Further, FSOs are finding that extended academic training leads to faster promotions and better onward assignments. As many of the academic opportunities are at military universities, FSOs who spend a year thinking broadly with a mix of colleagues from the military and other agencies gain insights (both academic and interagency) that may improve their performance, and thus help win promotions and desirable assignments.

Leadership

Most presidents move quickly to fill the scores of senior State Department positions listed in the Plum Book—the register of some 7000 jobs "subject to noncompetitive appointment," about 1400 of which require Senate confirmation. These political appointments, the residue of the Jacksonian spoils system, include ambassadorships and most of the top four layers of the State Department's bureaucracy—even including a few jobs at the level of deputy assistant secretary.

Some political appointees virtually buy their positions. For example, a West Coast venture capitalist donated more than $500,000 to the Obama campaign and gave $300,000 for his inauguration ceremonies before being named ambassador to picturesque Luxembourg. As ambassador, her management style was characterized by the Office of the Inspector General as "aggressive, bullying, hostile, and intimidating." The Inspector General also highlighted her questionable expenditures on travel, wine, and liquor.[39] FSOs serving in her embassy asked to be transferred to Iraq or Afghanistan. She may be an egregious example, but most FSOs presume political appointees to be "incompetent until proven otherwise."[40] A number have served with distinction.

About 30% of ambassadorships in recent years have been filled by political appointees; most of the rest go to career diplomats. Where does the typical campaign bundler want to go as ambassador? Somewhere safe, clean, healthy, scenic, and in Europe. Of the first 24 ambassadorial nominees President Trump named to European countries, only two were career diplomats. Not surprisingly, of Trump's first 18 nominees to African ambassadorships, only one was a political appointee (to Kenya).

Domestically, political appointees populate the State Department's policy-level ranks. They tend to have more government experience than politically appointed (non-career) ambassadors. During the Ford administration, fully 61% of top jobs (assistant secretary and above) went to FSOs, but by the Obama years, that number had fallen to about 25%.[41] President Jimmy Carter started the trend toward increased politicization when he took eight former FSOs (including Richard Holbrooke and Tony Lake) who had resigned during the Vietnam War era and made them assistant secretaries. Sometimes called the "Baby Eight," all were under the age of 38.[42] Of President Trump's first 35 senior appointees to domestic State Department positions, just four (11%) were FSOs.[43]

An ambassador represents the person of the president. In the title "ambassador extraordinary and plenipotentiary," extraordinary indicates only for a specific assignment and plenipotentiary means full of power. Technically, while in his or her country of assignment an ambassador, as the president's personal representative, outranks visiting cabinet secretaries. Sometimes, special envoys or advisors are given ambassadorial rank to provide status in dealing with foreign entities.

Ambassadors who are chiefs of mission receive a letter of instruction from the president specifying that he or she is not just responsible for the embassy's State Department component, but for the activities of all executive branch employees in country (with two exceptions). An excerpt from an ambassadorial letter of instruction sent by President George W. Bush emphasizes this point: "As Chief of Mission, you have full responsibility for the direction, coordination, and supervision of all United States Government executive branch employees in the State of Eritrea, regardless of their employment categories or location, except those under command of a US area military commander or on the staff of an international organization. Except for the activities of the personnel exempted above, you are in charge of all executive branch activities and operations in your Mission."[44] This chief of mission mandate over the entire executive branch is essential. As a former ambassador observed, "Since agencies cannot instruct each other, effective management of manifold overseas activities is often difficult from Washington...."[45] The key to a successful embassy is an ambassador who is on top of all US government activities in his or her mission.

During the Obama administration, State Department employees made up less than 50% of American employees at nearly 50 diplomatic posts. In total, about 40% of American employees at all posts worked for agencies other than the State Department.[46] In some consulates or embassies, employees of USAID, the Drug Enforcement Agency, or the Defense Department were the largest single contingent. Regional hubs attracted staffing from a host of executive branch agencies; only about 46% of Americans working in Paris, Bangkok, and Nairobi were State Department employees. Most Americans working at the eight US consulates in Canada were employees of the Department of Homeland Security (DHS), clearing America-bound passengers for flights to US airports. In Winnipeg, the ratio was 30 American employees of other agencies (mostly DHS) for each State Department employee. Thus, it is crucial that ambassadors direct and supervise all US employees, not just those of the State Department, to ensure effective interagency coordination at post.

Ambassadors, both career and non-career, rely heavily on their deputy chiefs of mission to help run the embassy. A typical guideline from an ambassador to a DCM is, "I'll tell you where I want this ship to go. Your job is to get us there."[47]

In many embassies, the DCM is the rating or reviewing officer of most Foreign Service personnel at post; thus, he or she is almost everyone's boss. Having no peer at post and lacking chief of mission authority over other agencies, a DCM's job requires finesse and firmness, especially at posts where State Department employees are in the minority. When the ambassador is temporarily away from post, the DCM serves as acting ambassador, called the *chargé d'affaires ad interim*. Being a successful DCM is the path to an ambassadorship; most career ambassadors have served as DCM once or twice.

Role in Foreign Policy Making

The State Department provides this clear (if oversimplified) description of how foreign policy is made and implemented:

> Under the Constitution, the President of the United States determines U.S. foreign policy. The Secretary of State, appointed by the President with the advice and consent of the Senate, is the President's chief foreign affairs adviser. The Secretary carries out the President's foreign policies through the State Department and the Foreign Service of the United States.[48]

Thus, the secretary has two roles. He or she advises the president on foreign policy and, once the president decides what the policy is, the secretary implements it via the State Department and Foreign Service. In reality, of course, the process is much more tangled.

Dozens of other departments and agencies are active players in the foreign policy process; at times, some wield more clout than the State Department. When President Trump proposed cutting State's budget by 31% in 2018, he also called for a $52 billion bump-up to the Defense Department's huge budget—an addition nearly equal to the entire foreign affairs budget. The Pentagon has 1.3 million active duty troops and over 740,000 civilian employees, making it the nation's largest employer.

To highlight the colossal size disparity between the State Department and Department of Defense (DOD), sometimes, diplomats claim that the Pentagon has more musicians than the State Department has diplomats. Not true, says *PolitiFact*, noting that the Defense Department has 6500 musicians, compared to the State Department's 7900 diplomats. However, *PolitiFact's* comparison specified "instrumental musicians" and did not include the military's many vocal musicians.[49] In any case, the Defense Department dwarfs the State Department in every respect.

The Intelligence Community, comprising 17 agencies (including State's small but highly regarded Bureau of Intelligence and Research), has an overall budget and workforce much larger than that of the State Department. In his book *War on Peace: The End of Diplomacy and the Decline of American Influence*, former State Department political appointee Ronan Farrow decries what he sees as "the steady dissolution of the State Department" and the "trend of sidelined diplomats and ascendant soldiers and spies ..."[50]

The "interagency," a term derived from the interagency policy process, is the hurly-burly of US government agencies competing for a piece of the national security or foreign policy pie. The National Security Council (NSC) staff, located in the Old Executive Office Building right next to the White House, serves both as foreign policy referee and as heavyweight participant. The National Security Council staff, ranging in size from around 75 professionals under George H.W. Bush to as many as 300 under Barack Obama, is made up of political appointees and individuals detailed from the State Department, Department of Defense (military and civilian), Intelligence Community, and other federal agencies.

Most policy decisions are taken at the level of the NSC's Deputies Committee (attended by deputy secretaries and the equivalent) or one of the lower Policy Planning Committees (PPCs) (assistant secretaries and the equivalent). Only the most important policy issues reach the Principals Committee (cabinet secretaries) or the entire National Security Council (which includes the president).

At a typical Policy Planning Committee (PPC) meeting on Venezuela, for example, the State Department's Assistant Secretary for Western Hemisphere Affairs (either an FSO or a political appointee with some regional experience) will be one of a dozen or so voices in the meeting, which is chaired by an NSC staffer. PPC members or their senior assistants often confer informally in advance and arrive at a general policy direction prior to the actual meeting. The State Department's view normally carries substantial weight in the deliberations, unless the issue is a specialized or technical matter squarely in another agency's bailiwick. Decisions reached at the PPC level usually constitute policy on issues of low to medium importance, whereas the Deputies Committee decides policy on topics of higher priority.

While the president is ultimately responsible for making foreign policy, diplomats play a key role in shaping the policy debate, influencing policy choices, and to some extent making policy as they administer it. This occurs in various ways.

In Washington, diplomats prepare policy background and briefing materials for senior State Department officials, serve as advisors and staffers to senior officials, and engage in interagency policy debates. Those who work in the State Department's Office of Policy Planning or who are seconded to the National Security Council are apt to be particularly influential in framing policy.

Embassy cables (formal written communications) are a prime source of information on numerous policy issues. After the 2010 WikiLeaks debacle, *New York Times* columnist Roger Cohen wrote: "Let's hear it for the men and women of the US Foreign Service! They are, to judge from the WikiLeaks dump of a quarter-million of their private or secret cables, thoughtful, well-informed and dedicated servants of the American interest who write clear, declarative English sentences."[51]

Reporting cables, which all go out under the ambassador's name, often conclude with a paragraph titled "comment" that gives post's view on the issue along with policy recommendations. An embassy cable's "so what" and "next steps" paragraph can be influential in shaping the State Department's policy position on a given issue, particularly those that relate to the bilateral relationship.

Visiting Congressional and other VIP delegations provide another avenue of influence for diplomats overseas, as visitors often look to the embassy's diplomats as the local experts on a range of policy issues. Presidential visits often come with an entourage numbering in the hundreds, requiring embassy staff to serve as control officers for senior delegation members, work as site officers and note takers at specific meetings, and follow up on action items at the conclusion of the visit.

Foreign policy can be made as it is administered, within limits. Diplomats facing emergency situations sometimes make snap decisions, only informing the State Department after the fact. On most issues, the timing and rank of the diplomat proposing a course of action can substantially affect the likelihood of its acceptance. Asking a first-tour political officer to telephone the Foreign Ministry on a Friday afternoon seeking host government action or approval is unlikely to be fruitful. However, if the ambassador were to meet in person with the Foreign Minister with the same request on a Tuesday morning, chances of acceptance improve significantly. Sometimes individual personalities impact policy outcomes, such as Richard Holbrooke's blustery engagement leading up to the Dayton Accords or Ryan Crocker's hard-nosed leadership in mustering diplomatic support for President Bush's 2007 surge in Iraq.

Preparations for the Future

"Diplomacy, then, is persuasion in the shadow of power," stated Colin Powell. "Diplomacy without power is just naked pleading," he added.[52] A diplomat from the miniscule Republic of Tuvalu, equally skilled in every way as her American counterpart, would be much less persuasive, given the vast differences in the two countries' abilities to coerce, induce, and attract others. In promoting America's interests and values overseas, American power gives US diplomats a huge inherent advantage compared to diplomats of most other countries.

Persuasion is also enhanced by trust, which is often fostered by friendships, respect, and mutual interest. Building relationships with foreigners has long been a strong suit of US diplomats. "Diplomacy is still largely about getting other governments to do what your government wants, and all governments are made up of people," said former FSO James Dobbins. "Identifying the right people to talk to and establishing a degree of mutual trust are the first steps toward almost any objective," he concluded.[53]

America's substantial soft power, arising from its attractiveness to other people, has added clout to US diplomacy, as does the country's hard power—the ability to coerce or induce others. Polls point to steep global declines in the approval of US leadership in the Trump era; this will likely diminish the country's soft power and the ability of US diplomats to persuade others to do what American wants.

How effectively are American diplomats promoting American interests and values?

"Our diplomatic corps is the finest in the world," testified R. Nicholas Burns to the House Committee on Foreign Affairs in 2017. Burns, a former diplomat now teaching at Harvard, noted that without "the respect and resources they deserve," our diplomats' ability to maintain their expertise and high standards of performance would be in jeopardy.[54] "In general, we are better staffed, better informed, and our networks are stronger than other embassies," observed an American diplomat with postings in Europe and Latin America.[55] Most FSOs would agree. As the world's largest diplomatic service, representing as it does the most powerful country in the world, something would be seriously amiss if America's diplomatic service was not able to successfully foster US interests and values around the globe.

Some, however, contend that the Foreign Service isn't as good as it should be. "Our diplomats punch below their weight and carry less influence than our country's power ought to deliver," claimed Kori Schake in her book *State of Disrepair: Fixing the Culture and Practice of the State Department*. In contrast to the effective US military, in Schake's view, "we choose to fund it [the State Department] penuriously, set no real standards for its performance, and populate it with leaders who do not invest in making the institution or its people successful."[56] Schake's critique deals with the State Department as a player in Washington's interagency foreign policy process, as well as around the world.

Nick Burns and Kori Schake could both be right, if the State Department's performance were judged as being good overseas but mediocre in Washington. A CSIS report on statecraft came just to this conclusion. "State is now often perceived as underperforming in Washington," while "overseas, State often performs above its weight, using its unrivaled presence and skills…"[57]

This "good overseas, mediocre in Washington" perspective could result from the difference in the types of employees serving overseas versus in Washington. Domestically, the Foreign Service has seen its relative size and influence diminished compared to that of both the Civil Service and political appointees.

In Washington, the top tiers of the State Department are packed with political appointees who get their positions thanks to political connections, not merit. They typically represent the State Department in the complex interagency policy process. The increasingly influential NSC staff comprises many outside experts coming from universities or think tanks along with officers seconded from the Pentagon and Intelligence Community (as well as FSOs, who, nonetheless, are in a distinct minority), and the State Department's Policy Planning staff likewise includes many "irregulars" alongside FSO "regulars." Furthermore, at "main State" in

Washington, FSOs are outnumbered by Civil Service employees by a ratio of more than four to one.[58] Civil Service employees, whose numbers have grown rapidly relative to those of FSOs serving domestically, dominate the bureaus handling administrative, management, personnel, financial, legislative, and other functional affairs.[59] Conversely, members of the highly selective, merit-based US Foreign Service are still the largest American contingent at most embassies and consulates.

A major challenge facing the traditional role of the diplomatic service and the State Department as a whole is the simultaneous diffusion and concentration of the foreign policy process.

The diffusion of foreign policy influence from the State Department to other government agencies and non-state actors is partly a result of the increasingly interdependent, complex world. More agencies have a stake in foreign affairs, from the Centers for Disease Control to NASA to the FBI, and their voices have joined the interagency policy-making mix. Many agencies, thanks to advances in travel and telecommunications, directly interact with their foreign counterparts, bypassing the State Department entirely. This is especially true for specialized or technical issues such as scientific affairs, cybersecurity, financial sanctions, nuclear energy, money laundering, and similar issues.

Non-governmental organizations and individuals use social media to influence foreign policy in ways unforeseen in past decades. A celebrity's visit to a refugee camp in a drought-stricken region or a non-governmental organization's (NGO) documentary on the plight of trafficked children fleeing a war-torn country can attract hundreds of thousands of followers, instantly moving an issue up the list of foreign policy priorities. NGOs are important actors dealing with transnational issues like HIV/AIDS, human rights, refugees, human trafficking, and biodiversity.

Meanwhile, the foreign policy process is increasingly concentrated in the White House. "I'm the only one that matters," proclaimed President Trump in November 2017 when asked about the unusually high number of senior vacancies in the State Department.[60] Beyond the person of the president and the inner circle of White House staffers, the prominence of the National Security Council staff has reached new heights in recent years. The growth in the NSC's size and role is reflected in the fact that it occupies the building next to the White House that once housed the State Department.

What is the future role, then, of the generalist Foreign Service Officer? American diplomats have struggled to adapt to the expanded interagency arena, a decade of expeditionary diplomacy, and the era of sharply polarized politics. The Foreign Service has failed to build a strong constituency in Washington and beyond to prevent the encroachment of others on what it sees as its traditional turf, despite efforts by the American Foreign Service Association. Some diplomats disdain even making such efforts, thinking they could remain above the partisan, bureaucratic fray. In Washington, the policy role of the diplomat is increasingly constrained by political appointees, outside experts, the Civil Service, and the expanding interagency process—all dominated by the White House. The State Department still has a comparative advantage in providing the "inputs" to foreign policy decision making, but its advantage is shrinking.

Overseas, the scope for impact and influence remains relatively greater. Consular operations will remain critical to the United States, as will efficient management of embassies as platforms for the projection of US influence. Straightforward reporting is apt to be less important, except from extremely isolated countries, as commercial and social media sources provide nearly instantaneous news from around the globe. Thoughtful diplomatic analysis, the "so what" explaining political and economic dynamics, should increasingly aid decision making. FSOs with strong cross-cultural, interpersonal, and language abilities are likely to find themselves repeatedly thrust into the role of concierge, matchmaker, or fixer during ever-more-frequent Congressional and other high-level visits. Enhanced networking, contact building, and social media skills would make embassies more effective advocates for the United States.

Building relationships of trust and respect with foreign governments and people, as Benjamin Franklin did in France, is the first step in persuading them to do what the United States wants. This is the essence of diplomacy. In past years, the State Department has, at times, lost focus of the need to recruit, mentor, train, and, most of all, empower diplomats to fulfill this fundamental role. If Colin Powell's leadership and training principles are further institutionalized (and not undercut by another decade of expeditionary diplomacy), the future of the Foreign Service remains bright, at least overseas.

Acknowledgment *The author wishes to thank the following diplomats and scholars consulted in researching and writing this chapter:* Shawn Dorman, Sharon Hardy, Julie Nutte, David O'Neill, Robert Scott, Patricia Scroggs, and Donald Yamamoto.

Notes

1. H.W. Brands, *The First American: The Life and Times of Benjamin Franklin* (New York: Doubleday, 2000), 7.
2. G.R. Berridge, *Diplomacy: Theory and Practice, Fourth Edition* (Houndmills, UK: Palgrave Macmillan, 2010), 7.
3. William Marcy, "Remarks in the Senate," January 25, 1832, *Register of Debates in Congress*, vol. 8, col. 1325. https://www.bartleby.com/73/1314.html. Accessed July 22, 2018.
4. Richard J. Behn, "Mr. Lincoln & Friends: Political Patronage," *The Lehrman Institute*, http://www.mrlincolnandfriends.org/presidential-patronage/. Accessed July 26, 2018.
5. John Kerry, "Remarks at the 90th Anniversary of the United States Foreign Service," May 22, 2014, U.S. Department of State, https://2009-2017.state.gov/secretary/remarks/2014/05/226496.htm. Accessed July 10, 2018.
6. Harry Kopp and John Naland, *Career Diplomacy: Life and Work in the US Foreign Service* (Washington: Georgetown University Press, 2017), 14.
7. U.S. Department of State, "History of the Bureau of Diplomatic Security of the United States Department of State," 122–129, https://www.state.gov/documents/organization/176702.pdf. Accessed July 11, 2018.
8. George Gedda, "Nixon Vowed to 'Ruin Foreign Service,'" *Associated Press*, January 3, 2007, http://www.washingtonpost.com/wp-dyn/content/article/2007/01/03/AR2007010301405.html?noredirect=on. Accessed July 20, 2018.
9. Thomas Pickering and Edward Perkins, "The Foreign Service is Too White. We'd Know—We're Top Diplomats," *The Washington Post*, May 18, 2015, https://www.washingtonpost.com/posteverything/wp/2015/05/18/the-foreign-service-is-too-white-wed-know-were-top-diplomats/?utm_term=.434757d64878. Accessed July 19, 2018.
10. U.S. Government, "Foreign Service Act of 1980, Section 101(2)," https://www.usaid.gov/sites/default/files/documents/1868/fsa.pdf. Accessed July 14, 2018.
11. Kopp and Naland, *Career Diplomacy*, 27.
12. Condoleezza Rice, "Remarks, Georgetown University, Washington, DC 13. January 18, 2006," *U.S. Department of State*, https://2001-2009.state.gov/secretary/rm/2006/59306.htm. Accessed July 6, 2018.
13. Kopp and Naland, *Career Diplomacy*, 113.
14. Shawn Dorman, ed., *Inside a U.S. Embassy: Diplomacy at Work* (Washington: Foreign Service Books, 2011), 156–157.

15. Mike Pompeo, "Welcome Remarks to Employees," May 1, 2018, U.S. Department of State, https://www.state.gov/secretary/remarks/2018/05/281365.htm. Accessed July 6, 2018.
16. U.S. Government, "Foreign Service Act of 1980, Section 101(b)(10)," https://www.usaid.gov/sites/default/files/documents/1868/fsa.pdf. Accessed July 14, 2018.
17. U.S. Department of State, "HR Factsheet: Facts about Our Most Valuable Asset—Our People As of 06/30/2018," https://www.state.gov/documents/organization/284259.pdf. Accessed July 13, 2018.
18. Alex Karagiannis, "Straight Talk on Diplomatic Capacity," *Foreign Service Journal* (May 2018): 22, http://www.afsa.org/sites/default/files/flipping_book/0518/22/index.html. Accessed July 8, 2018.
19. American Foreign Service Association, "Department of State—Full-time Permanent Workforce as of 03/31/2018," http://www.afsa.org/sites/default/files/0318_ftp_bureau_loc.pdf. Accessed July 26, 2018.
20. American Foreign Service Association. "Schedule B and Schedule C Employees at State," http://www.afsa.org/sites/default/files/Portals/0/sched_BandC_employees.pdf. Accessed July 26, 2018.
21. Allison Stanger, *One Nation Under Contract: The Outsourcing of American Power and the Future of Foreign Policy* (New Haven: Yale University Press, 2009), 66–68.
22. The author headed the Office of Afghanistan and Pakistan 2006–2007 in the Bureau of International Narcotics and Law Enforcement Affairs.
23. American Foreign Service Association, "Department of State—Full-time Permanent Workforce as of 03/31/2018," http://www.afsa.org/sites/default/files/0318_ftp_bureau_loc.pdf.
24. *U.S. Department of State, Bureau of Human Resources*, November 30, 2017, https://careers.state.gov/discussion/topic/application-numbers-for-2017/. Accessed July 15, 2018.
25. American Foreign Service Association. "The Drastic Reduction in Foreign Service Officer Hiring (1990 vs. 2018)," derived from AFSA records and emailed to the author July 7, 2018.
26. U.S. Department of State, "FY 2001 Program Performance Report, Human Resources," 147, https://www.state.gov/documents/organization/9816.pdf. Accessed July 12, 2018.
27. Foreign Affairs Council, "Secretary Colin Powell's State Department: An Independent Assessment," March 2003 (Section III, Human Resources, Action), http://www.unc.edu/depts/diplomat/archives_roll/2003_04-06/fac/fac.html. Accessed July 10, 2018.
28. Domani Spero, "Foreign Service Staffing Gaps, and Oh, Diplomacy 3.0 Hiring Initiative to Conclude in FY2023," *Diplopundit*, July 17, 2012, https://diplopundit.net/2012/07/17/foreign-service-staffing-gaps-

and-oh-diplomacy-3-0-hiring-initiative-to-conclude-in-fy2023/. Accessed July 10, 2018.
29. U.S. Department of State, "Foreign Service Generalists," oral briefing to the author and other Diplomats in Residence, July 26, 2011, Washington, D.C.
30. U.S. Department of State, "Foreign Service Promotion Statistics for 2017, Category: Generalists FS-04 to FS-03." https://www.state.gov/documents/organization/265924.pdf. Accessed July 11, 2018.
31. "Race and Ethnicity in the United States," *Statistical Atlas*, Clear Lake Ventures, Inc. https://statisticalatlas.com/United-States/Race-and-Ethnicity. Accessed July 14, 2018.
32. U.S. Department of State, "Education and Work Experience of Passers of the Foreign Service Selection Process at the U.S. Department of State." Unpublished document furnished to author and other Diplomats in Residence, October 8, 2009.
33. Kopp and Naland, *Career Diplomacy*, 48.
34. Rosemary Hansen and Rick Rife, "Defense is from Mars State is from Venus: Improving Communications and Promoting National Security" (Carlisle Barracks: Army War College, 1998), http://www.dtic.mil/dtic/tr/fulltext/u2/a351032.pdf. Accessed July 21, 2018.
35. U.S. Department of State, "2018 Foreign Service (FS) Salary Table," https://www.state.gov/documents/organization/277016.pdf. Accessed July 14, 2018.
36. U.S. Department of State, "Foreign Service Promotion Statistics for 2017 Category: Generalist FS-04 to FS-03," https://www.state.gov/documents/organization/265924.pdf. Accessed July 11, 2018.
37. Colin Powell, "Why Leadership Matters in the Department of State," U.S. Department of State, October 28, 2003, http://govleaders.org/powell-speech.htm. Accessed July 22, 2018.
38. Sharon Hardy, U.S. Department of State, Bureau of Human Resources, Interview with the author, July 17, 2018.
39. U.S. Department of State, "Report of Inspection: Embassy Luxembourg, Luxembourg Report Number ISP-I-11-17A, January 2011," Office of Inspector General, https://www.stateig.gov/system/files/156129.pdf. Accessed July 13, 2018.
40. Harry Kopp and Charles Gillespie, *Career Diplomacy: Life and Work in the Foreign Service* (Washington: Georgetown University Press, 2011), 63.
41. Domani Spero, "Department of State, Career Versus Other Appointments: Deputy Secretaries, Under Secretaries, and Assistant Secretaries," *Diplopundit*, November 4, 2014, https://diplopundit.net/tag/career-vs-political-appointees/. Accessed July 2, 2018.

42. Association of Diplomatic Studies and Training, "Charles Stuart Kennedy Interview with Stephanie Kinney," 2010, https://adst.org/2014/02/whither-the-foreign-service/. Accessed July 15, 2018.
43. American Foreign Service Association, "Tracker: Senior Official Appointments" July 20, 2018, http://www.afsa.org/tracker-senior-official-appointments. Accessed July 21, 2018.
44. The White House. Letter of instruction from President George W. Bush to the author, October 29, 2007.
45. Edward Peck, "Why U.S. Ambassadors Should Be Career Professionals," *Foreign Service Journal* (January/February 2017): 15, http://www.afsa.org/sites/default/files/flipping_book/010217/files/assets/basic-html/page-15.html. Accessed July 10, 2018.
46. U.S. Department of State, Bureau of Human Resources, unclassified, unpublished data, January 2012.
47. Ambassador Osman Siddique's instructions to the author, Suva, Fiji, November 1999.
48. U.S. Department of State, "Duties of the Secretary of State" https://www.state.gov/secretary/115194.htm. Accessed July 24, 2018.
49. Jon Greenberg, "Does the U.S. Have About As Many Military Band Members As Diplomats?" *PolitiFact*, March 31, 2018, http://www.politifact.com/global-news/statements/2017/mar/31/nicholas-burns/are-there-more-military-band-members-diplomats/. Accessed July 19, 2018.
50. Ronan Farrow, *War on Peace: The End of Diplomacy and the Decline of American Influence* (New York: WW Norton and Co., 2018): 295.
51. Roger Cohen, "American Diplomacy Revealed—As Good!" *New York Times*, December 2, 2010. https://www.nytimes.com/2010/12/03/opinion/03iht-edcohen.html. Accessed July 2, 2018.
52. Colin Powell, "The Craft of Diplomacy," in *The Domestic Sources of American Foreign Policy: Insights and Evidence*, fifth edition, eds. Eugene Wittkopf and James McCormick (Lanham, Md.: Rowman & Littlefield Publishers, 2008), 216.
53. James Dobbins, *Foreign Service: Five Decades on the Frontlines of American Diplomacy* (Washington: Brookings Institution Press, 2017), xiv.
54. R. Nicholas Burns, "Testimony to the U.S. House of Representatives Committee on Foreign Affairs, March 28, 2017," https://docs.house.gov/meetings/FA/FA00/20170328/105791/HHRG-115-FA00-Wstate-BurnsR-20170328.pdf. Accessed July 7, 2018.
55. Robert Scott, interview with the author, July 12, 2018.
56. Kori Schake, *State of Disrepair: Fixing the Culture and Practice of the State Department* (Stanford: Hoover Institution Press, 2012), 6, 140.
57. Robert Pollard and Gregory Hicks, "Economic Statecraft Redux: Improving the U.S. State Department's Effectiveness in International

Economic Policy," *Center for Strategic and International Studies*, July 28, 2014, https://www.csis.org/analysis/economic-statecraft-redux. Accessed July 9, 2018.
58. U.S. Department of State, "Department of State—Full-Time Employees and Locally Employed Staff as of 03/31/2018," http://www.afsa.org/sites/default/files/0318_ftp_bureau_loc.pdf. Accessed July 26, 2018.
59. American Foreign Service Association, "Department of State FS & CS Full-Time Permanent Employees, 1970–Present, 2013," http://www.afsa.org/sites/default/files/Portals/0/dosfscs_1970-present_ftdhe.pdf. Accessed July 22, 2018.
60. Donald Trump, "Fox News interview by Laura Ingraham, November 2, 2017," https://www.realclearpolitics.com/video/2017/11/02/trump_full_interview_with_ingraham_dossier_justice_department_immigration_dnc_primary__sanders.html. Accessed July 25, 2018.

References

American Foreign Service Association. 2012. Schedule B and Schedule C Employees at State. http://www.afsa.org/sites/default/files/Portals/0/sched_BandC_employees.pdf. Accessed July 26, 2018.
———. 2013. Department of State FS & CS Full-Time Permanent Employees, 1970–Present, 2013. http://www.afsa.org/sites/default/files/Portals/0/dosfscs_1970-present_ftdhe.pdf. Accessed July 22, 2018.
———. 2018a. Department of State—Full-Time Permanent Workforce as of 03/31/2018. http://www.afsa.org/sites/default/files/0318_ftp_bureau_loc.pdf. Accessed July 26, 2018.
———. 2018b, July 20). Tracker: Senior Official Appointments. http://www.afsa.org/tracker-senior-official-appointments. Accessed July 21, 2018.
———. n.d. The Drastic Reduction in Foreign Service Officer Hiring (1990 vs. 2018). Unpublished.
Association of Diplomatic Studies and Training. 2014. Charles Stuart Kennedy Interview with Stephanie Kinney. https://adst.org/2014/02/whither-the-foreign-service/. Accessed July 15, 2018.
Behn, R.J. 2003. *Mr. Lincoln & Friends: Political Patronage*. The Lehrman Institute. http://www.mrlincolnandfriends.org/presidential-patronage/. Accessed July 26, 2018.
Berridge, G.R. 2010. *Diplomacy: Theory and Practice*. 4th ed. Houndmills, UK: Palgrave Macmillan.
Brands, H.W. 2000. *The First American: The Life and Times of Benjamin Franklin*. New York: Doubleday.
Burns, R.N. 2017. Testimony to the U.S. House of Representatives Committee on Foreign Affairs, March 28, 2017. https://docs.house.gov/meetings/FA/

FA00/20170328/105791/HHRG-115-FA00-Wstate-BurnsR-20170328. pdf. Accessed July 7, 2018.

Cohen, R. 2010. American Diplomacy Revealed—As Good! *New York Times*, December 2. https://www.nytimes.com/2010/12/03/opinion/03ihtedcohen.html. Accessed July 2, 2018.

Dobbins, J. 2017. *Foreign Service: Five Decades on the Frontlines of American Diplomacy*. Washington: Brookings Institution Press.

Dorman, S., ed. 2011. *Inside a U.S. Embassy: Diplomacy at Work*. Washington: Foreign Service Books.

Farrow, R. 2018. *War on Peace: The End of Diplomacy and the Decline of American Influence*. New York: WW Norton and Company.

Foreign Affairs Council. 2003, March. Secretary Colin Powell's State Department: An Independent Assessment (Section III, Human Resources, Action). http://www.unc.edu/depts/diplomat/archives_roll/2003_04-06/fac/fac.html. Accessed July 10, 2018.

Gedda, G. 2007, January 3. Nixon Vowed to 'Ruin Foreign Service'. *Associated Press*. http://www.washingtonpost.com/wp-dyn/content/article/2007/01/03/AR2007010301405.html?noredirect=on. Accessed July 20, 2018.

Greenberg, J. 2018, March 31. Does the U.S. Have About as Many Military Band Members as Diplomats? *PolitiFact*. http://www.politifact.com/global-news/statements/2017/mar/31/nicholas-burns/are-there-more-military-band-members-diplomats/. Accessed July 19, 2018.

Hansen, R., and R. Rife. 1998. *Defense Is from Mars State Is from Venus: Improving Communications and Promoting National Security*. Carlisle Barracks: Army War College. http://www.dtic.mil/dtic/tr/fulltext/u2/a351032.pdf. Accessed July 21, 2018.

Karagiannis, A. 2018, May. Straight Talk on Diplomatic Capacity. *Foreign Service Journal* 22.

Kerry, J. 2014. *Remarks at the 90th Anniversary of the United States Foreign Service, 22 May 2014*. U.S. Department of State. https://20092017.state.gov/secretary/remarks/2014/05/226496.htm. Accessed July 10, 2018.

Kopp, H., and C. Gillespie. 2011. *Career Diplomacy: Life and Work in the Foreign Service*. Washington: Georgetown University Press.

Kopp, H., and J. Naland. 2017. *Career Diplomacy: Life and Work in the US Foreign Service*. Washington: Georgetown University Press.

Marcy, W. 1832. Remarks in the Senate, 25 January 1832. *Register of Debates in Congress* 8 (1325). https://www.bartleby.com/73/1314.html. Accessed July 22, 2018.

Peck, E. 2017, January/February. Why U.S. Ambassadors Should Be Career Professionals. *Foreign Service Journal* 15. http://www.afsa.org/sites/default/files/flipping_book/010217/files/assets/basic-html/page-15.html. Accessed July 10, 2018.

Pickering, T., and E. Perkins. 2015, May 18. The Foreign Service Is Too White. We'd Know—We're Top Diplomats. *The Washington Post.* https://www.washingtonpost.com/posteverything/wp/2015/05/18/the-foreign-service-is-too-white-wed-know-were-top-diplomats/?utm_term=.434757d64878. Accessed July 19, 2018.

Pollard, R., and G. Hicks. 2014. *Economic Statecraft Redux: Improving the U.S. State Department's Effectiveness in International Economic Policy.* Center for Strategic and International Studies. https://www.csis.org/analysis/economic-statecraft-redux. Accessed July 9, 2018.

Pompeo, M. 2018. *Welcome Remarks to Employees, 1 May 2018.* U.S. Department of State. https://www.state.gov/secretary/remarks/2018/05/281365.htm. Accessed July 6, 2018.

Powell, C. 2003, October 28. *Why Leadership Matters in the Department of State.* U.S. Department of State. http://govleaders.org/powell-speech.htm. Accessed July 22, 2018.

———. 2008. The Craft of Diplomacy. In *The Domestic Sources of American Foreign Policy: Insights and Evidence*, ed. E. Wittkopf and J. McCormick, 5th ed. Lanham, MD: Rowman & Littlefield Publishers.

Rice, C. 2006. *Remarks, Georgetown University, Washington, DC, January 18, 2006.* U.S. Department of State. https://2001-2009.state.gov/secretary/rm/2006/59306.htm. Accessed July 6, 2018.

Schake, K. 2012. *State of Disrepair: Fixing the Culture and Practice of the State Department.* Stanford: Hoover Institution Press.

Spero, D. 2012, July 17. Foreign Service Staffing Gaps, and Oh, Diplomacy 3.0 Hiring Initiative to Conclude in FY2023. *Diplopundit.* https://diplopundit.net/2012/07/17/foreign-service-staffing-gaps-and-oh-diplomacy-3-0-hiring-initiative-to-conclude-in-fy2023/. Accessed July 10, 2018.

———. 2014. Department of State, Career Versus Other Appointments: Deputy Secretaries, Under Secretaries, and Assistant Secretaries. *Diplopundit*, November 4. https://diplopundit.net/tag/career-vs-political-appointees/. Accessed July 2, 2018.

Stanger, A. 2009. *One Nation Under Contract: The Outsourcing of American Power and the Future of Foreign Policy.* New Haven: Yale University.

Statistical Atlas. Race and Ethnicity in the United States. Clear Lake Ventures, Inc. https://statisticalatlas.com/United-States/Race-and-Ethnicity. Accessed July 14, 2018.

Trump, D. 2017. Fox News Interview by Laura Ingraham, November 2, 2017. https://www.realclearpolitics.com/video/2017/11/02/trump_full_interview_with_ingraham_dossier_justice_department_immigration_dnc_primary_sanders.html. Accessed July 25, 2018.

U.S. Department of State. 2001. FY 2001 Program Performance Report, Human Resources, 147. https://www.state.gov/documents/organization/9816.pdf. Accessed July 12, 2018.

———. 2009. Education and Work Experience of Passers of the Foreign Service Selection Process at the U.S. Department of State. Unpublished.

———. 2011a. History of the Bureau of Diplomatic Security of the United States Department of State, 122–129. https://www.state.gov/documents/organization/176702.pdf. Accessed July 11, 2018.

———. 2011b. Report of Inspection: Embassy Luxembourg, Luxembourg Report Number ISP-I-11-17A, January 2011. Office of Inspector General. https://www.stateoig.gov/system/files/156129.pdf. Accessed July 13, 2018.

———. 2017. Bureau of Human Resources, 30 November 2017. https://careers.state.gov/discussion/topic/application-numbers-for-2017/. Accessed July 15, 2018.

———. 2018a. Department of State—Full-Time Employees and Locally Employed Staff as of 03/31/2018. http://www.afsa.org/sites/default/files/0318_ftp_bureau_loc.pdf. Accessed July 26, 2018.

———. 2018b. Duties of the Secretary of State. https://www.state.gov/secretary/115194.htm. Accessed July 24, 2018.

———. 2018c. Foreign Service Promotion Statistics for 2017, Category: Generalists FS-04 to FS-03. https://www.state.gov/documents/organization/265924.pdf. Accessed July 11, 2018.

———. 2018d. HR Factsheet: Facts About Our Most Valuable Asset—Our People as of 06/30/2018. https://www.state.gov/documents/organization/284259.pdf. Accessed July 13, 2018.

———. 2018e. 2018 Foreign Service (FS) Salary Table. https://www.state.gov/documents/organization/277016.pdf. Accessed July 14, 2018.

U.S. Government. 1980. Foreign Service Act of 1980, Sections 101(2) and 101(b)(10). https://www.usaid.gov/sites/default/files/documents/1868/fsa.pdf. Accessed July 14, 2018.

Conclusion

Robert Hutchings

One of the most striking things about our survey of diplomatic services in ten key countries is how different their histories and cultures are, despite the many structural and procedural similarities among them. With the exception of China's diplomatic service, all of them drew their structure and organization from a shared European tradition, Brazil's and India's originating in the colonial periods, and Japan's and Turkey's from the Westernizing reforms of the Meiji and Kemalist eras respectively. Yet each of these diplomatic cultures grew out of a unique historical experience.

More than a century after his death, the Baron of Rio Branco still hovers over *Itamaraty*, Brazil's foreign ministry, just as the Iron Chancellor, Otto von Bismarck, continues to stand over the German foreign office. In Japan, the "American school" of US-trained diplomats continues to dominate leadership positions in the foreign ministry (*Gaimushō*, in Japanese). Contemporary French diplomacy reflects the nationalist aspirations of Charles de Gaulle, and in India, the complicated legacies of Jawaharlal Nehru and Mohandas Gandhi continue to be a source of internal diplomatic tension. In China, despite the "great divide" of 1949 with the establishment of the Communist party-state, contemporary leaders regularly

---

R. Hutchings
Lyndon B. Johnson School of Public Affairs, The University of Texas at Austin, Austin, TX, USA
e-mail: rhutchings@austin.utexas.edu

© The Author(s) 2020
R. Hutchings, J. Suri (eds.), *Modern Diplomacy in Practice*,
https://doi.org/10.1007/978-3-030-26933-3

invoke two figures from the fifth century BC, Confucius and Sun Tzu. These cultural differences have made for a fascinating study, but they make comparisons and generalizations challenging.

The Ideal Diplomat

From these extensive surveys of ten very different services, is it possible to construct the Ideal Diplomat? Surely not: skilled diplomats come in various shapes and sizes. Some are master strategists, others are gifted linguists with deep regional expertise, and still others are experienced administrators and leaders. Diplomatic services need officers with these varied talents: the attributes one seeks for the head of the planning staff are not the same as those sought for the director of a regional bureau or a UN ambassador. *Vive la différence!*

There are, nonetheless, certain important features gleaned from our surveys that can be said to constitute the best of diplomatic selection and professional development. What are they?

To start with, our "Ideal Diplomat"—an imaginary figure who is a composite of the best of diplomatic attributes—comes out of a rigorous selection process that identifies and selects for excellence, yet is open to a broader pool of applicants than those coming through traditional pipelines like Oxbridge or ENA (the *École Nationale d'Administration*). In most cases, the Ideal Diplomat had academic training in a field directly related to international affairs. After selection, our Ideal Diplomat receives substantial, rigorous training in the arts of diplomacy and in the culture and operations of the foreign ministry and other government departments, so that before she takes up her first posting she is already a trained diplomat, prepared to represent her government competently. In cases where an entry level officer does not have an academic background in international affairs, she would be given additional academic training to prepare her for a diplomatic career. She does not begin her career by adjudicating visas, because in her ministry visa work is either outsourced or performed by those in a separate career track. Important as visa work is, having professional diplomats take on these tasks entails a high opportunity—as well as financial—cost.

Our Ideal Diplomat would receive periodic training throughout her career. Often these are short courses in key aspects of diplomacy: negotiation, cross-cultural communication, commercial diplomacy, management, strategy, coercive diplomacy, ethics, and others. These may be academic, experiential ("on the job"), or a combination of the two; some would be mandatory, while others would be elective, with the requirement that a certain number of electives be completed before she is eligible for promotion to higher levels. Additionally, she would routinely receive language and regional training before taking up a new post. At least twice in her career, our Ideal Diplomat would be afforded a full year away, to pursue advanced academic work, have a stint in another government department, be seconded to the staff of an international organization, or spend time in a think tank, foundation, or commercial enterprise. She would spend at least one tour back in her home country for every two tours abroad, and would be expected during these home stays to engage in public diplomacy at home so that she better understands her own country and so that her fellow citizens better understand her and her work.

Our Ideal Diplomat would be a member of a well-funded diplomatic service that enjoys a strong *esprit de corps*, a reputation for excellence among other parts of government (rivaled only by the finance ministry and office of the president, prime minister, or chancellor), and a general level of trust within the legislature and public at large. Mindful of the special stresses of a transient profession, her service would provide generous accommodation of tandem assignments and family leaves. The personnel or human resources department would be modern and mission-driven, led by career officers who put the needs of the service and its officers above adherence to standards. Rising diplomats would be given a sequence of early postings to afford them exposure to all aspects of the ministry's work, and they would engage with senior diplomats through a formal mentoring program as part of their career development.

Our Ideal Diplomat's rise might well be quite rapid, because her ministry's promotion boards, led by senior diplomats, prize excellence over time in grade. Also, she would not be competing with political appointees, because her ministry has none—only a handful of staff appointees in the minister's office and some select subject matter experts in the functional bureaus.

The ministry would be characterized by a culture of creativity rather than of conformity, in which officers are encouraged to exercise responsibility even at junior levels—and entrusted to do so, because they had been well versed in the culture and mission of the ministry starting at entry level and continuing throughout. Although the ministry's organizational chart might look hierarchical, its operating style would be characterized by "subsidiarity," the devolution of decision making to the lowest level feasible. Officers are not only permitted to act independently; they are expected to do so, and those who do not show themselves capable of exercising sound independent judgment would be winnowed out early on.

Through careful selection, mentorship, screening for promotion, and above all by socialization in the very culture of the service, our Ideal Diplomat would have developed the critical personality traits of humility, patience, emotional intelligence, empathy, and grace under pressure. Although such traits may have to be nurtured rather than taught, the service would have built into its training and mentoring programs innovative modules in role playing, resiliency training, psychological awareness, and crisis management.

The foreign minister would be a senior political figure with experience in party affairs as well as in at least one other ministry, and would have a national reputation. The minister would be recognized as the principal voice on foreign policy beneath the head of state or government and would have the stature to be an effective defender of the professional foreign service within government and before the public. The minister might not be a foreign policy expert but she or he would have had considerable direct experience abroad either in a party capacity or as a member of senior delegations. The minister would be supported by a small number of staff appointees, but below that level, the ministry would be staffed by career diplomats, career civil servants, or other professionals.

By the time our Ideal Diplomat is ready for promotion to the highest levels, she would have received an advanced degree (if she did not have one when she entered the ministry), acquired real expertise in one region and secondary expertise in another, developed competency in two functional areas (such as security, development, foreign trade, or public diplomacy), held senior leadership positions within the ministry, and gained broad experience with policy making at the inter-agency and political levels. She would speak multiple languages and have acquired expertise in negotiation, strategy, and other key elements of diplomacy. She would combine specialized knowledge with a strategic worldview and sense of national mission.

Above all, our Ideal Diplomat would have become a global citizen and leader, in keeping with the ethos and mission of her ministry. Recognizing that her country's interests cannot successfully be pursued from a narrow, nationalistic perspective, she would have become a representative and advocate not only of her own country but also of an international community of diplomats who share a commitment to diplomacy, empathy, and principled compromise as the irreducible elements of a cooperative global order.

The Real and the Ideal

Obviously, we have described an ideal type, but the traits described earlier are not fanciful or unrealistic. One encounters real world diplomats, past and present, who exhibit these attributes. Such individuals are rare, but they do exist. How well do the ten services nurture these qualities in their diplomats and in their diplomatic services? The record is mixed. None of them do all of these things associated with our ideal foreign service and ideal diplomat, but all of them perform well in at least some of them.

All are elite services and proudly so. Once the preserve of those of means and title, they have gradually traded the privileges of aristocracy for the more democratic but no less exclusive ones of meritocracy. They recruit from leading universities and institutes, many of them, like ENA in France and MGIMO (Moscow State Institute of International Relations) in Russia, specifically geared for the preparation of public servants. In most services, entry level officers have strong academic training in history, politics, economics, or law, as well as fluency in at least two languages. Brazil is a unique case in that every diplomat without exception is a graduate of the *Instituto Rio Branco* in Brasilia, creating a powerfully cohesive diplomatic corps (perhaps at the cost of insularity). The elite character of the services is of course a tremendous strength because they are populated by officers of high academic achievement and great skill.

Yet, there is a growing recognition in many countries that their elite diplomatic services are out of step with their more egalitarian political cultures. Many have made public commitments to diversity and most—Russia being an extreme outlier—have made strides in gender diversity. Ethnic diversity is another matter, and most services have made only scant progress. The United States and India, although far from perfect, are the clear leaders in this respect, and Brazil and the United Kingdom also have made serious attempts to improve ethnic diversity. The main impulse seems to be to promote equity and representativeness, so that public institutions better reflect the diversity of the populations they purport to represent, but this focus on diversity may also reflect an effort to build public understanding and trust by narrowing the distance between diplomats and the wider public. Interestingly, few of the services have stressed the rationale that a more diverse diplomatic corps would improve diplomatic effectiveness by strengthening cross-cultural familiarity and competency.

Most services do well in providing appropriate entry-level training designed to familiarize officers with the ministry as well as acquire diplomatic skills. While there is a diverse assortment of coursework and training lengths among countries, most require that entry-level officers take courses in foreign languages, history of the country's foreign service, and diplomatic language and protocol. The Brazilian, German, Indian, and Japanese services have the most extensive initial training, ranging from three semesters in the Brazilian case to as long as three years in the German. The German training period includes an internship and final examination before new officers are assigned to their first posting. France, Russia, and the United Kingdom do not provide the same level of initial training, relying instead on their rigorous selection process from elite institutions and the professional education entering officers received there before they joined the service. Russian diplomats in particular are known for their strong language and regional expertise. So are the Chinese, though the service has been criticized for promoting "translator diplomacy" over core diplomatic competency.

India's practice is unique among those we studied. New Indian diplomats are drawn from the highly selective Indian Civil Service examination process, which means that the Indian Foreign Service (IFS) recruits candidates alongside domestic counterparts such as the Indian Administrative Service. IFS officers begin their training with civil servants from across ministries and levels of government, and subsequently undertake almost two additional years of training on top of the induction they received as civil service recruits, including extensive rotations throughout the central government's ministries including military attachments. This training also includes innovative features meant to ensure that Indian diplomats are well connected to their country at the grass roots: a 10-day trek in the Himalayas followed by a 12-day visit to a remote village, and the *Bharat Darshan*, a tour of major cultural, commercial, and historical sites. Brazil has an analogous but less extensive practice whereby officers spend time in various states to experience something of the diversity of their country. China has a similar program required of newly appointed ambassadors.

Several services offer short and focused training courses at various points throughout a career, in addition to regular language courses. As noted in the introduction, Brazil and China link mandatory mid-career training courses to eligibility for promotion, and France requires mid-career management training after 15 years of service. The US Foreign Service also has a range of short courses in diplomatic tradecraft available at different stages of an officer's career. Until recently, China selected a large number of mid-career officers for a full year's academic training, often at American or European institutions, but this practice reportedly has been curtailed owing to security concerns. In Brazil, diplomats must complete the equivalent of a master's thesis before qualifying for promotion to the highest levels. In other services, opportunities for mid-career "sabbaticals" are very limited. Cost and staffing constraints are the reasons usually cited for not doing more, but it is worth noting that many other institutions, notably the armed services but also a growing number of private companies, build mid-career training or sabbatical opportunities into their professional development.

Penetrating the organizational cultures of ministries is difficult, but our surveys allow a few general conclusions. The German and French services seem to be the most advanced in promoting a "work-life balance" through generous family leave policies, flex time work arrangements, and job placement help for partners. Brazil's is perhaps the most professional, in that every diplomat, and usually the Minister as well, is a career diplomat and graduate of the Rio Branco Institute. France seems to the leader in cultivating a climate of creativity and innovation, and in nurturing in their officers the habits of strategic thinking. To regularize promotion procedures and make them more transparent, the British Foreign and Commonwealth Office has Assessment and Development Centers (ADCs), which administer a mix of written and interactive exercises, focused mainly on management and leadership. Similarly, Turkey requires meritocratic examinations between the sixth and ninth years of service.

A special feature in the United States is the presence at senior working level of many "irregulars" who come in from academia, the think tanks, or law firms to take up staff positions at the National Security Council, National Economic Council, the State Department's policy planning staff, and elsewhere. The ability of the US government to bring in such skilled outsiders, often mentioned by other diplomats with admiration, is a way of bringing a wider array of talent into the foreign policy decision making process. Of course, this practice needs to be done judiciously, lest it displace equally skilled foreign service professionals and limit their ability to influence policy at the highest levels.

On the other hand, the United States is a conspicuous outlier in the number of purely political appointees as ambassadors, even in key posts, and the growing politicization of the Department of State, with political appointees dominating the senior ranks (Secretary, Deputy Secretary, and Under Secretary levels) and extending all the way down to the Deputy Assistant Secretary level. Thirty percent of ambassadorial posts and around seventy-five percent of its top State Department positions are held by political appointees. Of course, there have been highly accomplished political appointees who have been superb ambassadors, but there have been many more patronage appointees with no relevant qualifications, having been chosen principally for their support in presidential election campaigns.

Ambassadorial posts in most other countries are almost entirely reserved for career diplomats. Japan has a few non-career officials from the corporate world serving as ambassadors in posts other than the most critical ones, and the United Kingdom is considering expanding the number drawn from outside the Foreign Office. The vast majority of ambassadors to key posts are career diplomats, have been ambassadors already (usually at lesser posts), have served before in the country to which they are accredited, speak the language fluently, and have served in senior levels back in their home ministries.

Reinventing Diplomacy

We are hesitant to draw sweeping conclusions about which practices are most relevant or most deserving of emulation by the United States or other services around the world. A "best practice" in one country is not necessarily best for another. What emerges from this ten-country survey is not a set of clear "lessons learned" but rather the troubling conclusion that the value of diplomacy itself is under threat in most if not all of the countries we studied.

Almost all of the diplomatic services we studied are underfunded, sometimes woefully so, in comparison with other government ministries and departments. Even venerable institutions like the British Foreign Office have fallen on hard times, ranking last among forty-eight UK government institutions surveyed in terms of satisfaction over pay. The US State Department had to fight back a Trump Administration proposal for a huge 31 percent budget cut. Underfunding of course leads to understaffing, fewer opportunities for mid-career professional training, diminished capacity to "surge" to respond to new priorities without compromising core functions, and less flexibility to bring in skilled outsiders or to contract out essential but more menial functions. Diplomatic services are forced to operate in perpetual crisis mode, scrambling to meet the latest emergency requirement, with little time to attend to the long-term vitality of the service or address the growing problems of morale and retention.

In the United States, there is a stark contrast between the Foreign Service and the uniformed military, whose services receive priority funding. Unlike Foreign Service Officers (FSOs), military officers routinely receive year-long training at least twice in a career, along with details to other services or government agencies. The armed forces consider that they have made a large investment in a career officer, and that it is important—for professional development and retention—to protect and nurture their investment throughout that officer's career. They also know that operational readiness demands regular training and retooling at every step of an officer's career. The very few Foreign Service Officers who are afforded mid-career academic opportunities most often receive their training at the Army War College, with the result that diplomats learn their strategy from the military rather than the other way around.

The role of diplomats abroad is also being eroded by the ready availability of information and analysis in today's globalized, networked world, and the many channels available for direct communication between capitals. Senior leaders tend to devalue the reporting cables from their missions abroad, though the more perceptive of them recognize the undiminished—perhaps increased—importance of reporting cables from their own trusted diplomats in vetting and putting in context the information they receive from other sources. Likewise, the ease of communication between capitals, many of which are connected by secure phone lines, makes it easy for senior leaders to speak directly with their counterparts in other countries, bypassing embassies altogether. These direct lines are convenient, but they raise dangers of miscommunication and misperception that could be prevented by relying on trusted ambassadors and their staffs, who are much more attuned to local circumstances, as intermediaries.

Meanwhile, many of the traditional roles of diplomatic services back in capitals are being eroded by the simultaneous fragmentation and centralization of policy making. Contemporary foreign policy increasingly involves a wide range of bureaucratic "actors" dealing with trade, finance, energy, justice, immigration, the environment, and many other issues; they vie with foreign ministries for a seat at the table and often take a lead role on a given issue. Coordination among these various actors as well as growing public scrutiny of foreign policy has led to growing centralization of decision making in the offices of presidents, prime ministers, and chancellors. In the past few years, several of the countries covered in this volume have created new coordinating bodies akin to the US National Security Council in an effort to gain control of decision making. Amidst these cross-pressures, top leaders are tempted to surround themselves with loyal staffers and create self-contained bubbles—not only in the United States under the Trump Administration but in other countries and other administrations as well.

With their privileged place in framing, shaping, and directly influencing policy decisions weakened, foreign ministries and the US State Department are struggling to redefine their roles in this crowded field. Foreign policy tends to be made incrementally, with different ministries or departments in the lead depending on the issue. Foreign policies become fragmented, ad hoc, and transactional, as different mixes of domestic stake-holders compete for the optimum outcome on the specific issue in play, with little sense of broader strategic purpose or the overall state of the international system. Foreign ministries need to be put back in the driver's seat for the sake of strategic coherence and a functioning system of relations among states.

An underlying problem that affects all others is that there is little public awareness of the role and value of diplomats, who typically have not seen outreach to legislatures or the public at large as among their responsibilities. In the past, they relied on governmental authority more generally for their protection; as governments themselves face growing populist pressure, foreign ministries find themselves with few advocates or defenders. This is certainly true of the US Department of State, but it is increasingly the case even for such revered institutions as *Itamaraty*, Brazil's foreign ministry. They very idea of diplomacy as an essential attribute of a country's security and well-being is under question.

Thus, our survey of the world's largest diplomatic services ends with an appeal: an appeal for diplomacy itself. The world has grown not only more complex, calling for a nuanced understanding of a larger array of global issues and actors, but also more violent, as nations and non-state actors resort increasingly to violence to settle their disputes or advance their agendas. International institutions at every level—from the United Nations and the international financial institutions at the global level to the many regional and sub-regional organizations—have been weakened by growing nationalism and diminished commitment on the part of national governments. The need for diplomacy and for skilled diplomats, committed not only to their own country's interests but also to those of a functioning international system, has never been greater.

Index[1]

A
Abe, Shinzō, 103, 107, 116–118
Acheson, Dean, xi
A-100 course, United States, 200–203
Akitaka, Saiki, 115
Aksoy, Hami, 146
Albright, Madeleine, 193
Algerian War, 45
Amorim, Celso, 2, 8, 9, 11–14, 15n2, 17n31, 18n37
Ankara University, 143, 148, 151
Assessment and Development Centres (ADCs), United Kingdom, 171, 172, 231
Ataturk, Mustafa Kemal, 144, 145
Audit berufundfamilie ("work-life balance"), Germany, 66
Auswärtiges Amt (German Foreign Office), 61–63, 77n51

B
Balcı, Ali, 145, 154
Baron of Rio Branco, (José Maria da Silva Paranhos, Sr.), 3, 4, 225
Beiwai (Beijing Foreign Language University), 22, 26
Belt and Road Initiative (China), 22, 23, 35
Bharat Darshan, 8, 88, 230
Bismarck, Otto von, 61, 74n4, 225
Blair, Tony, 173, 174
Bolsonaro, Jair, 5, 11, 14, 16n11, 16n12
Brandt, Willy, 61, 70
Braun, Harald, 69
"Brexit" (Britain's vote to exit the European Union), 60, 162, 167, 176, 178
BRIC countries (Brazil, Russia, India, China), 13

---

[1] Note: Page numbers followed by 'n' refer to notes.

238　INDEX

Bull, Hedley, xi
Burns, Nicholas, 213, 214
Bush, George H.W., 211
Bush, George W., 209

C

Cameron, David, 174
Cardoso, Fernando Henrique Cardoso, 10
Çavuşoğlu, Mevlüt, 151, 152
Cem, İsmail, 153
Chao, Wang, 32
Chilcot Inquiry, United Kingdom, 174
China Diplomatic Academy, 29
China Foreign Affairs University (CFAU), 23, 27–29, 31
Chinese Communist Party (CCP), 25, 32, 33
Christian Democratic Union (CDU) Germany, 60, 74
Christopher, Warren, 193
Churchill, Winston, 164, 176, 177
Churkin, Vitaly Ivanovich, 133
Civil Service, United States, 27, 47, 84–88, 95n20, 190, 193, 195, 196, 198, 205, 206, 214–216
Clinton, Bill, 193
Clinton, Hillary, 201
Confucius, 23, 36n3, 226
Council of Ministers, France, 50, 153
Crowe, Sir Eyre, 163, 164, 179n1

D

Darroch, Kim, 175
Davutoğlu, Ahmet, 144, 145, 153
de Gaulle, Charles, 45, 46, 51, 225
Department of External Church Relations (DECR), 136
Diplomatic Academy, United Kingdom, 170
Dom Pedro I, Emperor of Brazil, 3

E

École nationale d'administration (ENA), xiii, 47, 51, 226, 229
École polytechnique (IRA), 47
Enlai, Zhou, 25, 27
Erdoğan, Recep Tayyip, 145, 146
European Union (EU), 12, 44, 59, 60, 64, 71, 74, 162, 164, 174, 176, 178

F

Fifth Republic, France, 45, 51
Fischer, Joschka, v, 62, 70
Fletcher, Tom, 177
Foreign Affairs Committee (China), 165, 168, 170, 173, 175–177
Foreign and Commonwealth Office (FCO), United Kingdom, 161, 163, 174
"Foreign Office mind," 4, 163–165
Foreign Service Institute (FSI), 87–90, 190, 194, 202, 203, 207
Foreign Service Officers (FSOs), United States, 189, 192–209, 211, 213–216
Fox, Charles James, 163
Franklin, Benjamin, ix, x, xix, xxn5, 190, 202, 216
Fraser, Simon, 175, 176
Fundação Alexandre de Gusmão (FUNAG), Alexandre de Gusmão Foundation, Brazil, 3
"Future FCO" Report, United Kingdom, 166, 167, 169, 172, 177

G

Gabriel, Sigmar, 70
Gaimushō (Ministry of Foreign Affairs), vi, 105
Generalistenprinzip (generalist principle), Germany, 67

INDEX 239

Genscher, Hans-Dietrich, 64, 70, 71
German Diplomatic Academy, 64
Grandes Écoles, 3, 46, 47
Gromyko, Andrei, 135
Grundgesetz (Germany's Basic Law, or constitution), 70
G20 (Group of 20), 13, 154
Gusmão, Alexandre de, 3

H

Hague, William, 175, 184n82
Harriman, Averell, xi
Herwarth Report (Germany), 61
Holbrooke, Richard, 209, 213
Hunt, Sir Jeremy, 173

I

Ichirō, Fujisaki, 115
"Ideal Diplomat," the, 226–229
Indian Civil Service (ICS), 82, 85, 230
Indian Foreign Service (IFS), xvi, 8, 81–94, 96n29, 230
Itamaraty (Brazilian Ministry of Foreign Affairs), 1

J

Jackson, Andrew, 191
Japan Foundation, 105, 106, 114
Japan International Cooperation Agency (JICA), 100, 105, 114, 115
Jiechi, Yang, 33
Jinping, Xi, 22, 23, 28, 34, 37n12, 39n40, 39n44
Jintao, Hu, 23, 25, 37n12
Jisi, Wang, 35, 40n47
Joint Intelligence Committee (JIC), United Kingdom, 174, 175

K

Kasumigaseki culture, 107
Kennan, George F., x, xi, 192
Kijūrō, Shidehara, 101
Kiliç, Serdar, 152
Kinkel, Klaus, 71
Kislyak, Sergey, 133
Kissinger, Henry, xi, 12, 74n5
Kohl, Helmut, 71
Kōki, Hirota, 101

L

Lavrov, Sergey, 128, 134, 135
League of Nations, x, 13
Lincoln, Abraham, 191
Luiz Inácio Lula de Silva, 13

M

Maas, Heiko, 60, 70
Mahabharata, 82
Makiko, Tanaka, 118
Mamoru, Shigemitsu, 101
Matvienko, Valentina, 133
McCarthy, Joseph, 192
MERCOSUR (Common Market of the South), 13
Merkel, Angela, 60, 70, 73, 74
Metternich, Klemens von, 61
Ministry of Europe and Foreign Affairs, France (*Ministére de l'Europe et des affairs étrangéres*), 45
Ministry of External Affairs (MEA), Indian, 84–94
Ministry of Foreign Affairs, Russia, xvii, 125, 129, 130, 133, 135
Mission civilisatrice, continuing influence of, 44
Modi, Narendra, 92, 93

Moscow State Institute of
  International Relations
  (MGIMO), 130–132, 229
Muneo, Suzuki, 118
Musa, İsmail Hakkı, 152

N
National Security Committee
  (China), 34
National Security Council
  Japan, 102, 103, 118–120
  United Kingdom, 164, 166
  United States, 11, 32, 72, 174,
    211, 234
Nehru, Jawaharlal, 82, 83, 85, 88,
  92, 225
Neo-Ottomanism, 145
"New diplomacy," the, xi, 193
Nicolson, Sir Harold, xi, 164
Nixon, Richard, 192
Nobuhiko, Ushiba, 101, 117
Non-Aligned Movement,
  Indian role in, 83, 92
North American Treaty Organization
  (NATO), 60, 71, 74, 152,
  164, 178

O
Obama, Barack, 208, 209, 211
"Oxbridge"
  (Oxford and Cambridge), 226
Özal, Turgut, 152

P
Palmerston, Lord, 164
Pariota, Antonio, 13, 14
People's Liberation Army (PLA),
  China, 25, 29, 33

Pickering Fellowships, 200
"Plum Book," United States, 208
Pompeo, Mike, 195
Powell, Colin, 200, 207, 213
Putin, Vladimir, 125, 128, 133,
  135–137

Q
Quai d'Orsay, see Ministry of Europe
  and Foreign Affairs, France

R
Ramayana, 82
Rangel Fellowships, 200
"Review 2014," Germany, 72, 73
Rice, Condoleezza, 194
Ricketts, Lord Peter Forbes, 176
Rio Branco Institute (Brazilian
  diplomatic academy), 2, 7, 231
Rogers Act (establishing the Foreign
  Service), United States, 191
Rousseff, Dilma, 5, 14
Rühe, Volker, 71
Russian Orthodox Church, Influence
  on diplomacy, 135

S
Shigenori, Tōgō, 101
Shigeru, Yoshida, 102
Shin'ich, Kitaoka, 115
Shōtarō, Yachi, 118
Slavophile-Zapadniki split, 127
"Sofa government,"
  United Kingdom, 174
Steinmeier, Frank-Walter, 70, 72, 73
Strauss, Franz-Josef, 71
Su Wu, 23
Sun Tzu (Sun Zi), 23, 24, 36n2, 226

T

Takeo, Akiba, 112
Talleyrand-Périgord, Maurice de,
   legacy of, 44
Tanzimat (Ottoman) period, 144
Tiankai, Cui, 31
Trump, Donald, 103, 116, 117, 195,
   198, 200, 208–210, 213, 215
Tugendhat, Tom, 165, 176

U

Union of South American Nations
   (UNASUR), 13
United Nations (UN), x, 13, 38n34,
   44, 51, 60, 63, 65, 69, 91, 92,
   107, 114, 115, 152, 168, 191,
   205, 226, 235

V

Village Study Program, 87, 88
Vivekananda, Swami, 83

W

Washington, George, 190, 207
Weiqi (Wei-Ch'i), 24
"Westminster model," United
   Kingdom, 173

White Paper on Defense and Security
   (*Le Livre blanc: Defense et Sécurité
   Nationale*), 55n23
Wittig, Peter, 69

X

Xiaoping, Deng, 25
Xue, Li, 35

Y

Yakovenko, Alexander
   Vladimirovich, 133
Yeltsin, Boris, 128
Yeşiltaş, Murat, 145
Yılmaz, Ahmet Mesut, 153
Yoshida Doctrine, 102
Yoshiji, Nogami, 118
Yukio, Hatoyama, 118

Z

Zakharova, Maria, 136, 137
Zedong, Mao, 21–22, 24, 25, 30, 35
Zhang, Qian, 23
Zhongguo (Middle Kingdom;
   China), 23
Zongli Yamen (China's first foreign
   office), 24

The manufacturer's authorised representative in the EU is Springer Nature Customer Service Centre GmbH, Europaplatz 3, 69115 Heidelberg, Germany. If you have any concerns regarding our products, please contact ProductSafety@springernature.com

Printed and bound by CPI Group (UK) Ltd, Croydon, CR0 4YY

23/03/2026

02076738-0003